AROUND THE WORLD RALLY

Jimmy Cornell

LANDFALL NAVIGATION
354 West Putnam Avenue
Greenwich, CT 06830
Phone (203) 661-3176
Fax (203) 661-9613
Web Addr. http.//www.landfallnav.com

S

SHERIDAN HOUSE

Published by Sheridan House Inc.
145 Palisade Street
Dobbs Ferry, NY 10522

Library of Congress Cataloging-in-Publication Data

Cornell, Jimmy.
    Around the world rally / Jimmy Cornell
        p.   cm.
    Includes index.
    ISBN 0-924486-47-3 : $16.50
    1. Europa 92, 1992.   2. Yacht rallies.
   3. Yachts and yachting—Equipment and
supplies—Evaluation. I. Title
GV832.C67 1993
797.1′4—dc20   92-35944
                              CIP

Printed in Great Britain

ISBN 0-924486-47-3

CONTENTS

Dedication

To the participants in the first round the world rally, and in particular to the skippers of the 36 boats whose valuable comments in the equipment survey formed the basis of this book.

ACKNOWLEDGEMENTS

So many people and organisations have contributed to the success of the first round the world rally that listing them all here would run the risk of leaving some unmentioned. I am particularly indebted for the generous help provided by my many friends, new and old, in the ports of call of EUROPA 92. In almost every place the yacht clubs, tourism, port and municipal authorities went out of their way to make our stay in their midst as pleasant as possible. It was their unstinted support, more than anything else, which made it possible to run an unsponsored event of such magnitude.

Once again I must express my gratitude for the support provided by *Yachting World* magazine and in particular its editor, Dick Johnson. My sincere thanks are also due to the magazine's Deputy Editor, David Glenn, who gave me the inspiration to carry out a comprehensive equipment survey among participants in the round the world rally.

EUROPA 92 would have never succeeded without the dedication of the entire staff at World Cruising, our Operations Manager Andrew Bishop, coordinator Caroline Herring, the Race Officers Tony Mark, Erick Bouteleux and Tom Williams. None of the participants will ever forget Mary Mark's welcoming smile at the end of many landfalls, or that of Muriel Bouteleux.

As on many previous occasions, my deepest gratitude goes to Gwenda, who once again supported me through a very difficult project and whose efficient running of the London office miraculously managed to keep the event within budget. Like other projects in the past, EUROPA 92 appeared to be run at times by the Cornell family, with Gwenda editing the newsletters, Doina being in charge of press and public relations, and Ivan devising the computer program for the results. It was indeed a family effort and the success of EUROPA 92 was greatly helped by the fact that its route often coincided with the one sailed by us just over one decade earlier.

CAST OF CHARACTERS

Boat name	Design	LOA (ft)	Displ. (tons)	Rig	Year
Amadé	Levrier de Mer	52.5	9	S	1990
Ambler	Morgan Out Island	41	12	C	1986
Bluewater	Tayana 55	55	20	C	1986
Brydie	Hinkley 42	42.9	10	S	1989
Cacadu	Bénéteau 51	50	17	C	1990
Cheone	Clark	72	65	C	1937
Dafne	Nautic Saintonge	44	11	S	1981
Daughter of Baltic	Lunstroo	56	41	Sc	1985
Elan Adventurer	Elan 43	43	10	S	1989
Eye of Ra	Moody 419	42	9	S	1985
Gilma Express	Bill Lee 53	53	8	S	1985
Gulkarna II	Hallberg Rassy 45	45	16	C	1990
Gulliver	Swan 59	59	27	S	1990
Jakes Fantasia	Roberts 55	55	25	K	1980
Jolly Joker	Cetus 45	45	9.5	S	1989
Kite	Stevens 47	46	14	S	1982
La Aventura	Aventura 40	40	16	C	1989
Lady Samantha	Coppola	45	17	K	1985
Laura	Altura 422	42	14.5	K	1979
Libertad II	Amel Mango	53	27	K	1988
Locura	Deerfoot 72	72	22	K	1984
Midnight Stroller II	Trintella 53	53	19	S	1982
Octopus	Via 42	42	10	S	1989
Oingo Boingo	Gibsea 442	43.2	9.8	S	1989
Orchidea	Bill Lee 53	53	8	S	1989
Oyinbo	Nordia 61	61	42	S	1985
Pennypincher	Oyster 46	46	19	K	1988
Rockhopper	Roberts 435	43.5	18	K	1987
Scorpio II	Adams 50	50	20	C	1979
Sojourner	Tayana 52	52	17	C	1990
Soolo	Contest 43	43	13	S	1990
Tais	Rival 41	41	10	S	1978
Trillium	Mason 43	43	12	C	1982
Twilight	Sea Eagle 55	55	20	C	1989
Wachibou	Meridien	51	22	C	1985
Who Dares Wins	Swan 53	53	24	S	1988

Rig: S = sloop   C = cutter   K = ketch   Sc = schooner

Div.	Crew (Average)	Owner/Skipper(s)	Flag
C	4	Walter Gollhofer	Austria
C	3	John Papp	USA
C	4	Paul Skilowitz	USA
C	3	Bradford Bernardo	USA
R	5	Arne Blässar/John Blässar	Finland
C	6	Marcello Murzilli	Italy
R	4	Nicola Borsó	Italy
C	6	Ismo Nikola	Finland
R	6	David Miles/Julian Wilson	Great Britain
C	4	John Smith	Great Britain
R	4	Pasquale de Gregorio	Italy
C	5	Peter Bunting	Ireland
R	8	Francesco Casoli/Alessandro Mosconi	Italy
C	3	Jake McCullogh	Great Britain
R	4	András Jójárt/Janos Barzsantik	Hungary
C	5	Dick Wilson	USA
C	4	Jimmy Cornell/Ivan Cornell/Tom Williams	Great Britain
C	8	Enio Nardi/Giancarlo Damigella	Italy
C	3	Mario Filipponi	Italy
C	4	Christian Philibert/Richard Philibert	France
R	4	Leo Birkby	USA
C	5	John Rose	Great Britain
R	2	Karl Wilhelm Greiff	Germany
R	5	Roland Schlachter	Switzerland
R	6	Giovanna Caprini/Luca Repeto	Italy
C	6	Richard Goord	Great Britain
C	4	Alan Spriggs	Great Britain
C	6	Roger Gold	Great Britain
C	5	Wes Harris	USA
R	4	Rick Palm	USA
R	5	Pekka Hyryläinen	Finland
C	3	David Sutherland	Great Britain
C	3	Dutch Taylor	USA
C	6	Dino Blancodini	Italy
R	5	Guy Libens/András Jójárt	Belgium
R	8	Ian Kennedy	Great Britain

Division: R = racing   C = cruising

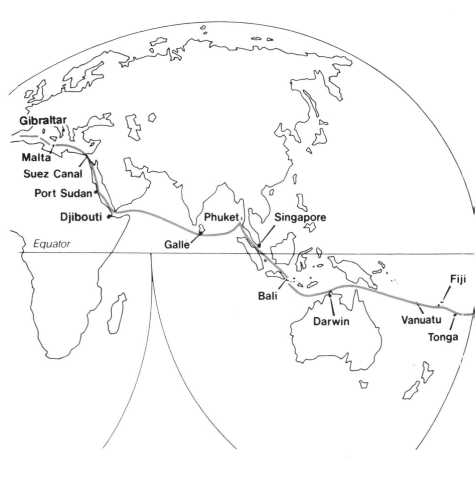

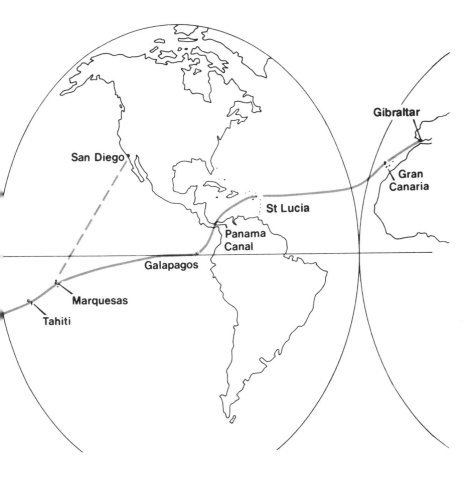

San Diego

Gibraltar

Gran
Canaria

St Lucia

Panama
Canal

Galapagos

Marquesas

Tahiti

1
PREPARATIONS

One of the most satisfying moments in my life was in Port Said in March 1981 when *Aventura* sailed out of the Suez Canal and recrossed her outward track thus completing a six year long circumnavigation. I can remember vividly the feeling of satisfaction I had in having sailed around the world on my own yacht. Today I still consider it one of the most significant achievements of my life.

To sail around the world on a small yacht is an immense accomplishment and many sailors harbour the secret dream of realising it one day. To help some sailors achieve this dream is one of the reasons why I decided to organise the first round the world rally. The other reason was to provide an alternative to the only other round the world sailing events which existed at the time: the Whitbread and BOC round the world races. As a keen sailor I have followed those two events from their inception with great interest, being gradually forced to admit that I would never take part in either of them. Both events have moved into the realms of super high technology which no ordinary sailor can dream of reaching in his own yacht.

I remember clearly the day in the spring of 1975 when a beautiful yacht flying the Mexican flag appeared in the now extinct London Marina, in Docklands, where I was fitting out *Aventura* with my own circumnavigation in mind. She was *Sayula*, the first and last production yacht to win the Whitbread. It never crossed my mind then that one day I would organise a race around the world myself. However, when I started planning EUROPA 92, I often thought of that first Whitbread, hoping that it would attract the same kind of amateur sailor, interested in sailing around the world in a competitive event rather than just winning at all cost.

No sooner was the event launched than the entries started pouring in, showing that the timing could not have been more opportune and that indeed there were many sailors waiting for just this kind of event. The success was similar to that of the ARC, the Atlantic Rally for Cruisers, which shares the same concept and is the fore-runner of the round the world rally. Not surprisingly, over one third of the skippers taking part in EUROPA 92 had also sailed in at least one ARC, and these former ARC participants formed the core of the new event.

Nearly one thousand yachts have taken part in the ARC since its first edition in 1986 and many of the valuable lessons learned from the ARC were applied in the round the world rally. The secret of the ARC's continuous success is that it combines in roughly equal proportions three basic elements – safety, enjoyment and competition. There is no doubt that crossing an ocean as part of an organised event adds an element of safety, and this was shown during the emergencies which have occurred in the ARC over the years. The enjoyment of the participants has always been a major priority and a rich social programme, both before and after the Atlantic crossing, gives everyone the opportunity to relax and meet fellow participants. Although conceived as a rally for cruising yachts, the competitive element has not been neglected, and over the years the ARC has shown that with few exceptions everybody wants to do well when sailing in the company of others, especially on a long passage such as the Atlantic crossing. An in-house handicap system is used in the ARC to give a rating to every yacht, but in recent years a new division was introduced for the more competitive minded participants. In order to ensure impartiality, the Channel Handicap System was chosen for this division. For the same reason, all yachts taking part in EUROPA 92 were CHS rated. The system is administered by the Royal Ocean Racing Club and has been perfected over many years of ocean races. It has the advantage of being easy to manage and obtaining a certificate is simple and inexpensive.

The choice of the route for the round the world rally was dictated by the attempt to provide an attractive alternative to other round the world races. Although I have profound admiration for anyone who sails around Cape Horn and the other southern capes, it seems to me that to sail around the world without seeing some of the most beautiful places on the way is to deny one of the reasons for setting sail in the first place. From earliest times the history of discovery and exploration has been intrinsically bound up with sailing and most sailors are explorers at heart. Even if one can no longer discover new lands, every landfall is, in its own way, a discovery and few sailors will deny the excitement of making landfall after a long passage. For these reasons the rally route was chosen to pass through some of the destinations that dreams, and tourist brochures, are made of – the Caribbean, Galapagos, Marquesas, Tahiti, Fiji, Bali, Phuket and a lot more besides. As all of these places are situated in the tropics, the logical and shortest route passes through the two man made canals: Panama and Suez. Unfortunately the balmy tropics are safe for sailing during only part of the year, so the timing of the rally had to be chosen carefully to avoid the hurricane and cyclone seasons *en route*.

Many other factors were also considered, but eventually a route emerged which took into account every relevant aspect. A serious threat to the entire undertaking was posed by the outbreak of hostilities in the Middle East shortly before the start of the rally. An alternative route was

The author's 40 ft steel *La Aventura* was designed and built with a circumnavigation in mind.

therefore devised, which would avoid the Middle East altogether by taking the fleet back to Europe via South Africa and the South Atlantic. In the event, the Gulf War finished while the yachts were still on the other side of the world and the rally was able to follow the original route.

The choice of name for the event was entirely due to my own commitment to the European ideal and, when the event was launched, I had hoped that we would attract participants from every one of the twelve Community members. In the end, although Europeans formed the majority of the participants, only half the EC countries were represented. Nonetheless, we kept the name and everywhere we stopped we made sure that everyone understood why the event was called EUROPA 92. In our own modest way we were the heralds of a Europe without frontiers, and it was a great satisfaction to notice the number of officials and journalists in the countries visited who understood the significance of the message and what the little blue flag with the twelve golden stars stood for.

Unfortunately our efforts were not appreciated by the Community itself and, in spite of countless letters and telephone calls, the event was treated with a lack of interest which was difficult to understand. Finally I managed to make an appointment with the director of sports in the relevant directorate in Brussels, but my visit proved just as fruitless as all previous attempts. It gave me, however, an insight into the workings of the European Community bureaucracy and brought me face to face with the inefficiency and ineptitude of the department whose principal aim is to inform the rest of the world, as well as the people of the Community itself, what this new Europe is all about.

A floating village is how the EUROPA 92 fleet has been described, while others have compared it to a television soap opera. Either is an apt description for the peripatetic 200 strong community, in which every household travelled snail-like with its home on its back. Nothing ever happened without everyone else knowing about it and moments of both sorrow and happiness were shared by everyone. Just like a television soap opera, every episode had a beginning and an end, the story of EUROPA 92 being told in 17 separate episodes – or sailing legs. In the following chapters, the story of EUROPA 92 will unfold in the same chronological order as the event itself. Every chapter will also include the findings of a comprehensive survey I carried out, which dealt with the technical aspects of the rally. This information is based on a series of detailed interviews with all of the skippers concerning the performance of their equipment, problems encountered, breakages suffered and any other subject that I thought may be of interest to anyone contemplating a similar voyage or indeed any offshore passage. The survey was similar in concept to other surveys I had conducted in the past, and it was significant that I started work on the most comprehensive of all my surveys in the same place where I undertook my very first survey 13 years earlier. A long stop in Fiji during my first voyage around the world gave me the idea to interview the skippers of 50 cruising yachts about various aspects of their voyage and equipment. The result of that first survey,

The skippers of the 36 yachts with HM Taufa'ahau Tupou IV, the King of Tonga.

and its unexpected success in the yachting press, showed me the value of obtaining this kind of information based on first hand experience.

In the following years, I was to follow that first survey with other surveys conducted in various parts of the world. Naturally, I realised that the round the world rally presented an opportunity which I shouldn't miss. I started interviewing the skippers of the 36 yachts taking part in EUROPA 92 in Fiji, where a long pause had been built into the schedule to enable participants to cruise at their leisure before taking on the second half of their voyage around the world. By the time they reached the halfway mark of the voyage the yachts had sailed some 12,000 miles since the start and the skippers knew so much more about both the good and the bad sides of their yachts and equipment. The detailed information they gave me in the lengthy interviews was later supplemented and updated right up to the finish in Gibraltar. The first subject to be discussed were modifications and improvements made to the boats in preparation for their forthcoming circumnavigation.

The yachts; modifications for the rally

Gibraltar provided a perfect meeting point for yachts arriving from North America, Northern Europe and the Mediterranean, and by New Year's Day, everyone had arrived for the long awaited rendezvous. As the fleet gathered in Marina Bay Marina, it was a great relief to see that even some of the latecomers would make it to the start and there would be no last minute withdrawals. Never before had such a large group of yachts sailed around the world together, and the boats were as different from each other as were their owners. With only one exception – the two Bill Lee designed Italian ULDBs – there were no two boats the same, and in its diversity the fleet provided a perfect cross section of current yacht design, with production boats and one-offs, new and second hand, fast light displacement racing yachts and solid comfortable cruising boats.

The sustained rhythm of the rally, which would take only fifteen months for the circumnavigation, called for serious preparation and on some yachts the crew were busy working until the night before the start. Most of the yachts had undergone some modifications for the proposed voyage, either to bring them up to world cruising standards or to provide a higher level of comfort than that provided by the manufacturer; more a necessity than a luxury for an arduous voyage totalling some 24,000 miles.

With a few exceptions, most yachts had confirmed their participation in the round the world rally at least one year before the start and therefore had sufficient time to prepare for the forthcoming voyage. A rather obvious observation, which I made later on in the rally, was that there was a relationship between the time spent on preparing the boat for the voyage and the number of breakages sustained later. Those who had had sufficient time to prepare, such as *Lady Samantha*, *Gilma Express*, *Kite*, *Locura*, *Sojourner* and *Bluewater*, suffered far less breakdowns than some of the others who decided to join the rally nearer the start. Similarly, yachts that had been cruised or raced extensively for several years, such as *Dafne*, *Oingo Boingo*, *Libertad II*, *Laura* or *Pennypincher*, had ironed out most problems and were in better shape than some of the yachts which had just rolled off the production line. Also in good shape were boats which had been fitted out by their owners, such as *Octopus* and *Twilight*, or extensively refitted by their new owners, such as *Tais*, *Oyinbo* and *Who Dares Wins*. Some of the best prepared were those who had bought new yachts expressly for the rally, most of these owners taking delivery during 1990. With only a few months left before the start of the rally, these yachts were sailed extensively during the summer of 1990, their owners anxious to discover if the yachts lived up to their expectations. It also gave them the opportunity to sort out any teething problems or make the kind of changes or improvements that only become obvious once a yacht is being sailed.

Even in the cosmopolitan world of yachting it was interesting to note that not a single owner among those buying new yachts expressly for the event decided to have his yacht built in his own country. Thus *Amadé*, a 53 ft aluminium Levrier de Mer, was built in France for the Austrian Walter Gollhofer. Late delivery meant that the yacht had to be sailed straight to Gibraltar, a stormy crossing of the Bay of Biscay providing a thorough shakedown passage for the light displacement yacht. Walter was to remark later that virtually all his problems stemmed from this delay, as he had to leave the yard immediately without the chance of being able to return to put things right.

Also built in France for its Finnish owner, Arne Blässar, was the Bénéteau 51 *Cacadu*. Delivered in the summer of 1990, *Cacadu* was sailed first north to Finland and then south again for the start. As in the case of *Amadé*, the few things that did not work had to be put right en route. Another new yacht commissioned with the rally in mind was by the Finnish owner Pekka Hyryläinen who chose the Dick Zaal designed Contest 43, *Soolo*, built in Holland.

With the two Finnish entries built elsewhere, the Italian Francesco Casoli had his Swan 59 *Gulliver* built in Finland, sparing neither effort nor money in equipping the yacht to the highest standard, his stated objective being that of winning the event at almost any cost. Other new yachts built on the shores of the Baltic were *Gulkarna II*, Peter Bunting's Hallberg Rassy 45, and *Jolly Joker*, a Cetus 45. The latter was based on a 1979 Admiral's Cup yacht design, which called for some substantial modifications for the intended voyage. The yacht was built in the Polish port of Szczecin and sailed to Yugoslavia by András Jójárt and his

Hungarian crew to undergo final preparations nearer home before back-tracking to Gibraltar for the start of the rally.

Julie and Rick Palm's *Sojourner* was undoubtedly the yacht to be built the furthest away from its eventual home port. The Taiwan built Tayana 52 was delivered to New York in April 1990, but early hurricane activity that year thwarted their plans to cross the Atlantic for the start in Gibraltar. Instead they joined the Caribbean 1500 Rally from Chesapeake Bay to the Virgin Islands and caught up with the round the world rally in St Lucia, as did *Brydie* and *Locura*.

There were several second hand yachts bought for the rally, such as the Belgian *Wachibou*, a Meridien built in 1985. Several former ARC participants bought larger yachts to take part in the rally, such as Alan and Penny Spriggs who bought Arne Blässar's previous *Cacadu*, an Oyster 46 in which Arne had sailed in ARC 88. Another participant in the same ARC, John Rose, upgraded his *Midnight Stroller* to a Trintella 53, *Midnight Stroller II*. With a more limited budget, Dave Sutherland acquired the elderly *Tais*, a Rival 41 built in 1978. The boat was thoroughly refurbished for the rally, including a complete osmosis treatment of the hull.

Modifications on these tried and tested yachts varied widely, with some requiring considerable work to bring them up to the required standards, while on others the treatment was largely cosmetic. *Wachibou* was one of several yachts to have most or all of its electronics upgraded. Because of the requirement to make regular position reports to rally control, several yachts acquired new SSB radios, most of them equipped with automatic antenna tuners. The entire navigation station was upgraded on *Midnight Stroller*, a Trintella 53 built in 1982, including a new GPS and chart plotter. Indeed, the one piece of equipment which was bought by almost everyone was a GPS satellite navigator, an acquisition which was to change everyone's attitude to navigation.

On several yachts, radar masts were added at the stern to carry the additional equipment. The most comprehensive was the one on Ian Kennedy's *Who Dares Wins*, a Swan 53 formerly raced extensively under its previous name of *Crackerjack*. Eventually the yacht ended up with two stern mounted posts, one of which carried antennae for the GPS, weatherfax and Inmarsat-C satcom, a foghorn as well as a permanently mounted video camera, while the radar scanner was mounted on a separate post. Arne Blässar found that *Cacadu*'s stern mounted radar scanner performed poorly when the boat was heeled over, so he suggested a gimballed arrangement, which would probably work better, although he did not have time to make this modification before the start.

Another intended modification which Arne was later pleased he did not insist on was to have only one steering wheel, instead of the two which are standard on the Bénéteau 51. The manufacturers had advised him against it and indeed he found that two wheels worked better than one large wheel. On the other hand, on *Gilma Express*, the owner

Pasquale de Gregorio decided to have the wheel replaced with a tiller. This made the steering of the 53 ft ultra light displacement yacht much more sensitive and was also less prone to break. Another advantage, which Pasquale was to become increasingly aware of later on, was that with the wind astern one could brace oneself more comfortably in the cockpit when steering with a tiller, whereas one must stand up when using a wheel. Sailing his Bill Lee designed yacht more like a dinghy, Pasquale insisted on steering himself for most of the rally, so a comfortable position deserved serious consideration. According to his crew, he spent almost all the time while on passage in the cockpit making sure that the boat was sailed efficiently at all times. This he undoubtedly did and *Gilma Express* won line honours in more than half the legs of the rally, often averaging over 10 knots.

The rig itself was also thoroughly modified on *Gilma Express*, which was converted from fractional to masthead rig as Pasquale de Gregorio wished his ULDB, which he had successfully raced in the Mediterranean for the previous five years, to be easily handled by a small crew. The boat was fitted with two jib furling gears so that in stronger winds the spinnaker could be replaced by two poled out genoas. This was the main reason for abandoning the $\frac{7}{8}$ rig, but also to have a better stayed mast, which was fitted with an additional pair of spreaders to hold the cap shrouds which ran to the top of the mast. For added safety, *Gilma Express* was also fitted with an inner forestay, which could be removed when not needed, but could be used with a small hanked on jib when close reaching in winds over 30 knots. The rigging itself was replaced with Norseman Dyform cable. Being aware of the vulnerability of an ULDB during a voyage of this kind, Pasquale had taken every necessary measure to ensure the safety of his yacht which had already been built to the highest standards. As organisers we had had serious misgivings about allowing ULDBs to join the event, but with the kind of serious preparations such as were made by Pasquale, these misgivings proved to be largely unfounded. However, the loss of *Orchidea*'s rudder in the North Indian Ocean, when the stainless steel rudder stock sheared close to the hull leaving the yacht without a rudder, may have been caused by excessive forces being exerted on the unsupported rudder.

Simpler modifications to the rigging were made on *Soolo* and *Dafne*, both having running backstays added to stop the mast pumping in big seas. A baby stay was also added on *Dafne* and an inner forestay on *Soolo* to balance the runners. On *Dafne* the baby stay allowed a staysail to be set under the spinnaker which resulted in a more balanced set of sails in stronger winds.

On *Rockhopper*, Roger Gold fitted new swaged terminals replacing the stemball fittings on his 1987 built Roberts 434, as he considered the existing system unsafe and difficult to repair in out of the way places. For similar considerations Peter Bunting replaced the stemball terminals on *Gulkarna II* with tang and clevis terminals, although he still ended up having problems with the rigging towards the end of the rally.

Rigging was undoubtedly the most thoroughly checked item during the preparations, showing the concern of most participants that it should stand up to the rigours of the long voyage. Indeed this concern was warranted as several rigging failures occurred later in the rally, fortunately none resulting in a broken mast, although there were a few very close calls.

Safety considerations played a major part in most people's preparations. Several boats acquired the Man Overboard Module produced by the Survival Technology Group, either before the start in Gibraltar or after the loss of a crew member in the Pacific, when several yachts re-examined their man overboard procedures and found them inadequate.

The ULDB *Gilma Express* was thoroughly modified for the round the world rally. The yacht is taking a group of school children for a sail inside the lagoon at Bora Bora.

The addition of a wheelhouse proved to be an inspired decision on *Soolo* and also provided the ideal space to install two solar panels.

Expecting inexperienced crew, Roger Gold had extra secure attachment points welded close to the companionway of his steel yacht so that the crew could clip on their harness as they came into the cockpit on watch. *Rockhopper*'s lifelines were also replaced with new cables before the start.

Expecting lighter winds in the Pacific and Indian Oceans, several yachts had light weather sails added to their inventory, while *Daughter of Baltic*, a staysail schooner built in 1985, had its rig altered to increase the sail area. Some of the yachts normally used for racing, such as *Jolly Joker*, had jib furling gears installed for the rally, while on *Who Dares Wins*, the yacht only reverted to furling headsails while cruising between competitive legs.

On several yachts the sail inventory was completely renewed. One modification which some skippers regretted making was to change over to a fully battened mainsail. The problems encountered with these sails will be discussed in detail in the chapter dealing with sails and furling gears.

Besides sailing efficiency and safety considerations, skippers also thought about some of the comforts needed for a voyage lasting well over one year. Indeed the comfort and general wellbeing of the crew later proved to be not only a key element in the success of some yachts' performances but, more importantly, proved to be essential in actually keeping the crew together. Thus, some yachts had washing machines, driers, hi-fi sets, deck showers, watermakers, television sets or video players added to their inventory. On *Midnight Stroller*, *Elan Adventurer*,

Kite and *Lady Samantha* bimini tops were installed over the cockpit to give protection to the person at the helm, while on *Who Dares Wins* the existing bimini was taken off, as Ian Kennedy expected it to be a nuisance when racing, something he later regretted. Several skippers found the lack of an awning to be a great discomfort in the tropics and some yachts, such as *Cheone* and *Twilight*, acquired awnings *en route*. A much appreciated modification on *Soolo* was the building of a small wheelhouse, which also carried two solar panels on its roof.

Comfort on long passages seems to have been a major priority with most skippers, judging from the type of modification made on many yachts. On the Deerfoot 72 *Locura* the bunks in the two aft cabins were changed from double to superimposed bunks, while on *Gulkarna II* all standard bunks were narrowed by installing lockers outboard. More storage area and locker space was also added on *Locura*, *Elan Adventurer*, *Eye of Ra* and *Brydie*, the latter having its cabin heater replaced with lockers, which owner Brad Bernardo considered to be more useful in the tropics. A host of modifications were undertaken on *Kite*, which underwent a two year refurbishment programme before leaving California, during which time owners Dick and Lona Wilson thoroughly prepared their ten year old Stevens 47 for the planned circumnavigation. The boat was equipped with windvane, solar panels, separate track for the trisail, chain gypsy on the windlass, mosquito screens on all hatches and portholes as well as countless shelves and baskets in and around the galley.

Better use of the existing storage space was made on *Elan Adventurer* by dividing a large and deep forward locker into two separate compartments. This was achieved with the help of a new watertight floor, which ensured that if the bottom compartment was flooded, the water emptied into the chain locker.

Ventilation on yachts is often a major problem, especially in the tropics, so several owners tried to make improvements either by adding more hatches, such as on *Jolly Joker*, turning them around to face forward to improve the air flow, as on *La Aventura*, or by installing air conditioning. On *Midnight Stroller* this was limited to the owner's stateroom, while on *Oyinbo*, a Nordia 61, the entire yacht was air conditioned, one more feature on Richard Goord's luxuriously appointed yacht.

A lot of thought had gone into preparing *Sojourner* to be easily handled by a small crew. The standard layout was modified both on deck and below, so that the boat could be handled without the need to go forward of the mast. The navigation station was moved to the aft section of the boat allowing the navigator to watch the radar and talk to the person at the helm at the same time. A second companionway was added which led directly from the cockpit into the saloon to be used in an emergency if the aft end of the boat was no longer accessible. For similar reasons, an additional entrance from the steering cockpit into the aft cabin was provided on *Gulliver*, which also had its main companionway altered to provide easier access.

Among the new boats which had some modifications made was *Cacadu*, where the standard galley was replaced with a U-shaped galley giving better protection to the cook and also providing more storage and working surfaces. More lockers were added in all cabins and also a separate generator room for the newly acquired generator and water-maker. On *Libertad II*, an Amel Mango built in 1988, the stern platform was enlarged and the pushpit widened thereby creating a larger area for fishing. The additional space also allowed the liferaft to be stored underneath the platform from where it could be launched without any effort.

Even if structural modifications were not necessary, most yachts had some of their hardware replaced or upgraded. *Eye of Ra*, a Moody 419 built in 1985, acquired two extra anchors and more chain so doubling its anchoring capacity. John Smith also installed a new wind generator, one of several skippers who increased their boat's generating capacity by acquiring wind generators or solar panels.

Cheone, the splendid old lady of the fleet, a 72 ft Clark design built in Scotland in 1937, had undergone a major refit under the loving care of her owner Marcello Murzilli, who succeeded in bringing her back to her former splendour. Both the interior and the deck were kept as close to the original design as possible with only four extra winches being added to help with sail handling. Even the new suit of sails, which were made to the original sail plan by Ratsey & Lapthorn, who had also fitted out the yacht over fifty years ago, had the unmistakably off white colour of traditional cotton sails. Personalised handpainted Wedgwood china and Murano glass goblets added a special touch to this beautiful yacht.

Minimal or no modifications at all were necessary on *Orchidea* and *Oingo Boingo*, the two yachts having been sailed and raced extensively before the rally. Nor were any modifications needed on *Laura*, owned by Mario Filipponi for eleven years and thoroughly tested over many sea miles including the ARC and TRANSARC rallies. Similarly, Enio Nardi's *Lady Samantha* was not in need of any basic changes after having already clocked up six Atlantic crossings before setting off on her circum-navigation. However, she did have a radar and watermaker added to her list of equipment, as well as a GPS, the latter being a piece of equipment which was being installed on several yachts on the eve of the start from Gibraltar.

2
THE START

Leg 1: Gibraltar to Las Palmas de Gran Canaria

At 1030 local time on Sunday 6 January 1991, Her Royal Highness Princess Pilolevu of Tonga gave the starting signal for the firing of a gun of the Gibraltar Regiment and the first round the world rally was on its way. Thirty one yachts flying the flags of thirteen nations crossed the starting line off Europa Point lighthouse, the southernmost extremity of the Rock of Gibraltar. In strong westerly winds the fleet set off briskly through the Straits of Gibraltar bound for Las Palmas de Gran Canaria. The great adventure had finally begun.

For many of the participants it was the culmination of two years planning and preparation. Some yachts had been waiting in Gibraltar several months and were raring to go, such as Dave Sutherland on *Tais* or Paul Skilowitz on *Bluewater*, who had sailed across the Atlantic from the USA during the summer to join the event from the start, as had John Papp on *Ambler*. On the other hand, some of the Italian boats such as *Twilight* and *Gilma Express* had only left their home ports the previous week. Fine dry weather on the eve of the start helped everyone making their last minute preparations and the docksides were continually busy.

Friends and family arrived from all over the world to see the yachts off and bid them goodbye. Farthest to come were friends of *Jolly Joker*, the Hungarian entry, who drove a van from Budapest laden with stores, only to find they were not allowed into Gibraltar at the border, in spite of having been told at the British Embassy in Budapest that Hungarians no longer required visas for the United Kingdom, which apparently did not apply to colonies such as Gibraltar. After spending a night in a hotel in Spain, special permission was obtained from the highest authority and the Hungarian support team was allowed to enter Gibraltar. A few days later, the family of one of the Italian crew had their passports stolen in Spain while on their way to see the start. Once again special permission had to be sought from the Governor for them to enter Gibraltar without documents, so as not to miss bidding goodbye to their relatives.

Flying in from California were Dick and Lona Wilson, the owners of *Kite*, and their crew Tom and Diana Sutter. *Kite* was one of three US yachts scheduled to start from San Diego in April and join EUROPA 92

in the Marquesas, but the Wilsons were keen to meet their fellow participants earlier and feel the atmosphere of the event.

H Sheppard & Co, owners of Sheppard's Marina, who were sponsors
of the first leg, provided a welcome party for everyone at the Royal
Gibraltar Yacht Club, which had granted all EUROPA 92 sailors temporary membership and acted as hosting club. In spite of the busy preparations, time was still found for social activities. A farewell cocktail for the
skippers was given at the Little Mermaid restaurant by Marina Bay Marina, and one of the highlights of this memorable week was the presentation of the skippers to HRH Princess Pilolevu, when she visited the
Royal Gibraltar Yacht Club during the skippers briefing.

Destination Las Palmas

After the starting gun was fired, the fleet made a brisk start in the westerly
winds which were gusting up to 25 knots. First across the line was *Cacadu*
followed closely by *Elan Adventurer*, a Gibraltar based yacht skippered by
David Miles. A long tack towards the Spanish shore rapidly brought into
the lead the Italian Swan 59 *Gulliver*, who after one hour was leading
the fleet, followed closely by the other Swan, Ian Kennedy's *Who Dares
Wins*. Also making a good start was the Italian ULDB *Orchidea*, skippered
by Giovanna Caprini, the only lady skipper in the event, who had tried
hard to line up an all female crew but eventually had to resign herself to
a mixed crew, but one in which the female element still formed the
majority.

Easterlies had been promised by the weather forecasters, but they did
not materialise; even so everyone managed to negotiate the tricky straits
safely. After leaving the Straits of Gibraltar the fleet encountered very
light winds, which dropped to nothing at nightfall. The winds remained
light and variable for the next three days and this persuaded more than
half the fleet to take advantage of the ruling which allowed yachts in the
Cruising Division to use their engines in calms or light winds. Occasionally the winds came from the SW, but only six days after the start did
they show any real improvement when they finally started blowing from
the NNE at 12 to 18 knots providing a perfect finish for those who had
had the patience to wait for the change. Due to the light winds, the first
arrivals in Las Palmas were yachts which had motored and the first to
arrive was Richard Goord's *Oyinbo*. A battle for line honours in the
Racing Division ensued and *Gulliver* managed to cross the finishing line
inside Las Palmas harbour only two minutes before *Who Dares Wins*.

In contrast to Gibraltar, where the fleet had been spread out between
Sheppard's and Marina Bay Marina, in Las Palmas a section of the main
wharf in the Muelle Deportivo had been cleared of other yachts and
reserved for EUROPA 92. This helped to create a convivial dockside
atmosphere and also gave the crews a better chance to get to know each

other. The first of many crew changes soon got underway, crew swapping becoming a regular phenomenon in every port of call. It took some crew several legs to find the perfect yacht, just as it took some skippers as long to find suitable crew. For some crew, however, yacht swapping had a purpose, such as the Italian journalist Simona Oreglia who was sending monthly reports to the Italian yachting magazine *Forza 7*. Simona started off on *Orchidea* and then gradually moved from yacht to yacht in order to see the event from a constantly changing perspective. Another journalist who sailed with the fleet from beginning to end was Michaël Clement, who started off sailing on *Libertad II* and sent regular reports to TV3 in France. The rally also had a large following in Finland where Folke West kept Radio One listeners informed on its progress, Folke sailing several of the legs on *Daughter of Baltic*.

The lighter than expected weather on the first leg meant that there were not too many breakages and problems to deal with, so participants could enjoy the social programme arranged by our many friends in Las Palmas. After starting the ARC from Las Palmas for the previous six years, there is little the authorities would not do for an international event such as EUROPA 92 and the warmth of the Canarian welcome was not easy to match later on. Living up to his reputation, Pedro Pérez, of the Texaco station in the port, was his usual helpful self and made everyone's life easy, from arranging gas bottles to be filled to bringing out mechanics at short notice.

Gulliver was one of several boats provided with a functional radar post at the stern.

Local sailors, who keep their yachts in the marina and who had recently formed their own sailing club, organised a Friendship Regatta and invited the visitors to sail as crew on their boats. The regatta was followed by a barbecue on the dockside and a presentation party. Two astronavigation classes also proved to be very popular, one a refresher course and one on emergency navigation. One morning at sunrise, the port saw the unusual sight of eighteen navigators lined up with their sextants on the breakwater attempting to shoot the sun.

Arturo Molina, Director of the Tourist Board of Gran Canaria, has been the main supporter of the ARC since its inception in 1986. A man full of surprises, he certainly managed to surprise all EUROPA participants when he transported them out of Las Palmas into the interior of the island for what they were told was going to be a picnic. The picnic turned out to be a splendid lunch at a restaurant in the grounds of the former residence of the Marquis of Arucas. Those with stamina followed this the next day with a tour of the Tropical brewery.

The port of Las Palmas is one of the busiest in the world, whether with container ships or oriental fishing fleets, but unusually for such a major commercial port, it actually welcomes yachts and sailing events. The president of the port, José Manuel Hernandez, hosted a reception for the skippers in his office overlooking the port and presented each skipper with a commemorative plaque. A special presentation was made to Enio Nardi, the skipper of *Lady Samantha*, who had visited Las Palmas on many occasions in his fourteen Atlantic crossings.

A farewell dinner was hosted by the Tourist Board of Gran Canaria at the Alpendre del Amo in the Playa del Inglés. A presentation ceremony was held after dinner, during which everyone was entertained by some superb Canarian folksinging. The atmosphere was excellent and even John Rose's 81 year old mother took to the dance floor. Ernest Felipes of Sheppard's Marina had flown in from Gibraltar especially to present the Sheppard's Cup to *Oingo Boingo*, a Gibsea 442 from Switzerland, skippered by Roland Schlachter, the overall winner of the first leg. *Oingo Boingo* was also the first recipient of the large yellow flag with the EUROPA ying-yang sign, which the overall leader would fly on the same principle as the yellow jersey in cycling. Racing Division line honours was won by *Gulliver*, while *Oyinbo* received the Commodore's Cup from the Federacion de Vela Latina for the first yacht to cross the line. In the Racing Division, *Cacadu* took the Gran Canaria Tourist Board Cup for Class A and *Dafne* the Real Club Nautico Cup for Class C. In the Cruising Division the first prize for Class A went to *Amadé*, that of Class B to *Oyinbo* and Class C to *Lady Samantha*, who also received a special prize as overall winner in the Cruising Division.

Most of the prizes had been donated by Alcorde, the largest and oldest ship's chandlers in the Canary Islands, who were sponsoring the second leg from Las Palmas to St Lucia. Alcorde had made a great effort to welcome EUROPA 92 participants and had dressed both the port and the main esplanade in Las Palmas with colourful banners to give a festive appearance. They also published welcome and farewell announcements in the daily newspapers which brought thousands of people into the marina to look at the yachts. As a farewell gesture, the Canaries Government put on a magnificent fireworks display over the port the night before the start.

During the Gibraltar to Las Palmas leg, the daily radio net had been controlled by Rafael del Castillo, a keen radio operator as well as sailor, who is based in Las Palmas. Rafael also participates regularly in a world-wide Spanish maritime net, so he was well qualified to run the EUROPA 92 net during the Atlantic crossing. The transatlantic leg from Gran Canaria to St Lucia showed both the importance and the value of the daily radio net. There were three net controllers within the fleet who took it in turns to record the daily position reports before passing them on to rally control ashore. For the first few days, positions were relayed to Rafael in Las Palmas, but when Operations Manager Andrew Bishop arrived in St Lucia, positions were relayed directly to him. The position reporting net took place in the morning, with a second, informal net being held in the evening.

Radio communications

In several incidents during the round the world rally, the radio net provided a lifeline to the outside world, such as when *Jakes Fantasia* was seized by the Eritrean People's Liberation Front. The net also brought help to those in emergency situations, such as during the loss of a man overboard in the Pacific, a medical emergency in the North Indian Ocean or the wrecking of a yacht in the Torres Strait.

Because daily position reporting was compulsory, every yacht was equipped with an SSB marine radio. On seven yachts there were additional amateur radios, several participants being keen amateur operators, with a total of twelve licensed operators in the fleet. In some instances the amateur radios had been installed as a safety measure, such as on *Cacadu* where the set was only to be used in an emergency as there was no licensed operator on board. There were several other amateur sets in the fleet, as well as marine sets capable of being used on amateur frequencies, but in every instance the operators stressed that they never used frequencies other than the international marine frequencies and would only use an amateur frequency if in serious need.

Most of the licensed amateur operators used their radios to keep in regular contact with their friends and families. Those on US yachts did this by being patched into the US telephone system. This method consists of an operator on a yacht establishing contact with an amateur operator in his own country, who then dials the required telephone number and 'patches' in the call from the yacht into the telephone system. It is undoubtedly a cheap and convenient way of making calls from abroad, but is permitted only in a few countries. As Dick Wilson of *Kite* pointed out, 'Unfortunately some sailors do abuse the system which should be used in international waters only, or, if the yacht is cruising in a particular country, only if there is a third party agreement between that country and the United States which specifically allows phone patching.'

As shown in Table 1, there were several makes of SSB radios in the fleet, although by far the most popular make, both among marine and amateur sets, was ICOM, with the ICOM 700 being the most common model. One of its attractions is that the operator can dial any desired frequency, not just the international marine frequencies, but also weatherfax as well as broadcasting frequencies, such as the BBC World Service. On some sets it is also possible to dial amateur frequencies. The ability to dial one's own frequencies proved to be a great advantage during 1991 when many international communications frequencies were changed and the owners of radios with pre-set frequencies had great difficulties in having their radio retuned.

When interviewed for the equipment survey, the 36 skippers were asked to rate their equipment from 1 to 10, with 10 being the highest rating. As shown in Table 1, ICOMs scored well both on performance and reliability. The lowest make to score was Skanti, its average being brought down by the low rating given by Marcello Murzilli of *Cheone*

Table 1   Radio communications

Make	Number	Performance	Reliability
SSB marine radios			
ICOM	17	9	9.5
Skanti	3	4.3	6.7
Stevens	2	8.5	8.5
Sailor	2	9.5	9.5
Furuno	2	9.5	9.5
Raytheon	1	8	8
Kenwood	1	10	10
Total:	28		
Amateur radios			
ICOM	6	9	9.3
Kenwood	5	9.7	8.5
Yaesu	4	7.5	8
Total:	15		

who was not satisfied by the performance of his high-priced SSB radio and was particularly incensed by the poor after sales service. Despite expensive repairs *en route*, he was left with a radio that could not communicate with the rest of the fleet over long distances.

The performance rating sometimes reflected the operator's difficulty at reaching distant stations, which in some cases may have been a shortcoming of the installation rather than the transmitting capability of the set itself. John Smith of *Eye of Ra*, who had difficulties in reaching farther stations, felt that his grounding plate was too small and indeed, when discussing this matter with a radio engineer, I was told that on many yachts the grounding plate was often inadequate.

For Pasquale de Gregorio's *Gilma Express*, the grounding plate caused problems of an unexpected nature when he discovered in St Lucia that the anode on his stern drive was badly corroded. As he had not noticed any ill effects of electrolysis in the past, he felt that there must have been a reaction between the anode and his copper grounding plates, two of which were installed at the stern, one for the radio and one for the antenna tuner, and a third plate amidships for all the instruments. He replaced all copper plates with zinc anodes and one year later there was absolutely no sign of corrosion and the radio worked perfectly.

In some cases, it was not the sets or their installation which were to blame for their poor performance, but the operator's lack of understanding of the importance of good propagation and how to make use of the best conditions available. This is a subject of which amateur operators have a much better understanding, and some of the amateurs in the EUROPA fleet managed to keep in daily touch with Europe even when the yachts had reached their furthest point in the South Pacific. Being obliged to contact our London office via Portishead Radio on several occasions, I tried to learn more about propagation and when I was more likely to find optimum conditions. The fact that I managed to reach Portishead in England from as far away as Panama, Northern Australia and Indonesia, was a measure of my success. What was frustrating was the several occasions when I managed to raise the operator in Portishead with great difficulty, only to be drowned out by a ship with ten times more transmitting power than my own set.

The total number of amateur sets in the EUROPA fleet was lower than I had expected, which is a recent phenomenon also observed in the ARC, where the proportion of amateur radios was much higher in the past. One of the main reasons why some sailors used to prefer to acquire amateur radios was their much lower price compared to marine radios. However, prices have been coming down steadily over the last two or three years and now a good quality SSB radio transceiver, including automatic antenna tuner, can be bought for around £1500 or $2000.

On most yachts, the antenna was part of the backstay, which is the usual arrangement, especially on sloops. The system appeared to perform

With more miles under his keel than any other sailor in EUROPA 92, Enio Nardi is also a keen radio operator and kept in daily touch with Italy throughout the event.

satisfactorily, mainly because all radios were provided with automatic antenna tuners and therefore the actual length of the wire was not so critical. Nevertheless, the antenna should be kept as long as possible, with the top insulator mounted as close as feasible to the masthead, while the lower insulator should be installed at a sufficient height which does not permit anyone to grab the live part of the backstay while transmitting.

As a precaution for emergencies, 30 yachts were equipped with emergency antennas both for their SSB and VHF radios, in a few cases the emergency antenna being a whip installed either on the aft rail, or more commonly on the radar post at the stern. Also with an emergency in mind, nine yachts had either a separate battery pack for the radio or had prepared a quick way of removing a battery, so as to be able to take the radio with them should the boat have to be abandoned. For similar reasons, on several yachts handheld VHF radios were kept fully charged in an easily accessible place or stowed in the panic bag itself.

There were altogether 42 handheld radios on board the yachts, with ICOM making up more than half. Table 2 shows the individual ratings for performance and reliability. The main criticism levelled at the popular ICOM, hence its lower average reliability rating, was the shorter than advertised time that the battery pack kept up its charge. Leo Birkby of

Table 2   Handheld radios

Make	Number	Performance	Reliability
ICOM	24	9	8.5
SMR	5	7.5	6.8
Standard	2	9	5.5
Sealine	2	7	10
Kenwood	2	9	10
Navico	2	9	9
Yaesu	1	9	9
Husan	1	10	10
Searanger	1	8	2
Sitex	1	7	7
Furuno	1	10	10
Total:	42		

Locura also complained that the batteries were recommended to be kept on charge for 15 hours, which is too long to keep an inverter going, and he suggested that manufacturers of handheld radios should provide a better charging system from a boat's own 12 V supply.

Table 3   VHF radios

Make	Number	Performance	Reliability
Sailor	10	9.9	9.9
ICOM	10	9.4	9.5
Standard	2	7	9.5
Shipmate	2	8.5	8.5
Raytheon	1	10	10
West Marine	1	10	10
Furuno	1	9	9
Mariner	1	5	5
Navico	1	10	10
Demek	1	8	10
SMR	1	4	3
Seavoice	1	6	10
Husan	1	10	10
Ray Jefferson	1	7	7
Searanger	1	6	10
Kelvin Hughes	1	4	5
Total:	36		

There were few complaints concerning the performance of the fixed VHF sets, with more than half the units bearing either the Sailor or ICOM label. Some of the lesser known makes scored low both on performance and reliability.

Weatherfax

Two thirds of the yachts (24) had weatherfax on board, of which 15 were dedicated units capable of functioning independently of the SSB radio. The performance of the independent sets varied widely and in four cases, the owners found that the units performed much better if connected to the SSB radio transceiver as this ensured improved reception, usually because the main radios were provided with better antennae.

Table 4 Weatherfax

Make	Number	Performance	Reliability
Furuno	12	7.6	7.7
Alden	4	9	9.5
ICS	4	8.7	8.3
Koden	2	5.5	6
Stevens	1	6	10
JMC	1	8	7
Total:	24		

Once the yachts left the Atlantic, the availability of weather facsimile became rather disappointing with far less information being accessible than expected, while those with Navtex fared even worse, as the system is geared primarily for European and North Atlantic waters. With so many weatherfax machines in the fleet, there was a constant exchange of information on the best frequencies to be used, and usually those who managed to obtain a good picture passed on this information to the other participants on the daily radio net.

Asked if the information obtained by weatherfax influenced their routeing, the answers were as diverse as the yachts themselves. In fact, only eight skippers stated that they took notice of the weatherfax when actually plotting their course, most of the others taking the weather as it came and only expecting the weatherfax to warn them if worse was to come. 'It's only the bad news that we're interested in, anything else we'll take in our stride' commented John Rose. Other skippers wanted to be sure that the information was indeed reliable before committing themselves, while others thought that forecasting local weather conditions from a general picture was both difficult and risky.

Pasquale de Gregorio admitted that usually he took little notice of the weatherfax except to confirm his own decisions. 'My philosophy is to take advantage of the existing wind conditions to gain on other boats rather than sail further to find better wind.' However, as he aimed to sail his ULDB as efficiently as possible, he rarely sailed dead downwind as the boat was much faster with the wind on the quarter, so there were occasions when he did take inspiration from his weatherfax as to which gybe to hold. Later in the rally, during the leg from Galle to Djibouti, he either misread the information or gambled on a shift of wind direction which never came, and ended up sailing too far to the north so that he finished behind both *Gulliver* and *Who Dares Wins*. 'Blame it on the weatherfax' he exclaimed bitterly when I asked him what he had been doing taking such a roundabout course. In fairness to Pasquale, I must admit that when I sailed the next leg from Djibouti to Port Sudan on *Locura*, the prognosis for our area did not tally at all with the actual weather conditions we experienced. Later on in the Red Sea on *La Aventura* wind predictions on the weatherfax were often inaccurate and bore little relation to existing conditions.

In contrast to *Gilma Express*, Alessandro Mosconi, the skipper of *Gulliver*, the other Italian yacht which won line honours in almost as many legs as Pasquale, admitted that he studied the weather very seriously. As the yacht's owner Francesco Casoli explained, 'Alessandro doesn't like to gamble and our routeing is dictated both by existing and expected weather conditions. On most occasions, this has paid off.'

Telex

There was only one telex in the fleet, on *Gulkarna II*, rated by its owner Peter Bunting with the lowest mark possible as it never worked properly. 'The instruction manual is only understandable if you have a PhD in electronics. Even people familiar with radios couldn't make any sense of it. I can only describe this device as a con trick on the yachting community.'

Table 5 Inmarsat-C

Make	Number	Performance	Reliability
Thrane & Thrane	2	9.5	9.5
Saturn C	1	8	8
SNEC C-Mate	1	4	4
Total:	4		

A much better service was provided by the Inmarsat-C type satellite communications system which started off by offering a telex service, but has now expanded to provide a whole range of additional services. Four yachts had Inmarsat-C on board, the two leading yachts in the Racing Division, *Gulliver* and *Who Dares Wins*, using their satcoms on an almost daily basis and both owners swore by them. It could be argued that *Gulliver's* eventual success in winning the event overall may have been due, at least in part, to the skipper's ability to be in constant touch with home base from where new sails or spare parts would be dispatched without delay to the next port of call.

There was also an Inmarsat-C unit on *Daughter of Baltic* which had some teething problems but once these had been sorted out, the unit was used extensively. Unfortunately the same cannot be said of my own experience with the C-Mate unit on *La Aventura* whose user-unfriendliness put my patience to a painful test. Nevertheless, the system holds great promise and once some of its shortcomings are ironed out and the price comes down accordingly, Inmarsat-C will undoutedly become as popular with long distance sailors as the weatherfax and SSB radio.

In fact, the telex service provided by Inmarsat-C will eliminate the need for much of the voice communications that yachts are currently forced to use if they wish to communicate with land based stations. Asked how often they used their SSB radios to communicate with home base, only one third of the skippers said that they did this on a regular

The common language became a strong bond for the German, Swiss and Austrian crews of *Octopus*, *Oingo Boingo* and *Amadé*.

basis. A proportion used international radiotelephone services while sailing in the North Atlantic, but their number decreased as the rally reached remoter areas.

The amateurs fared better in this respect, especially those who had set up a regular schedule with operators in their own country, such as the Italian yachts, who took part in a daily net run by Pierluigi Zini, an enthusiastic amateur from Ravenna, who has been providing this service to Italian long distance sailors for the last ten years. Pierluigi would pass on messages to the participants' families and he also contacted the organisers of the rally when emergencies at sea came to his knowledge first. The crew of *Octopus* had a similar arrangement with INTERMAR, an amateur net operating on 14313 KHz, which is run in German from 0600–1100 GMT and English at other times. Similarly, Dave Sutherland of *Tais* kept in regular contact with the UK maritime net operating daily at 0800 and 1800 GMT on 14303 KHz. The round the world rally had broken down many barriers, but as far as the airwaves were concerned, most people still preferred to talk in their mother tongue.

3
ATLANTIC CROSSING

Leg 2: Las Palmas to St Lucia

At noon on Sunday 20 January, 30 yachts made a brisk start to the second leg of the event from Las Palmas de Gran Canaria. Under blue skies, with a strong southerly wind blowing, the majority of the fleet turned north around Gran Canaria but found they had made a tactical error as they fell into the lee of the island. The few boats who had chosen to go south found this to their advantage, among them *Gulliver* and *Who Dares Wins*, the leading contenders in the Racing Division. After beating offshore they found clearer winds and could set a course across the Atlantic, their destination the Caribbean island of St Lucia, 2700 miles away.

Once clear of the Canary Islands, the next decision the navigators had to make was whether to follow the rhumb line to St Lucia or to go south in search of steadier trade winds. As it happened, the choice of route made little difference as there were good winds over the whole area almost from the start to the finish.

For the first few days the winds blew strongly from the ENE. Later, the wind became southeasterly and blew between 8 and 18 knots. The wind continued at this strength and became more easterly as the yachts passed the halfway mark to St Lucia. One frontal system affected the fleet and brought headwinds to those close south of it, whereas yachts which stayed on a more northerly course had winds of up to 40 knots while the system passed to the east. Steady trade winds then set in, although many boats were caught out by the frequent line squalls that persisted for much of the crossing, particularly at night. Several boats blew out spinnakers, including *Who Dares Wins*, *Gulliver*, *Ambler* and *Eye of Ra*, while others experienced damage to booms, spinnaker poles, mast tracks, halyards and rigging, including two broken forestays.

Although the strong winds took their toll on the equipment, it was evident that most crews enjoyed sailing their boats hard in the exciting conditions provided by a winter crossing of the Atlantic. It certainly made for some fast crossings and the first boat to cross the finishing line in Rodney Bay was *Gilma Express*, having completed the 2700 miles in just under 13 days and 9 hours. The average speed was 8.4 knots, although Pasquale recounted some exhilarating moments while experiencing speeds of up to 22 knots while surfing, which showed the true potential of this ULDB. It was interesting that this performance was without spinnaker as *Gilma Express* sailed across the Atlantic with twin headsails only.

The second boat to arrive in St Lucia ten hours later, and the eventual overall winner on handicap for the second leg, was Ian Kennedy's *Who Dares Wins*, who also completed the crossing in less than 14 days. This was in spite of having blown out both of their heavy spinnakers and sailing the last 1000 miles without one. While trying to douse their spinnaker during a squall, *Who Dares Wins* broached badly. The yacht was knocked down flat, with the mainsail on the water, the free flying spinnaker driving the yacht downwind. It was a tricky moment and some time before the situation was brought under control and the yacht was once again on her way to St Lucia. *Gulliver*, the third boat to arrive, also lost both of her spinnakers while still some considerable distance from St Lucia and this accounted for her poorer performance on this leg.

Jolly Joker was one of several boats that damaged their boom. On the first night after the start, *Jolly Joker*'s boom was broken during an accidental gybe and the decision was made to call in at Tenerife to get it fixed. András Jójárt spent several hours driving around the island with the boom on top of a taxi before eventually finding a small factory which was able to carry out the repair. Forty eight hours later, the boat was underway again, having managed to sail in and out of port in order not to be disqualified from the Racing Division.

Radio net

Despite all the exciting sailing, participants still found time to talk on the radio net. The net was held at 1500 GMT every day with the help of three controllers in the fleet, Arne Blässar on *Cacadu*, Dave Sutherland on *Tais* and Moira Gold on *Rockhopper*. The daily net came into its own during this first long passage and became an important part of the event. An informal net was set up within the fleet as well as private schedules between various boats. It was on one of these that a fierce battle of Trivial Pursuit raged between *Pennypincher* and *Midnight Stroller*. *Pennypincher* was the final winner by two clear games. Meanwhile, English lessons were given by *Oyinbo* to *Cheone*, reciprocal Italian lessons being promised for the following leg.

Marine life provided another pastime, whether observing or catching it. One boat that seems to have had more than her fair share of both was *Daughter of Baltic*. The crew reported that they were entertained by a whale which played with the boat for several hours, in the same way as dolphins do, by swimming alongside then diving under the keel to reappear on the other side. When not watching, they were catching fish and arrived in St Lucia with their freezer better stocked than when they left Las Palmas.

After such a long crossing, there were a couple of close finishes to entertain the timekeepers on the terrace of the St Lucia Yacht Club overlooking Rodney Bay. The first was between *Pennypincher* and *Gulkarna*. *Pennypincher* was tempted to turn the engine on after the wind dropped on rounding Pigeon Island, while *Gulkarna* preferred to finish under sail. During a friendly chat over the VHF, *Gulkarna* was heard to say that they had just slowed down a little to 'blue rinse' their hair before finishing a few minutes later.

Caribbean welcome

An area of Rodney Bay Marina had been cleared to enable all the yachts to be berthed close to one another. After the long crossing this togetherness was much appreciated by all the crews. The excellent repair facilities in St Lucia were put to the test as more and more yachts arrived with repairs to be done. Perhaps not surprisingly, the second half of the fleet had less breakages during the crossing, probably due to the fact that these were mostly in the Cruising Division and had not pushed their boats as hard as the more competitive earlier arrivals.

As time went by and more yachts arrived, the reception given to each arrival became more boisterous. Many crews appeared to be rather overcome when they heard the noise from the horns and sirens greeting them at the completion of an arduous and testing leg. The atmosphere in St Lucia helped weld the fleet together and from there on EUROPA 92 became a definite event with its own character and feeling of belonging.

A week after the first yacht arrived, some of the early arrivals headed off, either north or south, to cruise some of the Caribbean islands before reassembling in St Lucia for the start of the leg to Panama. It was one of the planned features of the rally that sufficient time was allowed to cruise in most areas between competitive legs. Meanwhile, the St Lucia Tourist Board hosted a reception at the St Lucian Hotel, attended by over one hundred participants. It was a highly enjoyable evening with people swapping stories from the recent crossing. The crews of *Brydie*, *Locura* and *Sojourner*, all of whom had sailed from the USA to join the event in St Lucia, also attended the party and met many of their fellow participants for the first time.

As a fitting farewell to the Caribbean, the prize giving ceremony for the transatlantic leg was held at Point Seraphine overlooking the harbour of Castries in the presence of the Deputy Prime Minister of St Lucia, the Hon. George Mallet. Some crews were joined by families and friends who had come to cruise in the Caribbean and over two hundred people were present to see *Who Dares Wins* receive the Alcorde Trophy for the overall winner of the leg. *Who Dares Wins* also took over the special yellow flag of the current overall leader.

The Commodore's Cup for line honours went to *Gilma Express*, while the winner of the Cruising Division was *Midnight Stroller*. Arch Marez, the owner of Rodney Bay Marina, presented a trophy to *Elan Adventurer* for their class win in the Racing Division, while *Soolo's* victory in their class earned the Barclays Bank trophy. Many other prizes were awarded and the crews were entertained by a steel band and limbo dancer to round off the evening.

Last minute jobs

The last day in Rodney Bay Marina became a hive of activity as several skippers found last minute problems that needed repairing or essential parts only arriving at the eleventh hour. *Wachibou* received vital parts for their furling jib only the night before the start and the entire crew worked solidly to carry out the repair, at one point three of them being up the mast at the same time. They managed to finish and left the marina only three minutes before the start. Last minute repairs also had to be effected to the transmission of *Daughter of Baltic* who just made it to the start in time.

There was a rush of activity on *Tais* after Dave Sutherland had discovered a crack in one of the spreaders while making a routine inspection the day before the start. The entire rigging had to be slackened and the spreaders taken off. With the help of David Miles of *Elan Adventurer*, who went up the mast and riveted the spreader brackets in place, the repair was effected and Dave declared *Tais* ready to go. The last yacht to be bedevilled by repairs was *Jakes Fantasia*, whose skipper discovered a broken gear shift cable on the morning of the start so putting their

A perfect start to the leg from St Lucia to Panama.

engine out of action. In spite of working nonstop throughout the day, they missed the start, although managing to leave six hours later.

The first two withdrawals from the rally were confirmed in St Lucia. Shortly after the start in Las Palmas, the Swedish yacht *Amelia Viking* had been forced to return to the Canaries with rigging problems. Unfortunately by the time these had been sorted out, it was too late for the yacht to catch up with the rest of the fleet. Ray Lotto, the skipper of *Hypatia*, was forced to fly home from St Lucia for an operation and so he too decided to withdraw from the rally. His decision did not go down well with his daughter Krista, who was enjoying the event fully, so she became one of the first crew changes, found a berth on *Orchidea* and carried on all the way back to Gibraltar.

At 1100 on 2 March, the 32 yachts taking part in the third leg left St Lucia bound for Panama 1140 miles away. In perfect weather, with 20 to 25 knots of NE wind, the first yacht to cross the line was *Soolo*, followed closely by *Elan Adventurer*, *Locura* and *Who Dares Wins*. The fleet set off briskly towards a mark which had been set close inshore off the capital Castries in order to give St Lucian spectators the unique opportunity to watch the international fleet in action. They were not to be disappointed. An exciting fight developed at the front of the fleet where *Cacadu* set a spinnaker and started gaining on the rest of the fleet. *Gilma Express* managed to catch up with *Cacadu* and beat them to the mark by half a boat length. These two were followed in quick succession by *Gulliver*, *Locura*, *Who Dares Wins*, *Dafne*, *Orchidea* and *Elan Adventurer*. The four and a half miles to the mark were covered in just over 30 minutes by the fastest yachts. Because of the gusty wind conditions, most skippers decided against using spinnakers, with the exception of *Dafne*, whose gamble paid off as the smaller Italian yacht managed to catch up with the leaders. There was a nailbiting moment as *Dafne* was on the point of broaching right in front of the Committee vessel. However, quick reaction by Nicola Borsó's crew averted disaster and 44 ft *Dafne* managed to round the mark one boat length ahead of the 53 ft *Orchidea*, who also put up their spinnaker. The newcomer *Locura*, who had joined the event in St Lucia, was well up at the front showing great potential for a boat with a shorthanded family crew.

Sails

With one ocean safely behind them, participants were able to assess their equipment more realistically. Many of those who had not sailed in the tropics before, or had not done a lot of offshore sailing, found some gaps in their preparations. The first items to come under scrutiny were the sail wardrobes. Although when questioned later, 20 skippers thought they had the right number of sails, some of them considered the composition of their wardrobe inadequate for the kind of voyage they were undertaking. Seven skippers thought they did not have enough sails, among them Mario Filipponi who commented, 'The sails on *Laura* are fine for the North Atlantic, but not in prolonged light wind conditions.' John Smith agreed, 'The number of sails on *Eye of Ra* is right but we could do with at least one more spinnaker.'

On the other hand, nine skippers thought they carried too many sails, such as Dick Wilson of *Kite*, 'We have too many sails to store, but not enough for racing.' Indeed, as Roger Gold pointed out, 'On this route there is little justification for carrying a trisail or storm jib. We are badly undercanvassed and a 150% genoa cut really low to the lifelines to increase windward performance would have been so much more useful.'

This was the old story of cruising yachts not having enough sails for light winds. There were indeed plenty of trisails and storm jibs, but not enough spinnakers. As it happened, the strongest recorded wind during EUROPA 92 were three relatively brief spells of 35 to 40 knot winds, and a longer spell of 30 knot winds later in the Red Sea. It wasn't long before even hardened cruisers admitted that a spinnaker would be a good idea, and in fact several yachts had spinnakers ordered and flown out. Several owners of yachts in the Cruising Division spoke of their frustration at seeing themselves regularly outpaced by even the smaller yachts in the Racing Division. In the frequently encountered light weather

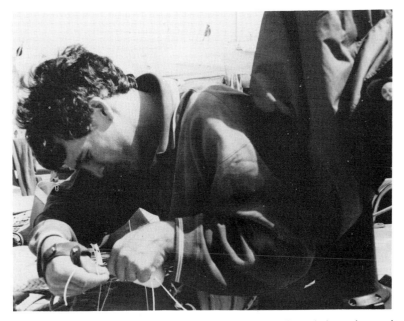

Chafe prevention was a continuous struggle to keep sails and sheets in good trim.

conditions, the heavily laden, often undercanvassed, cruising yachts were no match, and their only alternative was to turn on the engine.

Alan Spriggs, who only had a cruising chute and mizzen staysail on *Pennypincher*, admitted, 'We should really have a spinnaker as we always lose out in light airs.' It was a view shared by Wes Harris of *Scorpio* and Dutch Taylor of *Trillium*, both of whom were bedevilled by light winds on the way from San Diego to join the fleet in the Marquesas.

Altogether 27 yachts had at least one spinnaker on board. On 20 of these yachts all or some of the spinnakers were provided with dousers. However, not all skippers were convinced of the usefulness of the dousers. Richard Goord found that on *Oyinbo* the douser sock had holes chafed into it by its own douser line. Nicola Borsó was not too keen on dousers either and ended up using his spinnakers without. On *Who Dares Wins*, who carried three spinnakers, two of which had their own dousers, Ian Kennedy found that the douser buckets were too small and therefore difficult to use. He asked his sailmakers Williams & Lankaster to provide dousers with larger buckets and these worked much better.

During the Atlantic crossing, when several yachts used their spinnakers for days on end, some skippers were brought face to face with the problems that can result from long runs under spinnaker. As Julian Wilson was to remark later, '*Elan Adventurer* started off with three spinnakers and blew all of them out at some stage, not because of broaching but mainly due to halyards breaking. We lost two blocks at the masthead because of chafe at the sheaves and we also lost a spinnaker when the

A douser greatly simplifies spinnaker handling on short handed boats.

external U bolt sheared off. Twice the spinnakers went under the boat, but were rescued and stitched back into shape.'

These are the kind of reasons why some skippers preferred not to bother with a spinnaker. 'I believe we have a spinnaker', admitted Peter Bunting, 'but I cannot even remember when we last hoisted the thing.' Peter felt that on long passages a cruising boat was better served by sails which were easier to handle and more forgiving on the crew. 'Ideally, I would like to have twin headsails on some kind of furling gear, so that the two sails can be furled up together.'

Roller furling

Similar thoughts had led Pasquale de Gregorio to re-rig *Gilma Express* and equip her with two furling jibs. The one in front was a 150% light weather genoa, with a 120% genoa close behind it, the latter going to the $\frac{7}{8}$ position on mast, which is how *Gilma Express* used to be rigged before. When the wind went over 25 knots, Pasquale preferred to drop the spinnaker and use the two genoas poled out. 'In strong winds I like using the poled out genoas wing and wing, as they give a better average speed than the spinnaker, the boat is more stable and is easier to steer with the tiller.' However, Pasquale pointed out that occasionally he preferred using a spinnaker even in winds over 25 knots if there was too much swell and there was a danger of dipping the boom in the sea because of the rolling induced by the two poled out sails.

Another yacht with two jib furling gears was *Cacadu*, which had a 125% genoa on the forward furling gear and a smaller staysail on the inner one although, as Arne admitted, the boat was very seldom sailed as a cutter. 'Honestly, that staysail is useless. Having had two cutters already, I would never go for a cutter again. The same applies to ketches, of which I also have had my share, where a mizzen sail, if it is too small, is just as useless.'

In light winds, Arne used a light weight 150% genoa, hanked on a wire halyard which was used as a temporary forestay. The system worked very well, even when sailing on the wind, and when the sail was dropped it fell neatly on the foredeck.

As shown in Table 6, most yachts in the rally had jib roller furling gear of some kind, with six of the cutters having furling gears for both their foresails. Most gears performed well and this was reflected in the high ratings awarded for both performance and reliability. Indeed, there were few complaints about quality and remarkably few breakages. The electrically and hydraulically operated units performed just as well, with the exception of *Cheone*'s Reckmann jib furling gear which was put out of action by a burnt out Bosch electric motor.

Table 6 Jib furling gears

Make	Number	Performance	Reliability
Manual			
Hood	7	8.3	9.2
Profurl	5	9.6	8.4
Harken	5	9.6	9.6
Reckmann	3	9.7	9.7
Plastimo	1	10	10
Furlex	1	10	10
Goïot	1	7	8
Focmar	1	8	7
Elvstrom	1	8	8
Canglini	1	6	8
Electric			
Reckmann	1	10	5
Profurl	1	9	9
Hydraulic			
Rondal	1	10	10
Total:	29		

With the exception of the two Swans, all the others kept their furling gear mounted all the time. On *Who Dares Wins*, the Reckmann unit was installed only when the yacht was cruising between competitive legs. *Gulliver* also had a Reckmann gear, which was not installed if upwind work was expected during the forthcoming leg. Usually they started a leg without the furling gear and only installed it if needed. This was very easy to carry out as only the drum had to be removed.

Leo Birkby was one of those who thought he had too many sails on his 72 ft *Locura*. Sailing a large boat, often short handed, without any furling gear, he knew exactly what he wanted in the future: 'If I do it again, I would have roller furling for both jib and mainsail, and carry fewer sails.'

There were only five yachts equipped with mainsail furling gear and, in spite of their performance limitations, all owners were satisfied with them. Alan Spriggs had Hood Stoway system on both his main and mizzen, and rated the system 8 for performance and 7 for reliability, quickly adding 'when it works'. Apparently he had some problems with the ball bearings in the masthead assembly which caused the entire unit to jam. The bottom assembly also seized up once and Alan only managed to free it with a lot of WD40 spray and kettles of boiling water. Having been forced to sail once in *La Aventura* under full mainsail from halfway across the Bay of Biscay to Lisbon, after the bottom assembly had similarly jammed on my own Stoway, I could well sympathise with Alan.

The two jib furling gears ensured that *Gilma Express* sailed efficiently at all times.

Nevertheless, I am still a great believer in mainsail furling systems on cruising boats and the loss in performance is definitely made up by the comfort and safety of being able to reef the mainsail from the cockpit. These views were also shared by the other three owners of mainsail furling systems, the one on *Soolo* being perhaps the most ingenious as it combined a Furlex system with a fully battened mainsail. When upwind work was expected, Pekka Hyryläinen would use the fully battened mainsail made by North Sails, which he described as perfect. When sailing off the wind or short handed, he prefered to use the furling mainsail.

Fully battened mainsails

While the owners of furling mainsails generally agreed on their merits, there was far less consensus when fully battened mainsails came to be discussed. No other subject examined by the equipment survey was debated more vehemently and opinions were very much divided on the advantages of this kind of mainsail. Several skippers admitted that they had been talked into changing to fully battened mainsails, when a standard mainsail would have been much more suitable, especially on a voyage along the route taken by EUROPA 92.

Altogether 16 yachts had fully battened mainsails, while 15 had standard mainsails. The remaining five yachts had some sort of mainsail furling system, of which three were manual, one electric and one hydraulic. Among the yachts equipped with fully battened mainsails, the majority of skippers (10) were not convinced of their usefulness. One of the most outspoken critics was Brad Bernardo of *Brydie*: 'It might be OK for racing, but it's no good for our kind of sailing. There is a lot of chafe at the battens and although we have done everything to prevent chafe, such as putting on leather patches, it hasn't helped. I only went for a fully battened mainsail because three years ago that was the fashion and I was simply talked into it.'

John Rose was also talked into ordering a fully battened mainsail when he bought *Midnight Stroller II*. He had a lot of problems with the mainsail during the Atlantic crossing and broke several travellers. Even worse was the chafe, either by the carriers at the batten point, or the shackles on the batten holders, which eventually rubbed a hole through the aluminium mast. In St Lucia he reverted to his old mainsail.

Dafne had also been changed to a fully battened mainsail but Nicola Borsó found it very difficult to lower the sail when reefing. He believed that another system, with each batten having its own traveller, probably would have worked better. The system he had did not work with the wind aft, so the mainsail could not be reefed while the spinnaker was up and the yacht had to be brought into the wind to be able to lower the mainsail. Unfortunately the mainsail itself, made in Taiwan by Lee, was badly cut which made things even worse. Nor was Peter Bunting happy with his Doyle fully battened mainsail, which was so badly cut that he changed to a standard Hood mainsail. However, Dino Blancodini of *Twilight* considered his Doyle fully battened mainsail to be better than a similar sail made by Bianchi & Migliori. Dino preferred the Doyle mainsail as it had sliders both over and under each batten and worked better than the other system which only had one slider at each batten.

On *Locura* the fully battened mainsail was criticised for having too big a roach causing the sail to rub against the backstay, so large chafing patches had to be sewn on to protect it. Nor was Leo Birkby convinced about the merits of a fully battened mainsail. 'It is very hard to bring the sail down with this system. We have gone through two different systems and it still doesn't work. I feel that fully battened mainsails are simply not right for cruising boats.' Paul Skilowitz of *Bluewater* agreed whole-heartedly. 'We have serious problems with chafe when running down-wind as the batten pockets chafe against the aft lower shrouds, and although we have rod rigging, there is still too much chafe, which would not occur with a regular mainsail.' A similar verdict was given by Rick Palm of *Sojourner*. 'I wouldn't have a fully battened mainsail if I did this again. It chafes against the lower shrouds and we also broke several battens. Performance downwind is only minimally better.'

Enio Nardi was another skipper not happy with his fully battened mainsail, mainly because the travellers tended to jam when sailing before the wind. The quality of the battens was also poor, so he was pleased he had kept his old mainsail which was put back into use.

Although he liked the idea of a fully battened mainsail, John Smith was not entirely satisfied with his North mainsail, mainly because they had not worked out a system for keeping the battens in the pockets; they worked their way out and split their ends by hitting the mast.

Fortunately most of those who were not satisfied with their fully battened mainsail, had kept their old mainsails and so could use them instead. In spite of these criticisms, much of it caused by some sailmakers giving wrong advice to owners of cruising yachts, there were almost as many skippers who swore by the system, usually, although not always, among those who sailed their yachts more competitively. One of these was Walter Gollhofer, who had absolutely no doubts about the merits of the fully battened mainsail on *Amadé*. 'A fully battened mainsail with lazyjacks is ideal for reefing. The sail does not shake, its shape is always perfect and the performance is excellent.'

Another convert to the system was Arne Blässar, after he had sorted out his earlier difficulties. 'The problem is that most people do not use these sails properly, especially if there is no wind when the sail can slam terribly. In such conditions it is better to drop the sail altogether.' On *Cacadu*, the Harken system in use had individual travellers on each batten which allowed the mainsail to be reefed in any wind strength and on any point of sailing. However, Arne admitted that at the beginning he broke travellers as well as battens because the heavy sail was allowed to slam during calms. Arne commended the lazyjacks system for sail stowing, although he pointed out that usually the lazyjacks were mounted too high up the mast; on *Cacadu* he lowered them by mounting the blocks at one third of the height of the mast so that the lazyjacks were shorter, did not flog and the sail was easier to hoist and drop.

In fairness, it should be pointed out that just as owners have learned how to use their fully battened mainsails, so sailmakers and equipment manufacturers have also learned from their early mistakes. The systems in use now are superior in every respect to the earlier ones used on some of the yachts fitted out for the round the world rally.

Some of the above criticism was not always directed at the concept of a fully battened mainsail but at the sailmakers themselves. However, there was praise too, such as from Arne Blässar for the Finnish sailmakers WB who had done an excellent job on his sails, with not a single stitch gone in 20,000 miles of sailing. The eventual overall winner *Gulliver* started off with a full suit of sails by Diamond, but later switched to North Sails, whose Italian representative, Patrick Phelipon, flew out regularly with bags of sails to various locations along the route, sailing some of the legs and making sure that *Gulliver*'s sails were always in perfect trim. Similarly, John Conser of Tradewind Sails flew out from California to join *Locura* and also to admire the set of the two new spinnakers he had delivered personally. Among the less happy skippers was Jake McCullogh whose new cruising chute lasted for only a few minutes in 6 knots of wind before it ripped right across. 'We should have bought better quality sails, in other words we should have renewed our Hood sails rather than order them from a second class sailmaker in Emsworth, who was not prepared to back up his product.'

The sustained rhythm of the rally, the miles covered and the continuous exposure of the sails to the sun shortened the lives of most sails considerably. Towards the end of the event, particularly in the Red Sea when the yachts were experiencing some of the strongest winds of the entire rally, blown out mainsails and genoas were the order of the day. All those who had set off on the rally with used sails and no spares were keeping their fingers crossed praying that their sails would bring them back safely to the Mediterranean. Pekka Hyryläinen found that the Kevlar furling genoa he had ordered for *Soolo* could not stand up to the rigours of such a voyage and after less than one year in use it had reached the stage where it could be repaired no longer. 'The shape is perfect, but another time I would stay with Dacron.'

Some of the above examples highlight the advantage of dealing with one sailmaker on a voyage of this kind, as one establishes a working relationship with the same sail loft back home, so it is possible to order new sails from anywhere in the world and have them airfreighted wherever one happens to be at the time.

One yacht which sailed around the world with virtually one set of sails was *Oingo Boingo*, which eventually won Class II in the Racing Division. The performance of the Swiss yacht was the more remarkable as their sails had to be repaired continuously both at sea and in port. When *Oingo Boingo* arrived in Suez after having beaten against the wind for the entire length of the Red Sea, Fabienne and Roland Schlachter had to load several sail bags into an old taxi and drive 300 km to Alexandria to the only sailmaker in Egypt capable of repairing their sails. Earlier in the rally, at the start of the leg from Panama to Galapagos, a conversation was overheard over the VHF radio when *Oingo Boingo*'s crew was questioned by *Elan Adventurer* if it was indeed them who had just blown out a spinnaker. It was, and what made it worse was that it was the one spinnaker which *Oingo Boingo* had borrowed from *Elan Adventurer* to help them do better in the light winds expected on the leg to the Galapagos and which had lasted barely five minutes! Fortunately a delayed parcel bringing *Oingo Boingo*'s two new spinnakers to Panama, which arrived there one day after the start, was intercepted by George Day of *Clover*, who delivered the sails to the Galapagos. As Roland exclaimed with a bitter-sweet smile at the end of the rally in Gibraltar, 'The crew of *Oingo Boingo* virtually stitched their way around the world to ensure their victory in Class II!'

4
THE CARIBBEAN SEA

Leg 3: St Lucia to Panama

After a perfect start in St Lucia, excellent winds and little swell ensured exhilarating passages across the Caribbean Sea for all yachts, everyone clocking fast times to Panama. In order to avoid an area off the Colombian coast, where small boats had been molested in the past, a hypothetical mark was set 100 miles off the Guajira peninsula, which participants had to leave to port. No incidents were reported, although several yachts saw US vessels and aircraft patrolling the area in the war against drug traffic. They all seemed to be aware of the presence of the EUROPA 92 fleet as the US, Venezuelan and Colombian authorities had all been informed of the rally's route. *Jakes Fantasia* was intercepted by a US warship and, after having ascertained that it was a British yacht taking part in the round the world rally, the captain decided that there was no need to board. However, Jake McCullogh insisted that he would be happy to be boarded provided the boarding party included a specialist who could repair his broken generator. An armed boarding party, including two mechanics, was duly dispatched by the warship, who not only fixed Jake's faulty generator, but also delivered a drum of engine oil as well as other goodies. Their kindness was repaid with a gift of EUROPA 92 T-shirts, which were being carried on board *Jakes Fantasia* for the organisers.

In Panama the traffic controllers in Cristobal were treated to some exciting finishes as the EUROPA 92 yachts sailed across the finishing line, which was between the breakwaters marking the Atlantic end of the Panama Canal. The first to finish only $5\frac{1}{2}$ days after the start in St Lucia was *Gilma Express*, closely followed by *Gulliver*, both yachts averaging over 9 knots on the 1200 miles run. There were close finishes between several other yachts, *Cacadu* and *Locura* (8 minutes), *Dafne* and *Sojourner* (50 seconds) and *Twilight* and *Jolly Joker* (1 minute). In a questionnaire completed by the skippers at the end of the rally, the leg from St Lucia to Panama was voted by the majority as the best sailing leg of the entire event.

A champagne reception was awaiting *Gilma Express* and *Gulliver* on the newly constructed dock at the Panama Canal Yacht Club in Cristobal, where the Governor of Colón, Sr José Huc, personally welcomed the early arrivals. The first two leaders were followed in quick succession by *Orchidea* and *Who Dares Wins*. After the champagne ran out on the dock, Bill Speed, the club manager and self-proclaimed master of ceremonies, ordered the bar to stay open all night and serve free beer to EUROPA participants, a gesture which set the scene for the entire stay in Panama. The following Sunday the yacht club arranged a grand fiesta for participants, which started with folk dances and sampling of local dishes, followed by a dinner, to which various authorities had been invited.

The steady trade winds meant that all boats reached Panama within a short period of time and the Canal transits could start straightaway. The Gulf crisis had forced many ships normally sailing from the Far East to Europe via Suez to reroute and this had resulted in a record number of ships waiting to transit. In spite of working to full capacity, the Panama Canal Authority kept its promise to process the EUROPA fleet as quickly as possible, which meant that most yachts passed through the Canal the day after their arrival. Everything was done to ease this operation, with boats being cleared and admeasured within minutes of their arrival. The Director of Marine Operations, Capt George Hull, personally supervised the smooth running of the operation, as a result of which the most complex stage of the rally was accomplished with amazing efficiency.

Canal transit

The first batch of ten yachts transited the Canal in one group on Saturday 9 March, followed by a second group of 14 yachts on Monday. This was the largest number of yachts that had ever been locked through together in one operation. The yachts were rafted in groups of two or three and so only four long lines were needed per group which eased the process. As there was such a large number of yachts transiting together, it was not necessary to share the locks with a large vessel, as is normal practice, and this meant less turbulence in the locks. The operation passed off quickly and by nightfall all yachts were safely moored on the Pacific side at the Balboa Yacht Club.

A local Steering Committee chaired by Jaime Arias, Commodore of the Club de Vela de Panama, had drawn up an ambitious programme of social events, which started with a special presentation at the Municipal Council, whose members had passed an official resolution declaring all EUROPA 92 participants guests of honour of the City of Panama. A hand written parchment proclaiming this was handed over to the organisers during a special ceremony held in the magnificent municipal chambers and attended by the skippers of most EUROPA yachts. The Acting Mayor of Panama City, Sr Manuel Burgos, was present at all important functions, including a meeting with President Endara of Panama, which ensured support for the event at the highest level. All participants were issued by the Mayor of Panama with special ID passes, which allowed

A record number of 14 boats transit together at Miraflores Lock on their way to the Pacific.

them to go anywhere and to request help from any authority. The first to benefit from this was Race Officer Tom Williams, when he was stopped by the police for speeding on his way to meet the first boats in Cristobal!

On the evening when all yachts had reached the Pacific Ocean, the Panama Institute of Tourism invited everyone to a welcome dinner and display of traditional Panamanian dances and dresses. The prize giving dinner on Friday, 15 March was sponsored by the Panama branch of DHL, while many other Panamanian companies donated trophies and prizes to the winners of the previous leg. The wealth of prizes, mostly dinners at restaurants, meant that every single participating yacht received at least one prize. In the Racing Division, *Gulliver* and *Soolo* won their respective classes, while *Cheone* won the overall prize in the Cruising Division, the old lady's performance taking everyone by surprise, including her proud owner.

There were even prizes for the members of the newly created Benders Club, whose founding members included Peter Bunting of *Gulkarna*, whose feathering propeller got jammed in forward gear while the yacht was coming in to dock at the yacht club in Cristobal, so carrying out ahead of schedule the planned demolition of an old wooden dock. John Rose joined the club in a bending incident while mooring *Midnight Stroller* in Balboa, when his lifelines got entangled with the rigging of a small local boat, which was left without a mast as a result. A reluctant member of the same club was Dave Sutherland, whose *Tais* got its stanchions bent while rafting up alongside *Eye of Ra*. The fourth recipient of a consolation prize was Jake McCullogh, whose *Jakes Fantasia* got into trouble in the last lock while transiting the Canal and sustained some damage at the stern.

With so much bad luck at work, it was decided that fate should decide the winner of the most generous prize of the evening, a Yamaha 4 hp outboard engine donated by Econopartes SA. The Managing Director, James Reed, pulled the winning number out of a hat. The fortunate winner was yacht number 48, *Sojourner*, whose owner Rick Palm had just bought a new inflatable in St Lucia and the unexpected gift of an outboard engine could not have been more fortuitous.

One week in Panama proved to be much too short for everything on offer, nevertheless most participants managed to join some of the tours, while others went as far as chartering small planes to visit the San Blas islands. The success of the Panama stopover was mainly due to the efforts of Julie and Jaime Arias, who had managed to transmit their enthusiasm for the event to the highest authorities. They were ably assisted by Jane McColl, whose commitment to the event persuaded her to join *Midnight Stroller* initially for the leg to the Galapagos. Nicknamed Panama Jane, she stayed with EUROPA all the way to Gibraltar, and at the end of the rally planned to return home and work on improving yachting facilities in Panama.

Sailing instrumentation

Somebody once asked me what was the strongest wind I had measured during my first round the world voyage, '30 knots', I replied, as that was all my handheld plastic anemometer would register before it jammed. On my present *La Aventura*, an integrated Brookes & Gatehouse Hydra 330, interfaced with a Horizon GPS as well as a Helmstar autopilot, allows us to do things we would never have dreamt of doing before, such as sailing under spinnaker at night or being able to monitor bearing, distance and VMG to the next waypoint on the GPS display unit in the cockpit without leaving the helm.

My own case is a good example of the great changes which have occurred on cruising boats in recent years and this was more than obvious on the other 35 yachts taking part in the round the world rally. With one exception, they all had electronic wind instruments – and a whole lot more beside.

Every one of the 36 skippers was asked to describe in detail any problems encountered with their instrumentation and also to rate it for both performance and reliability. As shown in Table 7, the most satisfied customers were the few who had equipped their yachts with Datamarine products. Interestingly, this was also the finding of a similar survey I had conducted more than a decade earlier among another batch of yachts sailing around the world. Reading that earlier survey had made Brad Bernardo of *Brydie* contact Datamarine and ask them what instrumentation they would recommend for the world voyage he was preparing for. After two years of use, he rated his instruments a straight 10.

The best represented make, however, was Brookes & Gatehouse, which was installed on 15 yachts. Although most of the Brookes & Gatehouse customers were generally happy with their equipment, there were some aspects that attracted critical remarks. The biggest culprit appeared to be the visual display units, especially on the Hydra 330 and Helmstar autopilot, whose readings started fading after a while, necessitating the replacement of the entire unit. According to the manufacturers, this was caused by an early design malfunction which has now been corrected. As the faulty units on *Pennypincher*, *Wachibou*, *Eye of Ra* and *La Aventura* were under guarantee, they were replaced promptly and free of charge. Generally, the Brookes & Gatehouse aftersales service attracted praise from the end users and it is indeed the forte of this company which prides itself on giving a three year worldwide guarantee on most of its equipment. Brookes & Gatehouse also sent out an engineer to test and service all B&G equipment before the start of the rally in Gibraltar, as they do every year in Las Palmas de Gran Canaria for the participants in the ARC.

The best rated logs and speedometers were the Brookes & Gatehouse Hercules 190 and Harrier 6 models. The owners of some of the other models were not so unanimous in the praise, mainly those whose units

A Brookes & Gatehouse engineer services the equipment on *La Aventura*.

Table 7 Instruments

Make	Log			Speedo			Depth			Wind			Integrated		
	No	Perf	Rel	No	Perf	Rel	No	Perf	Rel	No	Perf	Rel	No	Perf	Rel
B&G Hornet 4	6	6.8	6.2	6	6.5	5.7	4	9	9	6	7.8	7.7	4	7.7	7.7
B&G Hydra 330	4	8.7	7.5	4	8.7	7.5	4	9.5	9.2	4	8	7	4	9	7.5
B&G Hercules 190	2	10	10	2	10	10	2	5	5	2	10	9	2	10	10
B&G Hercules 690	2	6.5	6.5	2	8.7	8.7	2	10	10	2	10	10	2	9.5	10
B&G Harrier 6	1	10	10	1	10	10							1	8	8
Datamarine	5	8.4	10	5	9.6	10	5	10	10	4	10	10	2	10	10
VDO	4	8.7	8.7	4	8.7	8.7	5	9.2	9.2	4	9.5	9.5	2	5	5
Navico	3	4.7	6.7	3	4.7	6.7	3	3.7	4.3	2	6	5			
Autohelm	3	9	9	3	9.3	9.3	3	9.7	9.7	3	9.7	9.7	2	9.5	9.5
NKE	2	4	5	2	4	5	2	7.5	6	2	8.5	9	2	5	5
Horizon	1	3	8	1	3	8	1	3	8	1	10	8			
Elcos	1	8	8	1	8	8	1	8	8	1	8	8			
Cygnet	1	8	8	1	8	8	1	10	10	1	10	10			
Danavigate	1	9	9	1	9	9	1	9	9						
Navsounder							1	10	10						
Seafarer							1	9	10						
Stowe							1	7	10						
Total:	36			36			37			32			21		

Perf = performance
Rel = reliability

had given almost as much trouble as faulty VDUs. In all cases, the problems were caused by the underwater units, whether the sonic type or the older paddle-wheel impellers. On *Oyinbo*, Richard Goord tried to overcome this by providing his Hercules 190 with twin mechanical impellers activated by a gravity switch. If one of the impellers got fouled or jammed, it was possible to switch over manually to the other one. Also, as the through-hull fittings could be shut off by a valve, the impeller could be cleared without letting any water in. While on *Oyinbo* the system worked perfectly, a twin impeller installation on *Octopus* did not prove to be much of an advantage, as both had seized up and the speedometer had been out of action for a while when I interviewed them in Fiji. As pointed out later, this could have been caused by some interaction with the aluminium hull.

Easy access to a fouled impeller is indeed of utmost importance as I know from my own experience on *La Aventura*, where the paddle-wheel impeller for the log and speedometer had been installed in a most inaccessible part of the bilge, the engineer who did the installation obviously not foreseeing the problems this could cause in the future when one would have to unpack a crammed locker before being able to extract and clear the fouled impeller. John Papp of *Ambler* explained that he had learned to overcome the problem of a jammed impeller by backing up under power when leaving so as to get the impeller going. 'It may look strange to onlookers, but it works!'

However, it was not just the mechanical type impellers which gave trouble. On *Amadé*, the electronic log transducer proved to be incompatible with the aluminium hull, so it had to be replaced with a mechanical impeller. Problems with the sonic transducer, for the Hornet 4 set on *Locura*, made Leo Birkby change to a paddle-wheel type impeller, a solution also adopted on *Gulliver*, which was equipped with a Hercules 690 system. Both Leo Birkby and Alessandro Mosconi complained about the difficulty of calibrating the sonic speedometer, another reason why they were happy to see it go.

Dino Blancodini had opted for the easiest solution. 'I no longer use my VDO log and speedometer on *Twilight* as I find the GPS much more accurate and reliable.' This could well become a solution adopted by many more in the future. What a pity that the increasingly popular GPS cannot indicate depth too, so as to do away with sounders as well. It would be a solution undoubtedly favoured by Roger Gold. 'My Horizon depth sounder is reliably bad. When it gets out of range it starts giving random figures and has almost caused me several heart attacks.'

Some wind instruments were also criticised for giving inaccurate readings, although in some cases this was due to air turbulence at the top of the mast or may have been caused by faulty installation. Typically, Pasquale de Gregorio had his own solution to this problem too. 'I have never used wind instruments in my entire sailing life. All I have is a

Windex on top of the mast with a light trained on it. It beats any instrument and never fails.' This is just the kind of statement one would expect from someone who sails his 53 ft yacht like a dinghy. The one instrument which Pasquale used on his boat, but was not too happy with, was his VDO depth sounder whose transducer had been installed inside the hull and therefore could not give readings to its rated depth.

Fluxgate compasses

Nearly half the boats had at least one fluxgate compass on board, with *Midnight Stroller* having three different makes. Although most performed satisfactorily, there were a few common problems such as the one pointed out by Alan Spriggs. 'The greatest disadvantage of this type of compass is that it cannot be calibrated or swung, so if the compass is giving a wrong reading, one has to learn to live with it and, if it is used for the autopilot, to set the pilot to steer a compensated course.' This problem was also encountered on both *La Aventura* and *Who Dares Wins*, similarly equipped with B&G Halcyon compasses. Although the *Pennypincher* solution may be acceptable for autopilot settings, when accuracy may not be of such importance, Ian Kennedy found that he could not always sail *Who Dares Wins* efficiently as his fluxgate compass consistently gave false wind instrument readings. To overcome the problem, on *La Aventura* we ended up rotating the compass in its mounting trying to match it to the heading given by the main magnetic compass.

Table 8   Fluxgate compasses

Make	Number	Performance	Reliability
B&G Halcyon	4	8.7	7.5
NKE II	2	6.5	9
Autohelm	2	10	10
Datamarine	1	10	10
Cetrek	1	10	10
VDO	1	10	10
Horizon	1	8	8
Navico	1	8	8
Robertson	1	8	8
KVH	1	4	4
Total:	15		

Integrated systems

Twenty one yachts were equipped with fully integrated systems with the Brookes & Gatehouse Hercules 190 and Datamarine units scoring the highest ratings. Most of the Brookes & Gatehouse models were rated high, four of the Hercules models attracting the highest ratings and some of the Hornets the lowest. The two Autohelm units were also rated high by their users.

The lowest ratings were given to the NKE and VDO units. The NKE system on *Amadé* had given a lot of trouble and although the aftersales service had been excellent, Walter Gollhofer was unhappy with the system itself. This was not the opinion of Arne Blässar who had a similar system on *Cacadu*, which he was happy with in spite of such shortcomings as the wind speed indicator occasionally giving erratic readings, or the depth sounder not working when going astern or sailing over soft mud.

Because of the relative newness of GPS, only seven yachts had their instruments interfaced with the GPS and an additional two with their Transit satnav. Autopilots were interfaced with the GPS on two yachts only, two more having their Transit interfaced with the autopilot and three their Loran as well. Finally, there was only one radar interfaced with the GPS, although several skippers expressed the intention to have their GPS interfaced with more of their equipment on their return. *Midnight Stroller* possessed one of the most complete systems, the chart plotter being interfaced with the GPS and autopilot, as well as with all three dedicated fluxgate compasses.

John Rose at *Midnight Stroller's* fully equipped navigation station.

Walter Gollhofer was one of the skippers who regretted not having had his instruments interfaced with the GPS and autopilot. Nearly losing *Amadé* on a reef in Tonga, he felt that the near disaster could have been averted had he been able to check the cross-track error and bearing to the next waypoint from the helm, as he was on watch alone in the cockpit when the yacht ran into trouble. Although he had tried to have the system interfaced before leaving, apparently this could not be done because his Autohelm 7000 autopilot did not have an interface port for the NMEA 0183.

Richard Goord was of a different opinion and on *Oyinbo* only the instruments were interfaced with the GPS, not the automatic pilot. 'I don't believe in having your autopilot interfaced with the GPS because if you programme your course to the next waypoint you can drive your ship on to the land. It is known to have happened.'

One of the main attractions of an integrated system is that it allows locating the display units in the most convenient place. However, several skippers complained about the location of their VDUs, which had been chosen by the boat builders or previous owners. On *Locura*, all the VDUs had been installed at the navigation station with only boat speed, depth and wind angle in the cockpit, which Leo Birkby found totally unsatisfactory, as it did not allow the boat to be sailed to its full potential. On the other hand, Julian Wilson of *Elan Adventurer* would have preferred some of the units displayed in the cockpit, such as log, speed and wind direction, to also have repeaters at the navigation station, enabling the navigator, or the skipper when off watch, to know what was going on outside.

Radar

A high number of yachts (31) were equipped with radar, some of which had been acquired especially for the rally. The most popular make, Furuno, attracted the highest average ratings for the 15 units, with only one dissatisfied customer, Richard Goord, who had thought that Furuno

Table 9   Radars

Make	Number	Performance	Reliability
Furuno	15	9.1	8.9
Raytheon	10	8.3	8.8
Koden	3	8	9.7
Goldstar	1	7	10
OKI	1	9	9
Vigil	1	5	6
Total:	31		

was represented everywhere in the world only to find that this did not include Tahiti. The ten Raytheon units were rated almost as high.

With only eight of the 31 yachts equipped with radar having a mizzen mast, the positioning of the scanner caused some difficulties. On 13 sloops, the scanner was mounted on the mast, usually in front of the lower spreaders. On the remaining ten sloops, the scanner was mounted on a stern post, a solution increasingly favoured on larger yachts as the post can also be used to carry antennae for the GPS, Inmarsat-C as well as spare VHF or SSB whip aerials. A separate stern post also avoids the risk of putting all this equipment out of action should the mast itself be lost.

However, not everyone was completely satisfied with having the radar scanner mounted on a post, and, as Giovanna Caprini observed, 'The performance and range are badly affected by the fact that the scanner is so low. On the other hand, as we only use our radar when close to a landfall, the range does not make such a big difference.' Leo Birkby, whose scanner was mounted on *Locura*'s mizzen mast, would have preferred to have it on a post where it would have been more accessible for servicing. Once, when his radar broke down and the fault was traced to the scanner, the engineer had to be hoisted up the mizzen mast several times.

Locura's scanner was the only open type protected by a cage and, in spite of its owner's misgivings about its location, it seemed to work very well. On the other hand, Pekka Hyryläinen, whose scanner was mounted just in front of the lower spreaders, contended that this was the best place for a radar scanner on a smaller sloop such as *Soolo*, as it provided a good range and the weight aloft was not excessive.

Only on three boats was the radar switched on all the time, while on an additional three it was always switched on at night. On the remaining 25 yachts the radar was used only in the approaches to a landfall, in coastal navigation or when sailing through known shipping lanes.

The positioning of the radar itself was commented upon by Roger Gold, who stressed the advantage of the radar screen being visible from the helm, which can be a great help on a yacht with a short handed crew. For similar reasons, Rick Palm positioned *Sojourner*'s radar so that the person watching it could talk to the helmsman at the same time.

5

ENCHANTED ISLANDS

Leg 4: Panama to Galapagos

The round the world rally broke new ground in almost every port of call, but nowhere more so than in Panama where there had never been an international sailing event of any description before. In order to give the people of Panama City the opportunity to watch the start of the fourth leg, it was scheduled for Sunday afternoon when many Panamanians take a stroll along the esplanade which fronts the city. The start was planned to coincide with high water so that the line could be set close inshore, and traffic was closed on the wide Avenida Balboa so the many spectators could watch without disturbance.

A good northerly wind contributed to a perfect start, the line being crossed first by *Jolly Joker*, followed closely by *Rockhopper*. The first mark was a yellow ship at anchor, which had to be left to starboard, but this was still not big enough to be seen by *Dafne*, who missed it and therefore received a time penalty of 3 hours. The next mark was set close inshore to give a perfect view to the VIP stand, *Amadé* leading the fleet around this gybing mark. As they rounded the mark, some of the boats set their spinnakers and the gap between the larger and smaller boats started widening. The Committee vessel, a twin-engined 45 ft sports fisherman, took up the chase, the owner refusing to believe that sailing boats could sail so fast. At the front *Gulliver* was leading, doing 14 knots with *Locura* in hot pursuit, having set their second spinnaker on their mizzen mast and appearing to be gaining ground. *Cacadu*, *Amadé* and *Who Dares Wins* followed closely.

In Panama, the fleet had been joined by two more yachts. *Clover*, a Mason 44, was taking George Day, former editor of *Cruising World* and *Sailing World* magazines, on a three year sabbatical cruise with his wife Rose and two sons. Also joining the event for the section to French Polynesia were former ARC participants Jennifer and John Joslin on the Oyster 435 *Dancing Wave*.

In the last few days before the start there had been lengthy discussions among participants as to which route to choose to the Galapagos. Some opted for the rhumb line, which was the shortest, while *Gulliver* chose a longer more southerly route in the hope of finding better winds. Alessandro Mosconi's gamble paid off and the Swan 59 had wind for most of the way including some thunderstorms which gave them an additional boost. All these factors helped *Gulliver* cover the 850 miles to the Galapagos in an excellent $4\frac{1}{2}$ days. The crew reported that they had three sail trimmers working flat out all the time to keep the boat moving.

Although everyone was trying hard to reach the Galapagos Islands as quickly as possible, to join the various excursions which had been booked on local boats, all the yachts in the Racing Division resisted the temptation to motor, most managing to cover the distance in very good times. They were also helped by a very strong current, a branch of the South Equatorial Current, which at times hurried the fleet along at 4 knots. After the good breeze at the start, the winds petered out during the first night and for the rest of the passage, they were mostly from the NE at between 5 and 10 knots.

Under such conditions, it is no wonder that there were no purists in the Cruising Division, where everyone used the engine for at least some of the time so as to reach Puerto Ayora by the deadline of 26 March. The only exception was *Jolly Joker* who caused the organisers some anxious moments as she became overdue. A general alert was put out by the Ecuadorian Navy to all vessels in the Galapagos area. Within minutes of the call being broadcast, an excursion vessel reported sighting a yacht south of Santa Cruz Island and indeed a few hours later the Hungarian yacht sailed in and joined the rest of the fleet at anchor off Puerto Ayora.

Academy Bay had never been so crowded with yachts in the entire history of the Galapagos and both the authorities and local population gave the EUROPA sailors an enthusiastic welcome. The warmest welcome came from the Port Captain, Lieutenant Carlos Rhor, who did his utmost to make the fleet's stay as pleasant as possible. Two sailors, Guerrero and Guacho, with a large inflatable boat from the Naval Base, were detailed to assist Andrew Bishop in the reception of the yachts. All facilities at the base were put at our disposal, so that arriving yachts could be received by Andrew's indefatigable crew around the clock.

The Galapagos Islands have been declared a National Park by the Ecuadorian government and, in order to protect the unique flora and fauna, access to the islands is strictly controlled. Only a very few yachts are given a permit each year and these can only cruise with an official guide on board. It took two years of negotiations with the help of the Naval Attaché at the Ecuadorian Embassy in London to secure a permit for the 38 yachts to stay more than the maximum 72 hours stopover usually allowed to yachts considered to be making an emergency stop. The EUROPA 92 fleet were finally granted permission for a 15 day stay on condition that all yachts remain in Academy Bay, on Santa Cruz Island, and all excursions to the other islands would be done on local boats. Even these local excursions are strictly controlled and only two boats a day are allowed to visit some of the islands whose wildlife is considered more at risk. Having been warned that the few boats may all be booked when we got there, arrangements were made one year in advance to reserve several boats during the period when the EUROPA fleet was going to be in Puerto Ayora. With the help of Fernando and Jaime Ortiz, two enthusiastic brothers belonging to one of the oldest resident families in Puerto Ayora, the arrangements worked perfectly and every participant managed to go on all the excursions they had requested.

In Darwin's footsteps

Most participants arrived in high spirits, obviously looking forward to their stay in the Galapagos, and the first excursion got underway even before all the yachts had arrived. Tom Williams, our race officer from Florida, was in charge of organising the excursions; this was a difficult job as most excursions started at the crack of dawn and it was not easy getting the right people on to the right boats at that hour of the day. There were countless cancellations and last minute changes, but in the end everyone appeared to get what they expected and left the Galapagos having gained at least a glimpse of the unique wildlife and scenery. Most participants chose to go on the various day excursions to the surrounding islands, which meant that they could return to their own bunks every night. A few people took a three day excursion, while the best deal proved to be the seven day excursion which called at all the remote islands of the archipelago, less frequented and much richer in wildlife than those nearer the populated islands.

Without fail, the highlight of every trip was the opportunity to swim with a group of sea lions, from a family of six at the Devil's Crown reef near Floreana, to a school of well over forty playful sea lions at Bartholomew Island. During a swim at Floreana, divers were shocked to see a small group of killer whales appear from the depths. Within seconds the sea lions had disappeared, as did the divers, who quickly retreated to the safety of their boat.

Diving with sharks at Caleta Tortuga on Santa Cruz was an unexpected excitement enjoyed by some, but an infinitely less dangerous pastime than the encounter with the real thing in mid-ocean which happened to *Pennypincher* on the passage from Panama. Just as they had crossed the equator and King Neptune had finished baptising an uninitiated member of the crew by dipping her into the ocean from the end of the boom, a dozen large sharks cruised by looking for their next dinner.

Also on the passage to the Galapagos, dinner arrived unexpectedly for the crew of *Tais* when *Octopus* reported on the daily radio net that their engine had stopped working and any boats in the vicinity were invited to help unload the rapidly defrosting freezer. Forced willy-nilly into the Racing Division, *Octopus* sailed on to Puerto Ayora where they managed to borrow *Oingo Boingo*'s spare starter motor for the next leg to the Marquesas. For the crew of *Ambler* the rich fauna of the area became too real when a large whale decided to scratch its back on their keel, luckily without damage. Soon afterwards, the crew noticed an unfortunate turtle entangled in the remains of a fishing net. John Papp turned the boat around, caught up with the poor creature and managed to cut it loose. For their noble deed they were earmarked for a prize at the presentation party in Puerto Ayora, which unfortunately was overlooked in the hubbub of a rather chaotic evening.

A rather more worrying encounter at sea involved *Pennypincher*. While sailing along at night, the crew on watch saw that they were being overtaken by a larger boat under power and not showing the correct lights. A collision with *Twilight*, whose watchkeeper failed to take avoiding action, was averted at the last moment, but Alan Spriggs felt strongly enough about the incident to lodge an official protest. This was upheld by the rally committee who investigated the matter and decided to disqualify *Twilight* for the Panama to Galapagos leg for infringing three basic rules: not showing the correct lights while motoring, not taking appropriate action as the overtaking vessel to avoid a collision, and failing to keep a proper lookout.

The stay in Puerto Ayora proved to be much more enjoyable than had been expected, undoubtedly helped by the exchange rate of the Ecuadorian sucre, which allowed everyone to have a good meal ashore for about three to four dollars. In spite of their remoteness, the Galapagos took everyone by surprise due to the availability of fresh fruit and vegetables, good drinking water from the newly installed desalination plant, an unexpected supply of diesel fuel and even a spare generator impeller for *Midnight Stroller*'s generator. The threatened dearth of supplies was nowhere as bad as predicted, and a local farmer arrived with an excellent supply of fruit and vegetables on the eve of the start selling large stems of bananas for $1.50 and juicy oranges for five cents a piece. The Naval Base kept its promise and refuelled all EUROPA 92 yachts, while a huge tank sent to the public quay by the desalination plant allowed everyone to replenish their water supplies for the long haul to the Marquesas. The only thing that could not be arranged by our obliging hosts was a telephone line to the outside world, as the Galapagos were not yet connected to the international telephone system. Participants had to accept the fact that for nearly two weeks they could not call their families or businesses, but in the laid back atmosphere of Puerto Ayora instant communications quickly lost their appeal.

There was a lot of entertainment ashore and the three local discos could hardly keep up with the unexpected influx of energetic sailors supplemented by a crowd of teenyboppers on Easter vacation from mainland Ecuador. On the last Saturday, the owners of Henry's Bar, La Panga Disco and Garapacha Restaurant closed the main street and put on a

Stacey and Scott Birkby, the youngest participants in the rally, check the mail at Post Office Bay on Floreana Island in the Galapagos.

huge outdoor farewell party, which only finished in the early hours of Easter Sunday. This followed hot on the heels of a well attended beach party in Tortuga Bay, where a EUROPA 92 team had taken on the Naval Base sailors in a tug-of-war competition, the latter winning the contest with a little help from their friends, who jumped in at the critical moment to tilt the balance in favour of the Armada de Ecuador. A special sundowner party for all EUROPA 92 participants put on by the Casablanca restaurant with a selection of cocktails from mainland Ecuador brought to an end an unforgettable stay in the Enchanted Islands.

Automatic pilots

Light winds on the way to the Galapagos and the deadline in Puerto Ayora persuaded many participants to turn on their engines, and autopilots were used to the full. Later, this subject was discussed with the skippers in conjunction with windvane selfsteering gears to find out how much these long distance sailors depended on them, under what conditions they were used and also how the various makes performed.

Automatic pilots proved to be one of the most popular pieces of equipment, with every yacht having one and five yachts having a second pilot as a backup. Added to the 41 pilots were 12 windvanes, which could almost lead one to believe that steering by hand on these world-girdling yachts was a rarity. This was hardly the case and on an average autopilots were used 41% of the time. This figure is perhaps misleading, as ten skippers pointed out that on their yachts the autopilot was never used, either because they were racing, or, such as on *Lady Samantha*, the crew were taking an offshore navigation course and were supposed to learn to handle the boat. Neither were the crew allowed to leave the steering to the autopilot on *Rockhopper*, whose skipper felt that it was better for the crew to steer by hand so that they would not lose their concentration. In contrast, on *Oyinbo*, 'We turn the pilot on at the start of a leg and turn it off at the finishing line.' Richard Goord was very fond of his Sigatron autopilot, which he considered to be the best piece of equipment on his yacht. He explained the background to these pilots manufactured by Mr Segers, a meticulous Dutch engineer, who only makes about 15 units a year and installs every one personally on board. On *Oyinbo*, the pilot was driven hydraulically directly off the propeller shaft so its energy requirements were provided by the movement of the yacht, which had a freewheeling propeller shaft. If the boat speed fell below 3.5 knots, the pilot switched automatically to its electric motor. Thus there was no drain on the batteries except when sailing below the cutoff speed, when the engine was likely to be turned on anyway.

Most skippers made the point that they would usually put on the autopilot when motoring, even if they didn't use it when sailing. On *Scorpio*, the engine was turned on when the speed fell under 3 knots and with it, the autopilot. *Scorpio* was one of the yachts which used the automatic pilot in conjunction with a windvane, reverting to one or the other depending on wind and sailing conditions.

Every skipper was asked to indicate the percentage of time when the boat was steered by either the autopilot or windvane. On ten yachts the steering was always done by hand, with neither pilot nor windvane ever being used. However, even on yachts where the pilot was never used during competitive legs or when sailing, it was used to steer the boat when motoring. By working out the average of the percentages indicated by the skippers of the 26 yachts on which the autopilot or windvane were used to steer the boat at times, a figure of 48% was arrived at. This is a fairly correct reflection of the true state of affairs as most yachts in the rally were only steered by hand approximately half the time.

Another thing which I tried to find out during the interviews was not only how much the automatic pilots were used, but also on which points of sailing. I was particularly interested to know if pilots were trusted to steer the boat when sailing under spinnaker. Paul Skilowitz explained '*Bluewater* is steered by autopilot most of the time and the performance of our Cetrek pilot is excellent. It copes well up to 12 knots of boat speed, when we would drop the spinnaker anyway.'

Altogether 18 skippers pointed out that they used their automatic pilots on all points of sailing including with the spinnaker, while an additional five stressed that although they trusted their pilots to steer the boat on all points of sailing, they only did this if the winds were light.

The next question referred to the use of autopilots in heavy weather. I was interested to find out how some models, which performed well under normal conditions, coped with strong winds and rough seas. Generally, during heavy weather conditions, skippers appeared to be more reluctant to let the boat be steered by the automatic pilot, especially if the boat was not equipped with one of the more powerful models.

Table 10 Automatic pilots

Make	Number	Performance	Reliability	Average Consumption (ah)
Autohelm 2000	3	8	6	1.2
Autohelm 3000	4	7.5	8.7	1.3
Autohelm 4000	2	9	10	3
Autohelm 6000	5	7.6	6.2	4
Autohelm 7000	8	8.9	9.1	4.6
Cetrek 727	3	8.3	7.3	4.5
B&G Helmstar	3	8.3	7.3	4.3
Robertson AP	3	8.7	8.3	4.3
Alphamarine Spectra	3	8.7	8.7	8.5
Sigatron	1	10	10	—
Neco	1	9	9	5
Navico	1	5	5	3
Benmar	1	8	8	10
Sharp	1	10	10	—
Nautiradar	1	9	9	20
Coursemaster	1	10	10	10
Total:	41			

The most popular make and model was the Autohelm 7000, of which there were eight in the fleet. On *Midnight Stroller*, the Autohelm 7000 had no difficulty in keeping an accurate course regardless of weather conditions. Walter Gollhofer was also very impressed with the performance of this model. 'Our Autohelm 7000 is excellent. This is especially noticeable when there is swell, as it makes allowances for the boat rolling, but doesn't make too many course adjustments and thus does not use much power.'

Leo Birkby, who was very pleased with his two Alphamarine pilots, would let them steer *Locura* on all points although he found that neither pilot could cope when reaching under spinnaker. Ismo Nikola was reasonably happy with his Robertson pilot, which steered *Daughter of Baltic* on all points of sailing, although it could not cope with winds over 30 knots. Before buying the pilot, Ismo tested a similar unit on a long keeled boat to ensure that it would be able to cope with a heavy displacement schooner such as his.

John Papp, who had two pilots on *Ambler*, found that the Autohelm 4000 worked better downwind than the 7000 which tended to wander, especially with the spinnaker up. *Rockhopper* was also one of the boats with two autopilots, an Autohelm 6000 and 3000, the latter being kept as a backup, although Roger Gold felt that it was not powerful enough for his boat. This was also the conclusion reached by Dave Sutherland who found that an Autohelm 3000 was undersized for his *Tais*. Dave admitted that he could only blame himself for this as he had been warned that the pilot may not be suitable for a 41 ft boat. Guy Libens had made exactly the same mistake when he bought an Autohelm 3000 in Gibraltar on the eve of the start, only to find later that a 51 ft boat like *Wachibou* could have done with a more powerful model.

Table 10 shows the average performance and reliability ratings given by the 36 skippers to their pilots and are a useful indication of the way the various makes and models performed during the rally. Some skippers welcomed the opportunity either to praise or criticise their automatic pilots and some valid and interesting points were made. Brad Bernardo was one of those not too pleased with his Autohelm 6000, which had been out of action for a long time after burning out a transistor. The plastic drive gears had also gone and Brad put this down to poor quality.

On *Eye of Ra*, the Aries windvane was affectionately called Mildred, but the real worker was George, an Autohelm 7000 which steered the boat for 95% of the time. George had once given up when the cockpit control box had to be replaced due to water ingression. 'Why can't they make them waterproof if they are supposed to stay out in the cockpit?' enquired John Smith, who nevertheless had only words of praise for his George, which he rated a straight 10 both for performance and reliability. His feelings were shared by Peter Bunting, also the owner of an Autohelm 7000, 'A great super machine', which he also rated a top 10. Another satisfied customer was Jake McCullogh, whose hydraulically operated Autohelm 7000 worked very well. Nevertheless Jake decided to question me in return concerning the type of selfsteering gear he should buy for his boat. 'Why do you want a windvane, when it may not even work on a heavy boat like yours?' I asked. 'Because I'm a salesman's dream!' he replied with hearty laughter.

Selfsteering gears

Salesmen of wind operated selfsteering gears have a lot of catching up to do if they are to match the number of automatic pilots sold to long distance sailors. Only one third (12) of the yachts taking part in the rally had windvanes and even this is a higher proportion than in the annual ARC transatlantic rally, where over the years I have noticed a gradual reduction in the number of yachts equipped with windvanes. There are several reasons for this, but I think the main reason is the ease and speed with which an autopilot can be set on a desired course, whereas a windvane can take several minutes to adjust. The undeniable advantage of windvanes is that they do not use any power, which is a major consideration on a long voyage, but obviously less important during a rapid circumnavigation such as EUROPA 92. Nevertheless, the skippers were asked to estimate the electricity consumption of their autopilots, the results being shown in Table 10, which indicates the average hourly consumption of the various models, as estimated by their owners. With ten yachts not using their pilots at all and one being run off its propeller shaft, the automatic pilots on the remaining 25 yachts had a total daily electricity consumption of 1746 ah, or a daily average of 70 ah per yacht. With the 25 automatic pilots being in use 60% of the time, or 14.4 hours every day, the hourly average consumption was 4.9 amps. Looking at these figures one can understand why engines or generators had to be run for several hours every day on yachts using their automatic pilots, and also why wind operated selfsteering gears are not a bad idea.

Amadé was one of the yachts equipped with both, although the windvane was hardly used. 'We only have it in case the autopilot breaks down. Anyway, the Windpilot does not agree with our boat and is quite erratic when steering. Especially when the boat is heeling, the windvane tends to take us into the wind.' In contrast to *Amadé*, a similar Windpilot on *Octopus* performed best in strong winds and reacted much more quickly than the automatic pilot. However, Wilhem Greiff pointed out that one had to reef early to make the boat more manageable or the windvane's auxiliary rudder came out of the water.

In several instances, the owners discovered that although the windvane probably would have performed well on a different type of yacht,

Table 11   Selfsteering gears

Make	Number	On wind	Performance Reaching	Running
Hydrovane	3	9.7	7	8
Monitor	3	8	7.5	8.5
Aries	3	8	6.3	4.3
Windpilot	2	7.5	3.5	5
Sailomat	1	10	8	6
Fleming	1	10	10	5
BWS	1	—	—	—
Total:	14			

La Aventura's Hydrovane selfsteering gear copes well under most conditions.

it was not suited to their own. 'Sailomat is a good windvane, but not on *Bluewater* which has a centre cockpit, so there are long line runs. Mainly because of that, as well as the stretch in the lines, the feedback from the steering wheel to the vane is affected' explained Paul Skilowitz.

The skippers were asked to rate the performance of their gear on various points of sailing and it was interesting to note the difference in performance, not just between different models, but also how the same windvane performed differently on different boats. The crew of *Jolly Joker* were very happy with their Hydrovane, especially with the wind from astern. 'We can sail at our maximum speed with a following wind and the vane steers the boat perfectly' explained János Barzsantik. John Papp, who also owned a Hydrovane, was not impressed with its perform- ance in light winds. I made the same observation on *La Aventura*, where I found that it took a lot of sail trimming to enable the Hydrovane to steer the boat when the winds were light.

Under normal conditions, *Kite*'s Monitor windvane performed very well before the wind, when the yacht was usually sailed with a boomed yankee and reefed mainsail. However, Dick Wilson pointed out that a lot depended on sail trim for the gear to work successfully. Rick Palm, also the owner of a Monitor, was not impressed with its performance either when reaching or running. 'I wouldn't have another one, not just because of its steering ability but also because one has this vulnerable piece of equipment at the stern, and we have already hit the dock twice when there was surge. An autopilot is definitely better and our Cetrek 727 handles the boat very well on all points of sailing. On reflection though, if I were just cruising and not pushing the boat so hard, I would use the windvane more.'

A recent convert to the advantages of a windvane was Dutch Taylor who acquired a Monitor gear for *Trillium* when he came to realise the serious drain put on his batteries by the autopilot. The windvane which served as inspiration for the Monitor was the Aries, a robust gear whose inventor and manufacturer Nick Franklin has sadly gone out of business. For many years, an Aries at the stern was the mark of a long distance cruiser and scores of circumnavigations were accomplished with its help.

Although in the EUROPA fleet windvanes were used relatively little, the gear which was used most was an Aries on *Tais*, where it steered the boat for 50% of the time. Another Aries, on *Pennypincher*, was only considered a backup to the automatic pilot, as the boat had plenty of battery power and so the skipper preferred to use the pilot, which steered the boat 95% of the time. Alan Spriggs was quite taken by the versatility of his autopilot, a Brookes & Gatehouse Helmstar 740. 'It is so clever it even makes tea, although we only use it to steer the boat.' However, the Helmstar did break down as they were leaving Las Palmas de Gran Canaria. 'So the Aries ended up steering the boat all the way across the Atlantic, proving what a good little boy it was!'

6
TRAGEDY AT SEA

Leg 5: Galapagos to Marquesas

After many hot windless mornings in Puerto Ayora, miraculously the wind sprung up on the morning of 2 April to give a good start to the fifth leg to Hiva Oa. A burst of machine gun fire from a rating on the Ecuadorean Navy Committee boat, kindly provided by Carlos Rhor, the Port Captain, sent the yachts on their way on the longest leg in the entire rally, 3060 miles to the Marquesas.

The northerly wind lasted throughout the first night but died at sunrise. For the next few days the fleet sailed through squally conditions with very light winds, rising rapidly to 20 knots during the rainy squalls. Eventually, the wind settled down and the expected southeasterlies set in, blowing between 12 and 25 knots. These, along with a strong favourable current, sped boats on their way.

Three days after the start, on 5 April at 2300 local time, the Finnish yacht *Cacadu* was hit by a squall which blew out the spinnaker. As the rain squall broke over the yacht, one of the crew on watch rushed below to close the hatches while the others tried to deal with the spinnaker. In the pitch black night, suddenly the mainsail gybed, breaking its preventer. The swinging boom hit 26 year old Panu Harjula, who was not wearing a harness, knocking him overboard. A danbuoy was immediately thrown in the water and the yacht was turned around to start searching for the man. The buoy was later retrieved, but there was no sign of Panu.

A Mayday was broadcast and this brought an instant response from several yachts, all of those in the vicinity altering course immediately to help *Cacadu* with the search. *Cacadu* continued to search the area all night and was joined in the morning by ten other EUROPA 92 yachts. All day long, the yachts coordinated their search operation, trying to cover the area as thoroughly as possible. Unfortunately nothing was found and by nightfall the search was called off and the yachts continued towards the Marquesas. Arne Blässar believes that Panu had been knocked unconscious by the blow of the boom and probably did not survive long in the water.

The tragic loss of Panu, who had only joined the yacht in St Lucia, greatly affected everyone and cast a sombre veil over the entire fleet. The day after the accident, a memorial service was held on board *Cacadu* and Arne spoke on the radio to his fellow sailors in EUROPA 92. On every yacht, the crew assembled on deck and one minute of silence was held in memory of Panu Harjula.

Unfortunately the accident occurred in one of the most remote ocean areas in the world and there was no outside assistance within range that could be called on. The organisers had been informed of the accident immediately and although the Ecuadorian authorities were duly alerted, there was very little they or anyone else could do. Throughout the hours following the accident and during the search for Panu, Pierluigi, the amateur radio operator based in Ravenna, kept in contact with the Italian yachts in the fleet. After the search had been called off, he linked me by telephone and radio with the fleet. I spoke in turn with all eight Italian skippers trying to reassure them as well as I could, although I was just as shocked by this unexpected tragedy as they were. They all wanted to know what we were going to do and if we were going to carry on with the rally. Calling off the event when the yachts were in the middle of the South Pacific would evidently serve no purpose, but I assured them that Panu Harjula would not be forgotten. Indeed a memorial trophy in his name was presented at the end of the rally.

Meanwhile, the faster boats, which had been well ahead of *Cacadu* at the time of the accident, carried the wind with them all the way to the Marquesas. *Gilma Express* was the first to arrive in Atuona, having taken only 13 days 21 hours. Seven hours later a close finish brought *Gulliver* over the line only 10 minutes before *Locura*, both boats taking 14 days 3 hours for the 3060 mile passage. *Orchidea* and *Who Dares Wins* arrived later the same day, also taking less than 15 days. It was then over 30 hours until the next boat crossed the line, *Bluewater* being the first arrival in the Cruising Division.

The time spent in the search for Panu Harjula had delayed the next batch of boats. Not only those involved in the search, but the entire fleet had been greatly affected by the tragedy and several skippers had second thoughts about pushing their boats too hard. Unfortunately for the slower boats, the good winds which had carried the larger yachts so swiftly to Hiva Oa petered out and the last third of the fleet was caught in light weather for the last few hundred miles to the Marquesas. Even so the majority of the fleet arrived within 21 days, everyone clocking up excellent average times.

San Diego feeder

Meanwhile, the three yachts sailing from San Diego to join the fleet in Hiva Oa were also getting closer. As *Trillium* had decided to leave earlier than the scheduled start on 6 April and *Scorpio II* had been delayed, Lona and Dick Wilson's *Kite* took the start from San Diego in solitary splendour. In spite of that, some fifty people gathered on Point Loma to watch *Kite* cross the starting line. A pleasant sail brought them into

Atuona only one day after the last boat arrived from the Galapagos, so completing the 2960 miles in exactly 20 days, which they sailed all the way.

This was by no means the case for Dutch and Pat Taylor, who had arrived in Atuona a few days earlier after 62 days at sea. The crew of *Trillium* had hoped to join the fleet in the Galapagos, but light winds frustrated their plan and, 200 miles short of their destination, they realised that they would miss the fleet, so they changed course for the Marquesas. Desperately short of fuel, they requested help over the radio and *Sojourner* made a diversion to come to their assistance and supply enough fuel to run their engine for essential purposes. After a delayed start, Wes Harris' *Scorpio* finally left San Diego and sailed directly to Nuku Hiva, arriving in Taiohae to join the fleet a few days before the start of the leg to Tahiti.

Only six yachts had arrived in Atuona from the Galapagos when another tragedy struck. A small Air Tahiti aircraft taking passengers from Hiva Oa to Nuku Hiva crashed into the sea on landing with the loss of ten lives out of the twenty passengers on board. Among the passengers was Ian Kennedy, owner of *Who Dares Wins*, who on arriving in Hiva Oa had decided to surprise his family in England and fly home for his son's birthday. Ian was among the lucky survivors and in fact he opened the emergency door and helped others to safety. With head and neck injuries, Ian was released after a few days from the small hospital in Nuku Hiva and the following week continued his flight to England.

There was a tragicomical sequel to these tragedies caused by an over-zealous radio amateur in Tahiti. Without checking the facts first, he relayed the news to Rafael del Castillo in Las Palmas, who in turn passed it on to the local newspapers. A garbled report was published the following day, which stated that after a participant in EUROPA 92 had been lost overboard in the South Pacific, the organisers chartered a small plane to look for the man. During the search operation, the plane crashed in the sea killing everyone on board except for myself who miraculously survived the accident. The report prompted some of my Canarian friends to call my home in London to express their relief that I had survived the crash. Not surprisingly this caused our children serious concern as they knew that at that moment Gwenda and I were on our way from Tahiti to the Marquesas to join *La Aventura*. Fortunately they managed to get hold of us and found out that we were safe and enjoying our cruise in the Marquesas. Nevertheless, the incident reminded me of similar misunderstandings caused by radio amateurs who are sometimes tempted to broadcast news before the facts are confirmed. We have had similar unfortunate situations in the ARC and one hopes to be spared such undeserved fame in the future.

The majority of those killed in the crash in the Marquesas, including several children, were from the small community on Hiva Oa and the island went into mourning with all shops and offices closed for several days. Understandably this meant that the reception of arriving boats was kept low key and the planned welcome festivities had to be cancelled. For several days the anchorage in Taahuku Bay at Atuona was afflicted by a large swell, which encouraged the early arrivals to start cruising around the rest of the islands. A popular anchorage was only a few miles away at Hana Moe Noa on the island of Tauhata, from where it was easy to sail back to Atuona for shopping, post office or other necessities.

Swell in the anchorages and sandflies on the beaches are notorious features of the Marquesas, but fortunately for the fleet the weather was unusually calm during the EUROPA 92 stay and swell in most anchorages was largely absent, although landing by dinghy was often a wet affair. Most of the yachts cruised to some or all of the other islands of Fatu Hiva, Ua Pou and Ua Huka before arriving at Nuku Hiva. Everyone enjoyed the dramatic scenery of these islands whose beauty and tranquillity had captivated the painter Paul Gauguin, who ended his life on Hiva Oa. His grave, in the small cemetery in Atuona, is close to that of Jacques Brel, the singer who also chose to end his life there after being told that he was suffering from an incurable disease.

Marquesan cruise

There was much to see in all the islands, with ancient religious sites and mysterious stone statues hidden in the luxuriant vegetation. Sailing between the islands, the fishing was excellent and most of those who trolled were rewarded with a good catch, the undisputed champion being *Midnight Stroller*, whose crew landed a 120 lb wahoo among other catches.

Everyone arrived in Taiohae with a tale to tell of the friendly reception and Marquesan welcome given by people in the various villages. The main village of Hakahau on Ua Pou put on several 'fêtes' with pig on the spit, singing and dancing. The main mover behind the feasts was Rataro, a Marquesan keen to preserve the traditional customs in his island and who arranged for Pasquale de Gregorio's birthday to be celebrated in great style. On the same island, Giovanna Caprini discovered a month old baby girl called *Orchidea*. After wrapping the baby in an *Orchidea* T-shirt, Giovanna was invited by the delighted mother to spend some time as a guest of the family. At Tauhata, Jake McCullogh took up an invitation to go shooting wild goat in the surrounding hills, an expedition which ended with a goat barbecue on the beach at Hana Moe Noa for the crews of half a dozen boats. The three young men living in this valley were delighted with the lively company and their barbecues became a regular feature on the EUROPA cruising circuit as most of the yachts made a point of calling at this welcoming spot. A small school in Anaho Bay on Nuku Hiva, recipients of some of the *Midnight Stroller* bumper fish catch, also put on entertainment for several of the boats anchored

Spectacular anchorage in the lee of Ua Pou in the Marquesas.

in the quiet, well protected bay, which had once harboured a large fleet of American warships during the Second World War.

Fortunately for EUROPA 92, the President of the Tahiti Yacht Club, Taro Tekuataoa, had recently returned home to reside in Nuku Hiva after twenty years divided between France and Tahiti. A yacht owner himself, his enthusiasm and knowledge of what sailors require did much to smooth our stay. With plans to form a yacht club in the bay of Hakatea, a few miles west of the main settlement of Taiohae, he made a start by leading out a hose with pure spring water to a buoy and most yachts availed themselves of this to fill their tanks. Hakatea, known affectionately as Daniel's Bay, after the resident guardian, proved to be one of the most popular anchorages in the Marquesas.

As the day for the next start approached, all yachts gravitated to Taiohae Bay, which had never witnessed such a large fleet of yachts at anchor. With a total population of only 7000 in the whole Marquesas, it was not surprising that the islands had felt the economic impact of a fleet of 40 yachts, the two restaurants in Atuona having taken in two weeks their normal income for six months, while in Taiohae fuel supplies, fresh produce and phone cards were totally sold out.

All the businesses in Taiohae contributed to the prize giving party, organised by Taro, who had donated two calves for the barbecue. The Administrator of the islands, M Jean-Jacques Fort, kindly lent the superb garden of his residence, which provided a beautiful setting for the informal prize giving ceremony for the winners of leg 5. The party got off to a slow start, due to the late arrival of the beer, the key to the cold store having been lost during the afternoon. However, a local group entertained everyone with Marquesan songs and continued without break until the end of the evening, ably assisted by the Italian contingent. Plaques were presented to the class winners in Polynesian style with a burst of music and tamuré dancing by the presenter. As the first to arrive in the Marquesas, Pasquale received an old carved Marquesan canoe paddle, donated by Taro, the paddle having belonged to his grandfather. For his fledgling Marquesas Yacht Club, Taro received a EUROPA 92 pennant and a poster signed by all the skippers.

Survival and emergency preparedness

The loss of Panu Harjula prompted all the skippers to examine the emergency procedures and safety equipment on board their boats. Although most yachts had been fitted out to the highest standards and, in accordance with the rally rules, were carrying all safety equipment considered necessary on a long offshore voyage, some skippers were shocked to discover serious gaps in their ability to deal with an emergency.

After the accident, most skippers went through their man overboard procedure and discussed with their crew what was to be done should such an emergency occur on their boat. From what I was told, the wearing of harnesses became a strict rule on many yachts, something which had not been insisted on before the loss of Panu. Although losing a man overboard is very rare on cruising boats, such accidents do happen. Incredibly, only a few days after the loss of Panu, a man fell overboard from another yacht taking part in the rally, but this was in daylight and the person was retrieved immediately. After the shock of Panu's loss, the incident was not made known on the radio and, at the request of the skipper, the name of the yacht will not be disclosed. In the ARC too there have been at least two cases of a crew falling overboard in the middle of the ocean. Fortunately in both instances the man was retrieved immediately. One of those who fell overboard was the skipper of the yacht *Windwalker*, and later he had to put up with a lot of teasing from his fellow sailors suggesting that he should change the name of his boat to 'wavewalker'.

EPIRBs

The retrieval of a man overboard, especially on yachts with high free-board and no easy access at the stern, can be a difficult operation. For this reason several of the yachts had been equipped with either a Jon Buoy or MOM (Man Overboard Module). Even more important than being able to fish a man out of the water is to be able to find him quickly. On *Gulkarna*, two personal EPIRBs (emergency position indicating radio beacons) fitted with polystyrene flotation collars were kept in the cockpit ready to be launched if a man fell overboard. The RDF unit on board, which was set automatically to the EPIRB frequency, would then be used to locate the EPIRB. A different system was used on *Tais*, where to his surprise, Dave Sutherland noticed that the armband transmitters, normally carried by the crew on watch, were found to be out of order when tested on a 500 kHz receiver. The personal transmitters were taken out of service and instead every crew joining the boat was given an armband strobe light and a personal flotation bag packed in a capsule to be carried around the waist. A lifejacket with a strobe light, which would come on automatically if immersed in water, was worn on *Octopus* by the crew on watch. As an added precaution on this short handed yacht, a 70 metre long line was tied to one of the lifebuoys to be thrown in the water if one of the crew fell overboard. As the line reached its end, a pull would release a floating strobe light.

EPIRBs were among the compulsory safety equipment carried by each yacht in the round the world rally. These lightweight transmitters operate on three different frequencies: 121.5 MHz, 243 MHz and 406 MHz. The 121.5 MHz frequency is used by commercial aircraft and ships and was chosen as the international distress frequency before the advent of satellites. The 243 MHz frequency is monitored only by military aircraft and is being phased out gradually. In spite of the proliferation of EPIRBs using the 406 MHz frequency, especially on commercial ships, the older 121.5 MHz frequency will be retained as it is monitored by aircrews and air traffic controllers. The satellite-based 406 MHz has several advantages, such as its better capability of locating the source of a distress signal. Also, the latest beacons give the user's identity and the data obtained from a distress signal is stored on board the satellite before its onward transmission. This last feature is very important as the 121.5 MHz distress signals are only retransmitted by a satellite as they occur and may go unheard if there is no station within range. In contrast, the 406 MHz system's storage capability means that global coverage is assured under any condition, and this is the reason why participants in EUROPA 92 were advised to acquire the later type of distress beacons.

Tested under rather more trying circumstances than the personal EPIRBs on *Tais* was one such 406 MHz EPIRB on *Jolly Joker*, whose crew tried to activate the set when the yacht was driven on to a reef while negotiating the tricky Torres Strait north of Australia. According to Janos Barzsantik however hard he tried to turn the activating lever so as to arm the unit, the lever would not budge. By this time the yacht had started breaking up and was almost full of water, so one of the crew dived into the cabin and handed out the VHF microphone through an open porthole. Fortunately their Mayday was picked up immediately by other EUROPA yachts sailing in the vicinity. The faulty EPIRB, made by Lo-kata, was later retrieved from the wreck and sent to the manufacturers who suggested that the only possible explanation for the malfunction was that the unit had been dropped before the accident, although the crew insisted that the EPIRB was undamaged when they attempted to use it.

Liferafts

Fortunately *Jolly Joker*'s liferaft inflated instantly and the crew could abandon the boat. Along with EPIRBs, liferafts were also compulsory and their capacity had to be equal to the maximum number of crew carried. Because of this requirement, but also as an added precaution, most of the yachts with larger crews had two liferafts. All liferafts were stowed in an easily accessible place within reach of the cockpit and no skipper estimated the launching time to take more than one minute. As a fully equipped offshore liferaft can be of considerable weight it is essential that it can be launched by the weakest member of the crew. One of the aspects checked by rally officials when carrying out individual safety inspections before the start of the rally was that liferafts were stowed in

The multi-functional stern platform on *Libertad II* provided an excellent place to store and launch the liferaft.

an accessible place from where they could be launched in the shortest time possible.

The best stowage was on *Libertad II*, where the liferaft was kept under a purpose built platform at the stern of this Amel Mango, from where the raft could be released in a matter of seconds. The liferaft also could be launched easily on *La Aventura* from its stowage place on the aft pulpit. On some yachts, the liferaft was stowed under the helmsman's seat, which has become a standard feature on some production boats. All liferafts stowed on deck were provided with a quick-release mechanism, although for good measure a knife was permanently strapped to the liferaft on *Pennypincher* in case of difficulties when launching.

Panic bags

A lot of thought had gone into the contents of panic bags meant to be grabbed if the yacht had to be abandoned in a hurry. At least one such bag, or more usually a watertight container, was to be found on every yacht. Their contents varied widely as did their size and weight, the largest being found on *Brydie* and weighed all of 70 lb (30 kg). Brad Bernardo had obviously tried to think of every eventuality and, apart from a spare GPS, hand operated watermaker, underwater camera and enough fishing tackle for an international tournament, he also kept in the bag all spare dry cell batteries for equipment on board as well as for equipment stowed in the panic bag. In this way, used batteries had to be replaced from those kept in the bag and there was no danger of forgetting the batteries on board if the boat had to be abandoned. On *Octopus*, several 12 V rechargeable battery packs were kept in readiness to be taken off in an emergency to be used with a VHF radio or search light. A Transpac GPS unit, with its own battery, was also kept in a handy place.

On most boats, passports, money and credit cards were either kept in an easily accessible place or in the panic bag itself. Besides the standard things that people put in their grab bags, such as flares, first aid kit, seasickness tablets, concentrated food and extra water rations, other items mentioned were: vitamins, glucose, survival blankets, sun block cream, sunglasses, mirror, flaying knife, whistle, compass, EPIRB, handheld VHF (with fully charged batteries), scissors, torch, survival manual, spare film, etc. Besides these more or less obvious items, EUROPA 92 participants came up with some very original ideas well worth mentioning. Items that could come in handy while marooned in a liferaft were: a roll of toilet paper (*Bluewater*), writing paper, pen and photocopies of the passports (*Amadê*), a chart of the area (*Gulliver*), inflatable diving vests (*Elan Adventurer*), strobe light (*Kite*), personal games (*Locura*), Verey pistol (*Orchidea*), empty plastic containers that float (*Oyinbo*) and medication taken by the crew (*La Aventura*). An excellent suggestion was made by Rick Palm who advised anyone wearing glasses to put a spare pair in the grab bag, as without glasses one could not read labels on medicine bottles, for instance. Rick also suggested putting in some US banknotes. 'It would be nice to be able to buy a beer for the guy who saved me.'

A couple of Kendal mint cakes were carried as emergency rations on *Jakes Fantasia*, 'Just as Captain Scott did in the Antarctic and Edmund Hillary on Mount Everest.' One of the most complete bags was on Marcello Murzilli's *Cheone* which even included a generous supply of shark repellant powder.

As liferafts carry only a limited amount of water in cans, most boats also had emergency jerrycans prepared on deck or close to the cockpit ready to be thrown overboard. On *Lady Samantha*, a crew member was designated to deal with this task should the yacht have to be abandoned. Enio Nardi held a detailed briefing every time there was a crew change and most other skippers made sure that every new person joining the boat was introduced to their emergency procedure. On *Octopus*, the two panic containers were tied to four jerrycans not completely filled with water so that they would float when thrown overboard.

A relatively recent piece of safety equipment are hand operated water-makers. Several of these had been acquired before the rally and were kept in the panic bags, while some of those without watermakers had acquired at least a solar still. On *Trillium*, the watermaker could also be operated from the 12 V supply and was in normal use on the boat. This watermaker was mounted on a sliding rack, from where it could be dismantled in a few seconds if the boat had to be abandoned, while the handle for its manual operation was always stowed in the panic bag.

Collision damage control

Various preparations for damage control in case the hull was holed had been made on the EUROPA 92 yachts and, as part of the recommended safety equipment, all carried a set of wooden plugs for their through-hull fittings. More than half the boats carried a good supply of underwater epoxy and also a selection of plywood to effect emergency repairs. On *Lady Samantha* bits of plywood provided with screws and glue were kept in readiness to deal with possible collision damage. The skippers of *Bluewater* and *Sojourner* had each prepared a 6 ft × 6 ft (1.80 m × 1.80 m) octogonal Dacron mat with grommets, which could be fitted over a dam-aged hull.

Brad Bernardo explained how a powerful 2 inch diameter Jabsco pump permanently mounted on *Brydie*'s main engine would probably control the influx of water until the crew managed to cover the hole from the inside with cushions. Once the flow of water had been reduced, a sail would be slipped over the hull from the outside. Rather than revert to cushions to plug a hole from the inside, Julian Wilson suggested inflating the dinghy seat to stem the flow of water. There was only one yacht, *Twilight*, which had been equipped with a flotation bag, which could be inflated from a diving tank and hopefully would keep the boat afloat.

All boats with large portholes or windows had plywood covers prepared in case of breakage, while Lexan covers had been prepared on *Bluewater* for all portholes as well as wooden panels for the cabin ports.

Seven boats were provided with watertight bulkheads forward, among them the steel hulled *La Aventura* on which the forward cabin was separated from the rest of the accommodation by a steel door. The watertight door was always kept closed on passage and access to sails and other equipment stowed forward had to be gained through a deck hatch. Five yachts, *Daughter of Baltic*, *Rockhopper*, *Locura*, *Oyinbo* and *Octopus* had been provided with watertight bulkheads both fore and aft. The most comprehensive system was on the Deerfoot 72 *Locura* which was divided into three separate compartments, each with its separate bilge and electrical bilge pump. An additional high volume pump on the main engine was connected to every one of the three bilges. On three metal boats, *Oyinbo* and *Rockhopper* (steel) and *Octopus* (aluminium), all tanks were integral thus providing a double skin for the hull.

7
POLYNESIAN INTERLUDE

Leg 6: Marquesas to Tahiti

On the morning of Saturday, 11 May, only a whisper of wind ruffled the bay of Taiohae. There was a little more breeze at the starting line, which had been set at the entrance of the bay between two islets called East Sentinel and West Sentinel. In tune with the entire stay in the Marquesas, which was marked by informality, the start was given from the smallest Committee vessel yet used, a small open fishing boat on which the starting flags were held aloft on long bamboo poles which Taro's son Jean-Yves had cut in the bush early that morning.

Born and educated in France, Jean-Yves had recently returned to his father's island, realising that neither metropolitan France nor Tahiti could offer him the fulsome life of the unspoilt Marquesas. During the stay of the EUROPA yachts in Taiohae, Jean-Yves worked wonders in satisfying the various needs of this floating community. On an island where there was no need for a market as everyone had their own garden, Jean-Yves drove around in his van asking his many relatives to supply some fruit or vegetables for the departing sailors.

The imposing humps of the two sentry islands guarding the entry to the picturesque bay made a splendid backdrop to the start line, which was crossed first by *Gilma Express*, followed closely by *Gulliver* and *Kite*. In the 8 knot breeze, spinnakers were broken out immediately on almost all of the boats, forming a colourful foreground to the luxuriant green island behind. Making good progress in the first 24 hours, the wind then fell away completely and boats reported sitting in a dead calm for hours on end, zero knots of wind and zero knots of movement forward. A light breeze eventually sprang up, but the SE trade winds, which should have been blowing at this time of year, were completely absent. As the yachts got nearer to the Tuamotus, everyone experienced lots of squalls with torrential rain showers. In order to pass safely by the aptly called Dangerous Archipelago, the yachts were instructed to sail north of the islands and leave all atolls to port before altering course for Tahiti. There was also a record of 3 days and 20 hours to beat for this passage, set by a Tahiti Yacht Club member in his Swan 65. The lack of trade winds however put paid to this challenge and *Gilma Express*, the first to arrive in Papeete, took 4 days and 10 hours for the 765 miles. For this leg

Pasquale was ably assisted by 10 year old Scott Birkby, who had jumped ship from *Locura* in the hope of being on the first boat to cross the finish line. For this he was rewarded on arrival with a flower garland given by a Tahitian vahine, as were the rest of the crew.

As on other legs, the early arrivals appeared to carry the better weather with them, and the day after *Gilma*'s arrival a small depression passed over the area bringing winds of over 30 knots and, turning through northwest, west and southwest, brought headwinds for the rest of the fleet, something that had not been anticipated at all. As the front moved over, boats were left with little wind and an unpleasant swell from all directions.

The disappointing weather was more than made up for by the welcome extended to every arrival by members of the Tahiti Yacht Club. Not only did volunteers from the club man the finishing line in their Committee boat, a sports fishing motor cruiser, but they also sent a small Boston whaler to guide every boat into Papeete harbour. There were many helpers and, over the three days of arrivals, there was always somebody from the club on hand even in the middle of the night. The club had been gearing up for a long time to welcome EUROPA 92 and the preparations were indeed impressive. Among the club members, Michel Alcon, Jeannette Bride, Benoit Soulignac, André Raoult and Reva von Schoenburg stood out for their warm hospitality.

Instead of docking at the normal yacht quay, the fleet was berthed at the Quai d'Honneur, right in the centre of Papeete. This is normally the berth of cruise ships and yachts had never docked there before, so

The EUROPA 92 fleet docked together in the centre of Papeete.

the Port Authority arranged for a chain to be laid down between the large bollards to take mooring lines, a wide boarding plank was supplied to each yacht and special adapters fitted to the large water outlets on the quay. The Port of Papeete did everything possible to make the fleet welcome and the Director of the Port, Patrick Bonnette, who was also chairman of the EUROPA 92 welcoming committee, was instrumental in the success of the programme in Papeete.

High society islands

The social programme kicked off with a welcoming cocktail in the garden of the Tahiti Tourist Promotion Board, in the presence of the President of French Polynesia, M Gaston Flosse and the High Commissioner, M Jean Montpezat. Unfortunately the light winds meant that five boats finished outside of the time limit and missed this first party, although *Jakes Fantasia* and *Tais* arrived in time to attend the presentation dinner at the Beachcomber Park Royal Hotel on Saturday 18 May, *Tais* arriving just in time to be whisked straight from the dock to the party. Not so well timed was the arrival of *Wachibou*, which arrived outside the port entrance and was unable to make its way inside as its engine refused to start. Just as the Minister of Maritime Affairs, M Gaston Tong Song, was getting ready to go on stage and welcome the participants on behalf of the Government, a VHF call from *Wachibou* requesting a tow was relayed to the organisers. The proceedings were delayed, while a rather reluctant volunteer was found among the yacht club members willing to drop everything and tow in the disabled yacht.

The weather smiled and a clear starry sky graced the evening, which was just as well as the tables were set out on the beach by the lagoon. The presentation was preceded by a Tahitian dance show given by the Claude Renvoyé group. In his welcome speech, M Gaston Tong Song, who was also the Mayor of Bora Bora, promised a special welcome to his island for the start of the next leg to Tonga. The prizes were then presented to the winners of the leg from Nuku Hiva, which was won by *Gulliver* in the Racing Division and *Bluewater* in the Cruising Division, while the Tahiti Yacht Club Commodore's Cup was presented to *Gilma Express*. The trophy was accepted on behalf of the skipper by Scotty Birkby who also received a special kiss from the youngest dancer in the group, a pretty Tahitian girl of his age.

The arrival of the EUROPA 92 fleet coincided with the long Whitsun holiday weekend and on Sunday an island tour of Tahiti was arranged with a picnic lunch in the grounds of the Gauguin Museum. This was followed on Monday by a barbecue given by the Tahiti Yacht Club in their pleasant premises at Arue, on the outskirts of Papeete. The following day, the Mayor of Papeete hosted a reception for all participants in the Town Hall, which had been beautifully refurbished for the centenary of the city of Papeete. The Mayor exchanged gifts with the skippers of the yachts representing their home towns, *Daughter of Baltic* (Helsinki), *Orchidea* (Ravenna), *Lady Samantha* (Treviso) and *Twilight* (Anzio), and presented them with special centenary medals.

The splendid hospitality and generosity of the Tahitian hosts prompted the crews of the British contingent in the fleet to club together and organise an impromptu party on the quay for Tahitian guests and rally participants. A special order for the popular Hinano Beer was made, the brewery lending a couple of large ice chests, and an impressive selection of snacks and dips was made by the ladies. This successful evening brought to an end the social activities and left everyone free to recover, get on with their repairs, maintenance and provisioning, or to cruise slowly towards the next gathering point at Bora Bora through the other Society Islands and some of the most beautiful cruising grounds in the South Pacific.

Electricity generation and consumption

'The generation of electricity on passage is the one aspect of our long term preparations which we did not look at seriously enough. I never imagined how much electricity can be swallowed up by the instruments, automatic pilot, radio and a large crew, some of whom have to be told repeatedly that a light switch has a dual function and can be turned off as well as on!' The feelings expressed by Guy Libens were shared by many of his fellow skippers, several of whom admitted that they had never realised the importance of electricity consumption and generation, nor was it something that many of the designers and builders of the yachts had paid much attention to either. This was also the main conclusion of a similar survey on the same subject conducted among the 121 participants in ARC 1990.

With virtually every yacht equipped with automatic pilot, sailing instruments, GPS, SSB radio, pressurised water system, and a high proportion also with radar, weatherfax, watermaker as well as other power hungry items, the consumption on most boats was indeed high. The

Table 12 Electricity consumption

Number of yachts	Consumption (amps/24 hours)
4	25–50
7	50–100
7	100–200
6	200–300
1	300–500
Total: 25	

skippers were asked to estimate their usual consumption while on passage and out of the 36 skippers interviewed, 25 were able to give a fairly precise answer, while the remaining eleven could not even guess. The individual consumption worked out at an average 156 amps per 24 hours, or 6.5 amps per hour.

Generators

To cope with such high average consumption, just over half the yachts (19) had separate diesel generators, which on average were run 3.55 hours per day. An additional 13 portable petrol driven generators were carried on other yachts, most of which were kept to be used in emergencies only and were not normally used for charging. The one exception was *Jolly Joker*, which was the only boat on which a portable generator was used routinely to charge the batteries. The Honda 500 was run for six hours every other day to charge the batteries, its petrol consumption being a meagre 2.5 litres for the six hours of use.

The rest of the fleet, usually the smaller consumers, used their main engines for charging, the engines being run an average 2.52 hours every day. Four of the biggest consumers ran their engines in addition to their generators, usually in two separate periods. One such big consumer was *Midnight Stroller*, on which an Onan 10 kW generator was run for two hours every day while the main engine was used for an additional two hours in the evenings to charge the batteries and keep the various systems running. The engine was also run in the evenings, immediately after sunset, on *Oingo Boingo*, when electricity consumption was highest. Julian Wilson also found it more practical to charge *Elan Adventurer's* batteries at night and the engine was usually started as soon as the lights started to dim. 'It may not be the most popular decision with the crew, but it works perfectly.' On *Bluewater*, the generator was run twice a day to coincide with the daily SSB radio net and position reporting schedules, when consumption was at its highest. At the same time, the Westerbeke 8 kW generator ran the freezer, fridge and watermaker.

On *Jakes Fantasia*, the generator worked automatically and an alarm sounded as soon as the voltage of the domestic bank dropped to 10.87 V. The alarm was only set at night when the automatic pilot was running off the batteries. On *Oyinbo*, the battery voltage was monitored continuously and the generator was started as soon as the voltage dropped to 23.9 V. *Oyinbo* was one of nine yachts with a 24 V installation. Enio Nardi explained that he had chosen this system for *Lady Samantha* so as to be able to use wire of a smaller diameter for the electrical installation and also because some 24 V equipment, especially anchor windlasses, were both more powerful and generally better built. John Rose of *Midnight Stroller* disagreed. 'It is a mistake having a 24 V installation for a voyage of this kind as spare parts are almost impossible to find in the places visited, whereas 12 V spares would have been more easily available.'

On boats where a mechanical compresssor for the freezer was fitted on the main engine, this had to be run for at least one hour every day, so the batteries were charged at the same time. A lot of thought had gone into the electrical system on *Twilight*, whose owner Dino Blancodini had fitted out the yacht himself and spent three years trying to get everything right. The yacht had a dual 12 V/24 V system, a bank of two 12 V domestic batteries being charged from their own 12 V alternator on the main engine and were used as an emergency backup. A second 24 V alternator on the main engine was used to charge a bank of eight 24 V batteries, which could also be charged by an Onan 6.5 kW generator. The latter was the main source of charging and was run for 6–7 hours every day.

On *Locura*, both the engine and the generator each had been provided with a second alternator which charged a smaller bank of batteries used for starting the engine and generator. The main engine on *Sojourner* had also been fitted with two alternators, one dedicated to the engine starting battery, the other charging all domestic batteries. Although the system worked well, Rick Palm found that the fuel consumption ($\frac{3}{4}$ gallon per hour) was unjustifiably high and with hindsight would have preferred to have a separate 12 V diesel generator rather than run a 80 hp engine just to charge the batteries.

Several yachts experienced problems with their generators, such as *Amadé* whose generator had not been installed correctly and could not be used when the boat heeled more than 25°. As the generator had been installed on flexible mountings, which were too soft, its flywheel would touch the soundproof casing when the boat was heeling. The generator also caused problems for a long time on *Gulkarna* until the problem was traced to a half closed seacock, which forced the generator to work flat out as it had to compete with the freezer with which it was sharing the same cooling water inlet. With the seacock fully opened, the running time of the generator was reduced by half.

A similar problem, which took some time to be traced, occurred on *Jakes Fantasia* which had acquired a portable Onan generator as a backup to the main generator of the same make. However hard they tried, the crew could not get the portable generator to charge until finally in St Lucia it was discovered that the on/off switch had been wired the wrong way around. Relying heavily on electricity, with cooking, water heating, fridge and freezer, and occasionally air conditioning too, all run by their Onan 4.5 kW generator, *Jakes Fantasia* had the misfortune of being left without power on several occasions when the cook had to make do with a one-burner camping stove. 'It does wonders for your waistline,' quipped Jake McCullough.

The automatic voltage regulator had to be replaced on *Midnight Stroller's* Onan generator in Tonga and John Rose congratulated himself on having bought the expensive spare before leaving Mallorca. He also noticed that the higher temperature of the cooling water in the tropics had considerably affected the performance of the generator. The high temperature caused the generator to cut out, so in order to overcome this, the soundproof box had to be taken off to keep the temperature down.

A generating system which did not satisfy its owner was on *Cacadu* which had been fitted by Bénéteau with a Geco generator producing 220 V. This was then stepped down to 12 V to charge the batteries on a trickle charge, similar to a shore charger. Arne felt that the generator should have had its own 12 V alternator, producing 12 V current directly, rather than the present configuration under which the actual output of the generator was less than 20 amps. So he preferred using the main engine to charge the batteries, as it was more efficient, and the generator was used to supply 220 V for the watermaker, microwave oven and icemaker. Arne would have probably agreed with Ismo Nikola, whose generator on *Daughter of Baltic* packed up completely in Panama and a new one had to be flown in from the USA. 'The more toys you have, the more problems,' commented Ismo.

The feeling might have been shared also by Dick Wilson who was not satisfied with his combined Balmar generator and watermaker on *Kite*. The unit was powered by an air cooled Yanmar diesel engine, which caused both excessive heat and noise, and should have been water cooled. The air cooled Yanmar diesel generator on *Ambler* was also found to be too noisy and so the main engine was preferred for charging the batteries and the generator was used in emergencies only.

Several yachts used their watermakers in tandem with the generators and when such combination had been thought out properly, the system worked very well. On *Orchidea*, the watermaker worked off its own dedicated alternator on the main engine, which produced 36 V to run the watermaker. Part of this output was stepped down to 12 V to charge an emergency battery. All other batteries were charged by a separate 12 V alternator, also run by the main engine.

The crew of *Trillium* experienced so many problems with the voltage regulator on their alternator that Dutch Taylor decided to bypass the regulator altogether and charge the batteries at the highest, unregulated, output of the alternator, although never for longer than 20 minutes at a time so as to avoid the batteries getting too hot. The output could be controlled from the cockpit with a switch, which cut the field on the alternator and thus deactivated it.

Although most generating needs relied on diesel driven engines or generators, several yachts used renewable forms of energy. Most of *Kite's* requirements while on passage were covered by its Aerogen wind

Eye of Ra sailing fast in a 20 knot breeze at the start from Fiji, but the apparent wind was not enough to turn the wind generator.

generator and three solar panels. Two of the latter could be orientated towards the sun while the third was of the flexible type and had been mounted on top of the dodger. On *Eye of Ra*, a Rutland wind generator and one solar panel kept the batteries topped up while cruising.

Probably the most contented owner of a wind generator was Pasquale de Gregorio, who rated his Salbini generator a top 10. The generator was most efficient at anchor where it produced sufficient electricity to cover all requirements without the need to run the engine to charge the batteries. Among the various unusual things done by Pasquale was to always anchor *Gilma Express* by the stern, primarily for better ventilation but also because this pointed the stern-mounted generator into the wind. 'It is only on passage that the generator is useless, as we sail so fast that the apparent wind is not enough to even turn it' explained Pasquale.

All wind generators performed poorly on passage, as the apparent wind was rarely sufficient to produce a useful charge. In order to overcome this shortcoming, several wind generators could be converted to be water driven, some systems being easier to convert than others. Generally, towing generators were less popular and several owners complained that at speeds over 6 knots the propeller tended to leap out of the water and skip the wave tops. This became particularly dangerous on *Locura* where the wave skipping caused the diving plane to break and eventually the skipper threw the whole lot overboard. On *Sojourner*, Rick Palm had a similar experience with his Hamilton Ferris towing generator which skipped the waves and on two occasions cut its own towing line. Rick tried to overcome this by weighting down the propeller, but without much success. Nevertheless, the unit was found very efficient at speeds of between 5 and 6 knots. One major disadvantage of this type of generator is that one cannot fish at the same time, so on *Sojourner* this was resolved by trolling in daytime and towing the generator at night, which had the additional advantage that the batteries were being charged when consumption was highest.

All towing generators were of the type that could be converted to be wind driven and the general consensus was that it would have been preferable to have one of each unit as the conversion was not as simple as it sounded. This was also the conclusion I drew on *La Aventura* where we have an Ampair wind generator that can be converted to be towed behind the boat. Converting the unit takes so long that we hardly ever use the generator in the towing mode, although this is its most efficient. Brad Bernardo complained about the poor attachment system of his Fourwinds towing generator, with only an Allen screw securing the unit to the stern deck plate, which came undone and the whole unit was lost.

The best alternative to a towing generator is one of the purpose built units which fit on to the free-wheeling propeller shaft. On *Libertad II*, a Motorola shaft generator supplied a minimum charge of 3 amps and had the added advantage of not interfering with the fishing exploits of the crew.

Batteries

Battery capacity on the various yachts was also examined and it was found that most owners had been generous in their allowance, with an average 825 ah battery capacity per yacht. The totals included all batteries carried, although on most yachts there was a separate engine starting battery which was kept apart from the domestic bank. For the sake of uniformity, when assessing the battery capacity on individual yachts, 12 V was used as a common denominator and the capacity of 24 V batteries was therefore doubled.

It should be pointed out that the majority of yachts (25) had a total battery capacity well below the mean of 825 ah, while on eight yachts the total capacity was in excess of 1000 ah. Therefore, a more meaningful figure would be arrived at if the yachts with the highest capacity were not included in the average. The average for the 28 yachts whose skippers had indicated a total battery capacity of less than 1000 ah was thus reduced to 564 ah, a figure which is closer to the actual battery capacity normally found on offshore cruising yachts on an extended voyage.

Table 13 Battery capacity

Number of yachts	Capacity (ah)
3	200–300
11	300–500
11	500–800
5	800–1200
6	1200–2000
Total: 36	

Asked if they were satisfied with their battery capacity, 31 skippers answered in the affirmative. Having started with a total of 480 ah, John Smith added another battery *en route* to bring *Eye of Ra*'s capacity up to 600 ah, which proved to be adequate. Dick Wilson found the six 85 ah gel cell batteries, which he had acquired in the USA before leaving California, to be excellent at holding their charge. The six batteries were split up into a four battery domestic bank, one dedicated to the windlass and one for starting the engine.

The domestic battery on *Octcpus* consisted of one 160 ah traction battery designed to be used in electric wheelchairs or forklifts and thus to give short bursts of high intensity. Wilhelm Greiff considered this to be particularly useful when using the battery for radio transmission. The battery regenerated rapidly during use and kept its charge very well. In between, two solar panels, with an estimated peak output of 1.5 amps each, kept the battery charged up. When the starter motor on their engine broke down in the Galapagos Islands and Wilhelm Greiff decided nonetheless to sail the 3000 miles to the Marquesas and rely solely on the solar panels to charge the battery, everyone in the fleet was amazed that *Octopus* managed to use their SSB radio every day and still have enough for their daily consumption. Wilhelm explained that he had put a lot of thought into managing his electricity consumption, which was indeed low, as only halogen bulbs were used for lighting. 'If anyone shows any doubts about the value of renewable sources of energy, I point out our own example. For three weeks we relied on one battery for all our needs as well as at least one hour of radio transmissions every day and when we arrived in the Marquesas, the battery was fully charged. And all thanks to our two solar panels!'

8
STORIES FROM THE SOUTH SEAS

Leg 7: Bora Bora to Tonga

Stretching from Tahiti to Bora Bora, the Society Islands are one of the most attractive group of islands in the world. The lofty islands surrounded by tranquil lagoons are a perfect cruising ground and after the busy social programme in Papeete, the EUROPA yachts had several weeks to explore them at their leisure before the start of the next leg in Bora Bora. The islands of Moorea, Huahine, Raiatea and Tahaa were visited on the way before the fleet reunited in front of the Club Nautique de Bora Bora. A yacht club only in name, Guy Clement's establishment is a favourite watering hole for itinerant sailors and the wide terrace of the restaurant and bar reverberated day and night with participants greeting each other noisily as if they had been separated for years not weeks.

In order to give the EUROPA sailors the opportunity to see some of the islanders' traditional activities, the Mayor had postponed the annual *Journée de la mer* festivities by two weeks to coincide with the presence of the fleet in Bora Bora. Most activities took place in a large tent in Vaitape, where a group of local ladies gave demonstrations of making basketwork, their dexterity impressing the onlookers as palm fronds were speedily transformed into sun hats, fish traps, fruit baskets or food trays. As part of our own contribution to the day's activities, several yachts took out groups of children on trips around the lagoon. *Gilma Express* temporarily ceased to be an ULDB as it left the dock with 35 excited children on board. Additional groups were taken by *Kite*, *Soolo*, *Dafne* and *Elan Adventurer*, all of whom had laid on good supplies of soft drinks and sweets.

That same evening, the Mayor of Bora Bora, M Gaston Tong Song, organised a special dinner for all participants as a farewell party on the eve of the start. It began in traditional style with a prayer in Polynesian and a hymn sung by the famous Bora Bora Mamas and was followed by a dancing group performing the less solemn tamuré.

James Michener called Bora Bora the most beautiful island in the world and few people disagree. The Otamaru mountain, with its distinctive double peak and slopes lush with vegetation, towers above the lagoon and provided a perfect backdrop for the start of the seventh leg. The morning of Saturday 16 June saw 36 yachts sailing to and fro in the lagoon, their white sails crisp against the green island. As the starting gun sounded at 12 noon, the yachts crossed the line and headed towards the south end of the lagoon. First across were the two Swans, *Who Dares Wins* and *Gulliver*, jostling for leadership of the Racing Division. The fastest boats started to draw quickly away, rounding a buoy at the far end of the lagoon, and within a few minutes were zooming past the Committee vessel to the wild cheers of a group of sailors from the Tahiti Yacht Club who had come to Bora Bora to prepare and watch the start.

The yachts then sailed out of Teavanui pass and set a course for Tonga, nearly 1400 miles away. Within a few hours the fleet stretched out on the rhumb line for Tonga, with the distance between the first and last boats rapidly lengthening. For a few days, the wind blew strongly from the SE at 25 to 35 knots. Later, the wind eased and went to the east and ENE, becoming increasingly lighter and lighter. The daily radio net came into its own, the favourite topic of conversation being the weather, as the trade winds petered out. As the days passed, the winds came from every point of the compass, if they came at all. Eventually some of those in the Cruising Division started to motor, catching up with the Racing Division yachts, which had leapt ahead in the first days of stronger winds and now wallowed in perfectly calm seas.

The daily radio chat show livened up the day. Several participants told of whale sightings and Brad Bernardo kept everyone enthralled as he recounted meeting a pod of whales that swam close to the boat, diving under *Brydie*'s keel and surfing on the waves alongside. There were also tales of huge fish that got away. Some whiled away the time asking each other Trivial Pursuit questions or riddles over the airwaves.

Elaine Thompson of *Yachting World* had joined *La Aventura* for this leg to write a report on the rally, with my daughter Doina making up the rest of the crew. One beautiful afternoon as we were sailing slowly past the Cook Islands, with the spinnaker drawing nicely, Doina read us a short story she had made up incorporating the names of all the yachts in the rally, some of which were indeed rather strange. I persuaded her to read the story on the evening radio net and a competition was launched to compose a story, supposed to be short and sweet, using all the names of the boats participating in the rally. The first entries were read out by their authors the following day, the quality of some compositions taking everyone by surprise.

Exactly one week after the start, while the stories were being read out on the air, *Locura* crossed the finishing line at Tongatapu, the main island of the Polynesian Kingdom. In the light winds *Locura* eventually decided to motor, while *Gilma Express* and *Gulliver*, close behind, found themselves barely moving. *Gilma Express* finished shortly after *Locura*, but as night fell, so did the wind, and *Gulliver* lay becalmed 10 miles from the finish. It took *Gulliver* several frustrating hours to sail the last few miles, all the while being watched by the crew of the Tongan Defence Force vessel, the *Neiafu*, anchored at one end of the finishing line. The *Neiafu* spent five days on station, while a smaller boat commuted between the finishing line and Nuku'alofa guiding the newly arrived yachts into port.

A bruising encounter

Drama struck at 2300 hours on 25 June when *Amadé* ran aground on one of the outer reefs while approaching the finishing line. *Who Dares Wins*, which was a few miles from finishing, immediately turned around on hearing *Amadé*'s Mayday and went to assist as did the patrol vessel *Neiafu*. Two crew from *Who Dares Wins*, Magnus McGlashan and Gordon Kay, made their way to the stricken vessel through the breaking surf. As they climbed on to the yacht heeling at 45° and pounding on the reef, they were amazed to hear Brunhilde greet them normally and ask if they would like coffee or tea. In the meantime, the rest of *Amadé*'s crew were transferred to the *Neiafu*, but Brunhilde and Walter insisted on remaining on board hoping that their yacht was not going to be lost. Several times the *Neiafu* tried to pull *Amadé* off the reef, but without success, as in the dark the tow lines kept snagging and the rescue attempt was abandoned until dawn. When daylight came, the Tongan sailors could see exactly where the ropes were snagging on the coral heads and dived to free them. The *Neiafu* was then able to pull *Amadé* into deeper water immediately. In spite of spending the entire night bouncing up and down on the coral reef, the aluminium Levrier de Mer had fortunately suffered little damage, and was able to make her own way into Nuku'alofa. Walter explained later that it had been caused by a simple navigational error, as he had failed to take into account the strong current setting towards the reef. Being alone on watch, he could not check the GPS as frequently as he should have done, and when the yacht struck the reef under full sail, it took some time for the rest of the crew to come up on deck and help him drop the sails. Until they got all the sails down, the yacht was being driven further and further on to the reef and Walter admitted that at that time he felt everything was lost.

News of *Amadé*'s grounding reached the rest of the yachts still at sea on the following morning's radio net and after the high spirits that had prevailed earlier, a sense of apprehension swept through the fleet. At the back of my mind I had almost expected something like this to happen once the yachts started sailing through the reef infested waters of the South Pacific. I had been very apprehensive throughout the leg from the Marquesas to Tahiti, while the yachts were sailing close to the Tuamotus, but all I could do was warn participants repeatedly at the skippers briefings about the danger of navigating through areas of reefs and strong unpredictable currents. The danger was probably compounded by the false sense of security derived from knowing one's position exactly at all times thanks to the GPS. In fact, most of the charts in use have not been corrected yet to agree with the latest data obtained from satellite measurements so, although the position of a vessel is known with perfect accuracy, the charts themselves can contain grave inaccuracies. This calls for as much prudence as before especially in dangerous areas such as the South Pacific.

A few days after the first arrivals, the bulk of the fleet began arriving in Nuku'alofa. The smaller racing boats were particularly affected by the calm weather, while the yachts in the Cruising Division took advantage of their motoring allowance to reach Tonga. The only exception was *Tais*, whose crew had no choice. After the water pump on his engine had broken in Tahiti, Dave Sutherland decided to sail with the rest of the fleet instead of waiting for the new part to arrive from England. As *Tais* was eventually towed into Faua harbour, she received a noisy welcome of cheers and foghorns. A similar reception awaited *Jolly Joker*, who, after a frustrating leg during which the yacht suffered several breakages, was the last to sail into Faua.

All boats were helped into port by a group of New Zealand and Australian sailors who took lines ashore and presented a basket of fruit and fresh bread on behalf of the Tongan Visitors Bureau. Most of the yachts had taken part in the South Seas Regatta for cruising yachts, which sails from New Zealand to Tonga every year. Particularly helpful were Pam and Ted Pasma of the yacht *Conandale*, who also allowed their radio to be used by Andrew Bishop for the daily radio net. Smoothing the way through all formalities was Don Mundell, who after organising the South Seas Regatta, stayed behind to coordinate everything for EUR-OPA 92 on behalf of the Tongan Visitors Bureau.

Royal anniversary

With the fleet dressed overall, Faua looked very festive, which was fitting as EUROPA 92 had been timed to arrive in Tonga for the Heilala Festival, a week of celebrations marking King Taufa'ahau Tupou IV's 73rd birthday. Various activities were going on throughout the week, from beauty competitions to canoe racing, leading up to the birthday celebrations on 4 July. Special events were also laid on for EUROPA participants; a welcoming party at the Nuku'alofa Yacht Club, tours of the island and a visit to the Tongan National Centre where crews found themselves participating in the traditional ceremony of kava drinking. A special set of postage stamps was issued to commemorate the arrival of the rally.

A reception and prize giving ceremony was held at the Dateline Hotel during which Baron Vaea, acting Deputy Prime Minister and Minister for Tourism, presented locally made trophies and prizes to the winners of the last leg as well as to the winners of the story competition. Pasquale de Gregorio won not only line honours but, for the first time in the rally, *Gilma Express* also won the leg overall on handicap. Class II in the Racing Division was won by *Oingo Boingo*, while a special prize was awarded by the Tongan hosts to *Locura* for being the first to reach Tonga, although she had been disqualified from the Racing Division by motoring. In the Cruising Division, Class I was won by *Bluewater*, Class II by *Libertad II* and Class III by *Daughter of Baltic*.

In the story competition, in spite of being dominated by the English speaking participants, Astrid Breuer-Greiff won the prize for the most succinct, the crew of *Elan Adventurer* for the most original and Peter Bunting for the most literary story. The choice of winners was not easy as all entries displayed much originality pointing to considerable literary talent among EUROPA participants. The prize giving was followed by a dinner and dance, with a floorshow of Tongan dancing.

It was pouring with rain the following morning, but this did not prevent the skippers turning out in their best dress for the group photograph to be taken with His Majesty King Taufa'ahau Tupou IV. The previous day the VHF radio had been alive with desperate appeals for spare jackets, and frantic searches for the one tie known to be lying somewhere at the bottom of a locker. The rain eventually stopped, and as the sun came out the skippers formed a neat group in front of the palace, with the King sitting in their midst.

The following day boats were already moving on, the majority planning to sail north to Ha'apai and Vava'u, Tonga's other island groups,

It has taken Astrid and Wilhelm Greiff over five years to get *Octopus* ready to sail around the world.

before making the passage across to Fiji. As the cruising break coincided with the summer holidays in the Northern Hemisphere, many yachts were joined in Tonga and Fiji by families and friends who had flown in from all over the world for a month of leisurely cruising before the start of the next leg in Musket Cove.

Radio story competition

EUROPA 92 – The Latest Lovestory

At *Midnight*, *Oyinbo* restlessly *Strolled* around looking for an *Aventura*: At an *Amble* he walked to *Wachibou* where a dance party was taking place. He wanted to hear *Oingo Boingo* and hoped to meet one of his *Brydies*: *Dafne* or *Gilma*. *Express*ly none of his *Fantasias* appeared, only good old *Jake*. At least the *Sojourn* is free, thought the old *Pennypincher*. He felt inclined to commit a *Locura* and asked *Lady Samantha* to dance. But she took the *Libertad* to refuse pretending she didn't like *Amade*'s music. So he did a *Soolo* instead, envying *Tais* waltzing with *Gulkarna*. Then he saw *Laura*. Her *Rockhopper*like shape made him feel like *Gulliver*. Well, *Who Dares Wins*, he said to himself, picked up an *Orchidea* and invited the *Daughter of Baltic* for a walk to the *Bluewater* zoo. At *Twilight* he showed her an *Octopus* fighting with *Scorpions*, a *Cacadu* necking with a *Kite*. With *Elan* he took her in his arms. I love you, *Cheone*, he whispered. I love you, too, you *Jolly Joker*. And in the *Eye of Ra* they enjoyed a gorgeous *Trillium*.

Astrid Breuer-Greiff
Octopus

Quest of the Maidens

Lady Samantha de *L'Aventura* and her twin sister *Elana Adventurer* had both come of age. They now had one week to prove themselves worthy of a noble marriage or else become the slaves of the cruel *Jakes Fantasia* and wed him, or suffer circumnavigation. So they set off over *Bluewater* and *Dancing Wave* to the land of *Gulkarna*l knowledge. They searched out the father of *Gulliver*, the last available nobleman, to discover what trials had to be overcome. This is how Signor *Gilma* *express*ed the quest:

'First *you-ropa 92* wild yachtsmen and tie them up, eat two dozen *Brydie*s, which will leave a bad *Tais* in your mouth. The only remedy can be obtained from the elusive French witch doctor, known locally as *LeCurra* (*Locura*). Search out the

Orchidea and the distant *Hypatia* in the darkness of *Libertad* together, for the doctor will need the petals of both.

Next, C*ram-a-day*s work into twelve hours. Then each make a *Soolo* blindfolded *Sojourner* through the land of a *Trillium Scorpios*, swim in the lake of *Wachibou*, battle the giant *Octopus*, avoid death by *Oingo Boingo* from the savage *Oyinbo* tribe. When you see *Penny, pinch her Kite* but don't get caught. Take this key and search out the three secret doors, but you only get one chance and the *Key only* (*Cheone*) fits one of the doors. Past the door, bring back the chicken with the strange *Cacadu-doodle-doo*. But, beware the full moon as the *Midnight's* troll-appears. *Rock-hop-*around the quagmires, outwit *Laura*, the *Jolly Joker* and pass through the *Eye of Ra*.

First R*ambler* back will face combat with *Dafne, Daughter of Baldric* and *Amelia Viking*. She *Who Dares Wins* through this far must then light this brazier, but they have to *Twi-light*ing it with this box of wet matches.'

This was the challenge issued from the Court of Cornell.

Elan Adventurer

A Cautionary Tale

The men of the village were round the fire in O'Spriggs Public House. The turf glowed red on its grey base of ash, an occasional flare lighting the hearth as a twig, millenniums old, caught a-light and died.

'Tell us, John, another of your tales,' said the landlord's great friend Brian – hoping for a story he could repeat to his wife and so divert her anger from his eventual later return. John Driscoll shifted his great hooked pipe across his mouth and reached for his empty glass. The gesture was not wasted on his audience and a pint of Guinness was soon on the stained oak table at his side.

'Well, youse know I've just come back from a daring and intrepid voyage around the world with Docker Dave – me and young Ian?' The men knew this and nodded. They loved his stories of St Lucia, Panama and the many remote anchorages he had visited and they particularly loved the flourishes and embellishments each story got in the constant re-tellings.

'Now' said John, settling himself comfortably 'it so happened that passing through London – that's a town in England – I heard tell of a sad tale which by the quaire coincidence involved some people with exactly the names of the ships which took part in Cornell's great expedition.

If youse'll be quiet and just fill that empty glass of mine, I'll tell youse all about it.' And John's story began.

Lady Samantha was calling at *Jake*'s house to see her friend *Brydie*. *Brydie* was usually called *Daughter of Baltic*, being the child of a well known Finnish lady-about-London and an Irish seaman, provenance and whereabouts unknown.

'I have an appointment in Ealing,' said *Lady Samantha*, 'Would you care to join me for a little *Elan Aventure?*'

'Do ask *Dafne* or *Laura* instead,' DOB replied, 'I must stay a *Sojourner* in this house, *Jake* won't let me leave for I am part of *Jake's Fantasia* world and he clings to me like an *Octopus*.'

'Do try and come,' urged her friend, '*Who Dares Wins* and surely he cannot *Wachibou* closely all the time?'

DOB gazed sadly back through her beautiful eyes, the colour of deep *Bluewater*. 'Alas,' she sighed, '*Tais* true, he does.'

So *Lady Samantha* had to set out alone. She booked a third class ticket to Ealing – being something of a *Pennypincher* – and paid for it with her new credit card, the *Gilmour Express*, which did very nicely.

Lady Samantha's appointment was with *Gulliver* and she hoped they might spend the afternoon indulging in a little *Oingo Boingo* to their mutual satisfaction. Oyngo Boyngo is, of course, an old Irish country game, usually played by two people.

Gulliver had arranged for a friend to join them at lunch as a 'blind date' for the DOB. Now, *Gulliver* was something of a *Jolly Joker* and had invited a rather sinister character known as the *Midnight Stroller*. This name followed from his custom of wandering the streets of remote Yorkshire mill-towns from *Twilight* till the first *Cacadu*-dule-do of the roosters as they awakened in the backyards and allotments of the grey stone terraced houses. The lunch appointment was at a quaint old Ealing landmark, the *Ambler* Inn.

When *Lady Samantha* arrived at the tryst, she was conducted to a private dining room by *A made* in the costume of another century – it was that sort of establishment. *Gulliver* was surprised that *Lady Samantha* was *Soolo* and wondered what he would do with *Midnight Stroller* when he arrived. Nevertheless, smiling, he handed her the *Orchidea* which he had brought.

As events turned out, *Midnight Stroller* had spent the previous rather cold night prowling in the country, terrorising the moor-dwellers of Yorkshire and was suffering from hypothermia and more seriously *Hypatia*. *Hypatia*, as is not well known, is a rare form of foot infection contracted through stepping in the droppings of the *Rockhopper*, a bird whose *Locura* are the Yorkshire moors and Antarctica. As a result of these misfortunes, he was unable to attend and embarrassment was spared to all.

While this was going on, DOB had made her escape from

the house of Jake and gained her *Libertad* too – or deux as the French say. Realising that the *Ambler* Inn was not too far off and she might yet be in time for lunch, DOB rushed to the nearest taxi rank, taking the *Cheone*-ly cab there. Unfortunately the driver did not know the way and she had to give instructions.

'Turn left at Station Road, right at the next corner – watch for a pub called the Gull and drop me at the *Gul-karna* . . . ' she directed. As DOB alighted she heard the *Trillion* at the church of St James the Seafarer sound the hour and pressing 10p into the hand of a surprised, small boy attempting to fly his *Kite* on the pavement, she entered the *Ambler* Inn.

With great anticipation DOB burst into the Salle Privé only to find her friend in the arms of *Gulliver*. *Gulliver* turned pale – '*Oyinbo*' he cried, which is an old Nigerian swear word, picked up in his days as a spaghetti farmer in Africa.

'It's you, *Brydie*,' he whispered, giving a fascinating glimpse of the obvious. He was trembling violently, as for years he had been the secret lover of the DOB and frequently vowed eternal faithfulness. DOB shook with rage and glared at the couple from *Eyes of ra*-th. 'And you told me you were sailing around the world, having the *L'Aventura* of a lifetime! Oh you wretch, you snake, you *Scorpio*!'

Still in shock, she stormed out of the room and returned to Jake's house in high dudgeon and a passing no. 11 bus.

The lives of all these people who have featured in this little drama were forever changed by the events of this sad afternoon.

Gulliver descended further into a life of crime and debauchery. He qualified as a chartered accountant, joined the firm of Coopers & Lybrand, was seconded to *Rockhopper* and sailed endlessly around the world in the position of Chief Stoker.

Daughter of Baltic, aka *Brydie*, returned to the security of *Jake's Fantasia* world and never again carped the Diem. The real world was not for her.

As for *Lady Samantha*, she had lost a good friend and a splendid partner for *Oyngo Boyngo* and settled, in her declining years, for gin and afternoon television, becoming an authority on old American 'B' category movies and Ronald Reagan.

'Well boys,' said John 'That's me story. Now it's someone else's turn' and finished with a term he had grown familiar with on his travels. 'Cambio!'

Peter Bunting
Gulkarna II

9
TRADE WIND PASSAGE

Leg 8: Fiji to Vanuatu

The long break of five weeks between the finish of the leg in Tongatapu and the start of the next one in Musket Cove, on Fiji's west side, allowed participants to spend some time in Vava'u, Tonga's northern island group. Scattered around one large central island are scores of uninhabited islets. The entire group is protected by a barrier reef which stops the ocean swell and ensures perfect sailing conditions in this large lagoon. With few visitors coming to Vava'u except those arriving by yacht, the locals are very welcoming and there were several beach parties organised by villagers with pork baked in the traditional earth oven and barbecued fish freshly caught in the lagoon.

While Tonga has most of its best cruising concentrated in one small area, the entire Fijian archipelago is one immense cruising ground. While sailing on to the next rendezvous, most participants managed to get a taste of Fiji's offerings, but time was too short to enjoy its many attractions to the full. Initially the rally was supposed to restart from the Fijian capital Suva, whose Royal Suva Yacht Club has the reputation of being one of the most welcoming clubs anywhere in the world. As some of Fiji's best cruising areas are in the west, that is to say downwind from Suva, this could have posed serious logistical problems when the time came for the yachts to make their way back against the prevailing winds and current to join the start. This is when Dick Smith, an Australian entrepreneur who has lived most of his life building resorts in Fiji, stepped in and offered EUROPA 92 the facilities of his present resort with absolutely no strings attached — except that we start the leg to Vanuatu from there. Musket Cove on Malololailai Island is already the venue of an annual fun race to neighbouring Vanuatu, which attracts some sixty cruising yachts for the 500 mile run to Port Vila. Dick Smith, who once roamed the South Pacific in his own yacht, founded at Musket Cove some years ago the most informal yacht club in the world, which can be joined by paying the grand sum of one Fiji dollar for life membership, the only condition being that the would-be member arrives in Fiji from overseas by yacht. The names of all existing members have been carved into the beams of the bar and restaurant, and a special beam was dedicated to the EUROPA 92 participants, all of whom were made honorary members of the Musket Cove Yacht Club. The main attraction of Musket Cove is its perfect location close to the picturesque Mamanutha and Yasawa groups of islands, while at the same time being within striking distance of Fiji's international airport at Nadi, to which it is linked by its own small aircraft. Fiji's second biggest town, Lautoka, is also close by with very good provisioning and repair facilities. A new boatyard, with its own travelift, had been opened in time for EUROPA 92's arrival, the owner Max Volau being so worried that he may not be ready in time and would miss this golden opportunity that he started his operation a bit too early with the result that the hastily built travelift pen collapsed just as *Who Dares Wins* was being hoisted out of the water. Fortunately the yacht was not damaged, but Ian Kennedy had had enough and decided to try his luck elsewhere. Other skippers were not daunted and many used the yard's improvised facilities, amongst them *Amadé* whose mangled rudder had to be completely rebuilt after its argument with the Tongan reef.

Formality and informality Fijian style

While some skippers were busily repairing or antifouling their yachts, others were cruising the neighbouring Yasawas and coming to learn first hand the etiquette of Fijian village life. By tradition, on arrival the skipper and crew are supposed to visit the village chief and make him a symbolic gift, normally a bunch of kava roots. Ground up and mixed with water, the roots of this plant produce kava, or yaqona as it is known in Fiji. This slightly narcotic drink, which is drunk throughout Polynesia, also has a ceremonial function akin to smoking a pipe with a North American Indian chieftain or taking part in a tea ceremony in Japan. While visiting Fijian islands most skippers took their ceremonial duties quite seriously, but some of those who ignored such rules of hospitality were surprised to be asked to leave the area of the offended village.

For the first time since leaving Gibraltar, participants had to sail on their own to another country and deal with the various clearance formalities themselves, something which was normally done by the organisers. Most yachts cleared into Fiji at Suva, where formalities were complicated and time consuming. Later Alan Spriggs confronted me directly. 'Jimmy, you must have done this on purpose, leaving us to deal with all these boring and lengthy formalities ourselves, only so as to appreciate more what you are doing for us in all the other places.'

Meanwhile, the fleet was gathering at Musket Cove, where yachts had to anchor in the lagoon as the marina being built by Dick Smith had only progressed as far as a dredged channel leading to the fuel pump. The private resort on this small island was very different to anywhere the fleet had assembled before and there was little to do except relax on the cool verandah by the bar.

The Italian participants invite everyone to a huge spaghetti party at Musket Cove.

In response to the British party in Tahiti, the Italian yachts invited all participants, as well as the staff of Musket Cove resort, to a spaghetti party. Dinghies full of spaghetti and parmesan cheese were ferried ashore, while Dick Smith provided the ingredients for the sauces. Every crew prepared a different sauce from their own region and the variety took many by surprise, several non-Italians remarking afterwards that spaghetti will never taste the same again.

Mini Olympics

Two days before the start, a mini Olympics was held when about fifty participants joined in a variety of fun events including beach volleyball, biathalon, golf, a three-legged swimming race and a beer drinking competition. For the less inhibited there was also a chance to get close to their friends with a game of pass the banana. Both teams managed to squash two bananas before a winning team emerged. The afternoon was ended with a tug-of-war in which the Europeans pulled against the Americans. The Europeans were heading for a convincing victory until six burly Fijians came to the aid of the Americans, crushing the stronger team. The matter was protested and the jury declared the Europeans winners. At least the Americans had the compensation of winning the volleyball tournament. The winners in the other events were:

Golf driving: Tom Sutter (*Kite*) and Rhonda Peterson (*Kite*);
Biathlon: Enroy Robinson (*Brydie*) and Jody Windmiller (*Tais*);
Three-legged swimming: John Nichols (*Sojourner*) and Liz Gilley (*Twilight*).

The same evening there was a traditional welcoming ceremony for the EUROPA 92 fleet prepared by the villagers from neighbouring Kawa Kawa on Malolo Island. This ceremony is rarely performed, being kept for very special occasions, the last occasion being two years previously. The formality of the occasion was quite impressive and every one of the skippers, sitting crosslegged on mats before the chief, was proffered a bowl of kava. The evening was rounded off by a magnificent meal of Fijian specialities to which our generous hosts, Dick and Carol Smith, had invited everyone in the fleet. It was a memorable evening that will remain in most participants minds as the highlight of their visit to Fiji.

True to his word, on the morning of Saturday 10 August, Dick's aircraft brought in a team of customs and immigration officials from Lautoka to do the clearing out formalities on the spot, which duly impressed everyone, Alan Spriggs included. With *Rockhopper* and *Jakes Fantasia* delayed at Max Volau's boatyard, 33 yachts lined up for the start of the leg to Port Vila. Sadly one yacht was not on the line; having been with the rally since Gibraltar, Richard Goord of *Oyinbo* had decided to spend more time in the South Pacific.

Excellent winds at the start, which had been set inside the lagoon in the lee of Malolo Island, allowed participants to sail the yachts at their full potential while racing for the wide passage through the reef. Unfortunately such seeming perfection was severely undermined when the Committee vessel, marking one end of the line, started dragging its anchor in the fresh winds. While the Committee vessel was rapidly falling off, shortening the start line as it did so, the crew were making frantic attempts to regain their earlier position. With less than five minutes left and the pre-start signal already given, it was decided it was too late to postpone the start and at the stated time, the starting signal was given. In the confusion caused by the moving Committee vessel, some yachts started incorrectly, leaving the vessel to starboard rather than to port, as stated in the Sailing Instructions.

After clearing the islands the yachts found themselves in a strong SE airflow with winds of 25 to 30 knots, gusting to 40 at times. Although strong, these excellent conditions made for a very fast and exhilarating sail to Vanuatu where the first to arrive was *Gilma Express*. The ULDB covered the 515 miles in 2 days 3 hours 39 minutes at an average speed of just under 10 knots; her top speed on the crossing was 21.2 knots. This time set a new record, breaking the 62 hours made by *Blizzard* during the 1988 Musket Cove to Port Vila Race. Seven other EUROPA yachts also broke the record and most yachts reported excellent times. There were no major equipment failures, although several yachts had to be towed in when their engines failed to start after the windy passage.

Port Vila

All the yachts were moored stern to the sea wall in the centre of Port Vila, creating a colourful spectacle and there was hardly a moment when there were not people walking along admiring the fleet. For the first time the crews from 30 yachts were able to attend the early arrivals party, so quickly did they all finish. On Sunday 18 August seven of the EUROPA yachts took part in a fun race organised by the hosting club, the Vanuatu Cruising Yacht Club, whose Commodore Ross Wilson had been organising the reception of the EUROPA fleet. A pursuit race of 18 miles around Mele Bay provided an excellent opportunity for the local boats to sail against the visitors. Most EUROPA yachts sailed with mixed crews having supplemented their own with some of those who were not taking part in the race. The winner was a local boat, with *Oingo Boingo* coming a close second. Afterwards a sausage sizzle at the Waterfront bar enabled participants to meet more members of the local sailing community. Twelve secondary school children were delighted to be taken for a sail on *Elan Adventurer* and *Kite* as a reward for having taken part in a T-shirt design competition to commemorate the arrival of EUROPA 92 in Vanuatu. The winner was James Alvine, whose design was made into an attractive T-shirt.

Although the stay in Port Vila was relatively short, some participants found the time to see more of this fascinating country. Undoubtedly the most interesting visit was to Tanna, a smaller island in the south of the country, where a live volcano has been active for some time. This is one of the most accessible live volcanoes in the world and the spectacle which met participants who made their way to the top and spent the night there was stupendous.

The excellent atmosphere in Port Vila was marred by the tension following a protest lodged by *Who Dares Wins* and *Pennypincher*. As a result of the confusion at the start in Fiji, the two yachts protested all the yachts which had started incorrectly. A Protest Committee was formed and it decided to give all yachts that had started incorrectly a 6 hour time penalty. As a result, *Who Dares Wins* won the leg on corrected time in the Racing Division and unseated *Gulliver* from the overall lead.

A prize giving, attended by the Deputy Prime Minister, the Hon. Sethy Regenvanu, was held at the Rossi Hotel. The number of prizes, donated by the local business community, reflected the generosity experienced by everyone during their stay in Vanuatu. It was particularly fitting that John Papp's *Ambler* won Cruising Class III, as he had decided to withdraw from the rally to spend longer in Australia.

Satellite navigation

Sailing one dark night through the reef-infested waters of Fiji's Lau Group I remembered passing through the same area in the mid-seventies on my previous 36 foot yacht *Aventura*. The crew was the same, my wife Gwenda, our daughter Doina and son Ivan, although now we were all 15 years older. *La Aventura* was also quite different to her earlier namesake which had safely carried us around the world, her sum total of electronic equipment consisting of RDF and a depth sounder. Now I had a lot more electronic gadgetry, including a brand new B&G Horizon GPS unit. It was the latter which eased our passage through this difficult stretch of water in contrast to my anxiety fifteen years previously when cloudy skies had prevented the taking of sights.

Being able to plot a safe course amid the reefs and unlit islands filled me with both admiration and gratitude for my GPS and I could understand the similar feelings expressed by my fellow sailors in the rally. One of the aims of the equipment survey I carried out was to find out how many yachts were equipped with GPS and to assess the role played by GPS in offshore navigation.

Some interesting facts came to light during the survey and I was surprised to find that only three boats (*Laura*, *Elan Adventurer* and *Jolly Joker*) did not have GPS, their owners finding the older Transit system sufficient for their needs. However, with hindsight, the loss of *Jolly Joker* in the Torres Strait may well have been avoided had the crew known their position more exactly, rather than relying on an earlier satnav fix and their DR. An accurate GPS fix might have shown them just how close they were to the reef, thus allowing them to take avoiding action before a steering failure rendered the boat unmanoeuvrable. On the other hand, being equipped with GPS did not prevent *Amadé* from running aground on a reef in Tonga, although a display unit in the cockpit may have made a difference as Walter Gollhofer was alone on watch at the time.

Another incident, when *Cacadu* lost a man overboard during the leg from the Galapagos to the Marquesas, caused Julian Wilson of *Elan Adventurer* to regret not having GPS. 'We had to alter course several times to search a specific area and more accurate position fixing would have made this much easier.' Altogether ten other EUROPA yachts joined in the search operation and, as all the others were equipped with GPS, they were able to coordinate their search areas very precisely.

As shown in Table 14, there was a large number of GPS makes and models in the EUROPA 92 fleet and every owner was asked why he or she had acquired that particular model. Because most GPS units were acquired when the price was still relatively high, the choice of make was often dictated by price considerations. This was the main reason why several people chose the Magellan 1000 Plus, which on the eve of the start of the rally was the cheapest model on the market. Several owners admitted that in the early days of GPS, they preferred to buy a cheaper model to see how it worked and also to use it as a backup for their existing Transit system. It did not take them long to realise the superiority of GPS and, in some cases, these cheaper portable units were relegated to the panic bag and the boat equipped with a fixed GPS unit.

Table 14   Satellite navigation equipment

Make	Number	Performance	Reliability
GPS			
Trimble Transpac	6	9.7	9.5
Trimble Navtrac	2	10	9.5
Trimble 10X	1	10	10
Furuno GP500	2	10	10
Magellan 1000	7	9.3	9.3
Pronav	1	10	10
Raytheon Raystar	4	9.7	9.5
Navstar XR4	3	8.7	9
B&G Horizon	2	6.5	9
Koden	2	9	9.5
Magnavox 4200	1	10	10
Philips	1	6	8
Shipmate 5300	1	10	10
Micrologic	1	10	10
Total:	34		
Transit			
Navstar 2000S	9	8.9	9
Magnavox 4102	5	8.6	8.4
Walker	5	7	7.6
Furuno	4	7.7	9.7
Shipmate 5100	1	10	10
Si-Tex 310	1	10	10
Total:	25		

The owners were asked to rate their satellite navigation equipment from 1 to 10 both for reliability and performance. In a few cases, the reliability rating of GPS units was influenced by the non-availability of a suitable satellite constellation to produce an accurate fix, or the temporary closing down of the entire GPS operation, neither of which should have been blamed on the actual performance of the various models.

Some models, however, were consistently rated high on both counts and, in spite of the obvious shortcomings inherent in a handheld unit, the Magellan 1000 Plus attracted more praise than criticism. Some of the Magellan's popularity was due to its portability and independence from the boat's electricity supply. For this reason, on five boats a Magellan 1000 was carried as a standby, was not in normal use and consequently was not included in the above statistics, while on *Brydie* it had been packed in the panic bag in case the boat had to be abandoned. I experienced the advantage of a second portable GPS, brought along by a crew member, while sailing at night between Hibernia and Ashmore reefs on the way from Darwin to Bali. Although we knew where we were, the strong currents sweeping through the area caused us some concern, so it was a great relief for the helmsman to be able to keep an eye on the cross-track error and make the necessary adjustments to our course without having to leave the cockpit. This point was also made by Walter Gollhofer who felt that *Amadé*'s grounding probably would have been avoided if he had been able to check his GPS without leaving the helm.

For similar reasons, a clear display which could be read easily from a distance persuaded some skippers to buy the Raytheon Raystar whose display was rated the best. Among other reasons given for choosing a particular model of GPS were the reputation of a particular make, or one owner's preference for a big ship model which, he hoped, would be easier to have serviced around the world if necessary. This was the reason why Rick Palm equipped *Sojourner* with a Shipmate 5300, but he was disappointed to find that when the unit was sent back for repair to the manufacturer, the repair cost exceeded the price of one of the handheld units available on the market.

The advantage of using GPS when sailing through an area affected by strong currents clearly impressed Enio Nardi, whose many Atlantic crossings and over 200,000 miles of ocean sailing made him probably the most experienced sailor in the fleet. 'GPS will radically change the current methods of navigation. GPS now gives the possibility of making night passages through difficult areas, such as the channel separating the Fijian islands of Viti Levu and Beqa, where our GPS gave us constant information on the state of the current. It is this kind of night passage that I would have never even dreamt of doing in pre-GPS days.' Given people's increasing dependence on GPS, Enio suggested that the GPS unit should have a separate power supply so as to make it totally independent and reliable.

Gulkarna II was one of the yachts equipped with a second portable Magellan, because owner Peter Bunting felt that with the main GPS running off the ship's batteries, it was a relief to know that the Magellan would be available instantly should the main electrics fail. 'Once you use these things, you become dependent on them, so as a prudent mariner you should have a backup.'

One of the best satellite navigation installations was on *Bluewater* where the existing Magnavox 4102 Transit unit was interfaced with the GPS through a black box supplied by Magnavox for their 4200 model. Both units were kept on all the time, and as the 4102 stored all information automatically, if the GPS went down for any reason, data would be available instantaneously from the Transit system.

Half the boats kept their Transit satellite navigators on all the time as a backup to the GPS, while on other boats the Transit was switched on occasionally to check if it was working or to compare its accuracy with that of the GPS. On *Jakes Fantasia*, one of the boats on which both satnavs were kept on permanently, the GPS and Transit were permanently cross-checked to detect any possible discrepancy.

Most boats kept their GPS on all the time, with only two exceptions, *Octopus* and *Pennypincher*, where the GPS was only switched on when required. Power management was an obsession with Wilhelm Greiff, the skipper of *Octopus*, who had worked wonders in keeping his electricity consumption to an absolute minimum. On *Octopus* the GPS was only switched on when a fix was needed, and even then the availability of satellites was checked first so as to ascertain that the existing constellation would ensure an accurate fix. Similarly, Wilhelm always checked to see if his GPS would be able to provide an accurate fix for an intended landfall and take whatever necessary measure if this was not the case.

Generally, participants in EUROPA 92 experienced far less interruptions in GPS coverage than they had anticipated, which was due mainly to the Gulf War because of which the Pentagon kept the system going all the time. During the few breaks in coverage, participants reverted to their faithful Transit units, although in some areas the satellite coverage by the older system was erratic and there were days when one had to wait several hours before obtaining a fix.

In spite of this, Alan Spriggs was so happy with the accurate performance of his Walker 412 Transit satellite navigator that he continued to use it in preference to his Trimble Transpac GPS, whose internal antenna caused it to pick up less satellites than would have been the case with an externally mounted antenna. According to Alan, the difference between positions obtained by the two units rarely varied by more than one mile, so he preferred to stick by his old satnav which was installed at his navigation station, rather than have to take the portable GPS into the cockpit. On *Libertad II*, the two units were used for different purposes and, as Christian Philibert pointed out, 'When sailing offshore and absolute accuracy is not so important, the permanently mounted Transit unit is much easier to use than the portable GPS. However, as we close with land, the Magellan takes over, although it has to be used in the cockpit.'

Astronavigation

Because one of the rally rules stated that at least one person must be able to fix a yacht's position by non-electronic means, every yacht was equipped with sextant, sight reduction tables and the current almanac, or at least a calculator which had the almanac data stored in its memory. Exactly half the boats carried calculators with dedicated astronavigation programs. Among the yachts equipped with a personal computer, ten had the necessary software for working out sights.

Although everyone looked well prepared to do their navigation with the help of heavenly bodies, the reality was very different. On the majority of boats, offshore navigation depended entirely on satellite navigation, while the sextants gathered dust in a locker from where they emerged on very rare occasions, if at all. Most skippers admitted that they carried their sextants primarily for emergencies and only about half made a point of occasionally taking a sight, either to keep their hands in or just for their own pleasure.

Although astronavigation was rarely used for position fixing, most of the skippers of boats which had frequent crew changes, such as *Oingo Boingo*, *Daughter of Baltic*, *Rockhopper* and *Lady Samantha*, gave new crew members a few lessons in astronavigation. On *Lady Samantha*, astronavigation formed part of the curriculum.

Although the majority of navigators were happy to let their GPS do all the work, there were a few yachts on which the sextant was used daily, $4\frac{1}{2}$ skippers answering this question in the affirmative. The half discrepancy was caused by *Locura*, on which the sextant was used every other day. Usually taking three sun sights, Leo Birkby was very pleased to find that his sights often put him within two miles of his GPS position. Perhaps the most assiduous navigator was John Driscoll who sailed on *Tais* for the first half of the rally and took at least three sun sights daily as a matter of routine.

Among those totally dependent on GPS was Peter Bunting. 'I'm horrified to find that I'm not using the sextant at all. A friend warned me I wouldn't use it any more and it's true! We are the very first generation of sailors to use GPS exclusively.' This was a point with which Marcello Murzilli was in complete agreement. 'Before all this I used to work out our position every hour, now we rely 100% on the GPS.'

Looking at the daily navigation routine of the 36 yachts surveyed, 23 of their skippers said that they based their offshore navigation entirely on GPS. Satellite navigation was also the principal means of position fixing on seven more yachts, two of which were equipped only with Transit, while the other five cross-checked the GPS and Transit all the time. On the remaining yachts a mixture of everything was used including the occasional sun sight. On *Oyinbo*, the sextant was used about three times a week, either for sun sights or occasionally star sights.

Although the majority of navigators appeared to rely entirely on their GPS, on several yachts positions were still marked regularly on the chart. On *Daughter of Baltic*, the course was marked on the chart frequently, the GPS being used only to check the accuracy of the DR either when a waypoint was reached or for cross-track error. On *Gulkarna II* the positions obtained from the GPS were marked on the chart at every change of watch. A similar practice was followed on *La Aventura* where the latest position was marked on the chart and the person coming off watch also recorded wind strength and direction, barometric pressure and other data of interest in the ship's log.

Because of their frequent crew changes, on *Rockhopper* the crew on watch had to make accurate log entries every two hours. Before joining the rally, Moira Gold had worked for the international firm of accountants Coopers & Lybrand, Deloitte who agreed to support *Rockhopper* during their circumnavigation. Thus, the yacht was joined at every leg by four different employees of the company, which has branches all over the world as well as in almost all the countries visited by the rally.

On *Twilight* the position was marked on the chart every hour and, as Dino Blancodini remarked, this was a good practice as it forced the person on watch to be more attentive as the boat was steered by autopilot. *Twilight* was one of three yachts also equipped with chart plotters, and in areas where electronic charts were available, the unit was kept on all the time. The absence of such charts for some areas on the EUROPA 92 route made Pasquale de Gregorio have serious doubts about the usefulness of a chart plotter on a voyage of this kind and personally he preferred plotting his course on a paper chart. 'In offshore navigation my Navmap is not really useful. In coastal navigation in order to see any detail, one has to zoom in but once you're zoomed in, you can no longer see the general picture to be able to relate to the rest. So I find electronic charts useless for both offshore and coastal navigation.' On *Midnight Stroller*, the chart plotter was interfaced with both the GPS and the autopilot, so an accurate DR was available at all times.

As Ian Kennedy explained 'Navigation on *Who Dares Wins* is planned for racing and therefore we depend on GPS to tell us how efficiently we're keeping to the desired course.' Understandably enough, their main purpose was to sail as fast as possible to gain an advantage over their rival *Gulliver*. After the outcome of the protest in Port Vila, the fight between the two Swans became even more heated and the leg to Darwin, perhaps the most difficult and demanding of the entire rally, was to provide *Gulliver* with a perfect chance to regain on the race course what had been lost at the protest table.

10
THROUGH THE
TORRES STRAIT

Leg 9: Vanuatu to Darwin

The temptation of neighbouring Australia and its Great Barrier Reef proved too much for four yachts, whose owners decided to make a detour to Cairns in Queensland before rejoining the rally in Darwin. On Sunday 25 August, 31 yachts took the start from Port Vila. Light westerly winds made for a cautious start as the yachts prepared to beat their way out of the beautiful bay fronting Port Vila. The Vanuatu Navy patrol vessel *Tukora* acted as the Committee vessel and in the light winds the starting line was crossed first by the two Finnish yachts in the Racing Division. A perfect manoeuvre gave Arne Blässar the satisfaction of *Cacadu* just beating Pekka Hyryläinen's *Soolo* across the line.

The yachts had a long and difficult passage ahead of them during which they had to negotiate the Torres Strait, one of the most treacherous stretches of navigable waters in the world. The winds remained light for the first 24 hours, then picked up and blew at 12 to 18 knots from the ESE, providing perfect sailing conditions across the Coral Sea all the way to Bramble Cay, at the entrance to the Torres Strait. The front runners changed several times, *Gilma Express* being in the lead for the first 36 hours. *Gulliver* then took the lead, holding on to it through the Torres Strait until relinquishing it to *Gilma Express* halfway across the Gulf of Carpentaria. During this time, a high pressure system over the east coast of Australia accelerated the winds in the Torres Strait to 25–30 knots. Combined with the strong tidal streams running through the strait, this made the transit more testing than had been expected.

The loss of *Jolly Joker*

On the night of 3 September a Mayday was picked up by John Rose on *Midnight Stroller*. The crew of *Jolly Joker* reported that they had been driven on to a reef and were abandoning the boat. No further communication was heard from the crew, so John Rose immediately turned his yacht around to head for *Jolly Joker*'s last known position. Other yachts in the area also joined in the rescue attempt or stood by. Due to the high winds and large swell, it was decided that any rescue attempt at night would put the yachts in too much danger. This decision was backed by the Australian search and rescue authorities who had been alerted and were coordinating the operation, although they also were unable to do anything until first light. While some yachts were released and advised to carry on, *Elan Adventurer* and *Wachibou*, the nearest yachts to the scene of the accident, remained standing by throughout the night.

At dawn a search and rescue operation was mounted by the Australian authorities who dispatched a helicopter to the area. It was ascertained that *Jolly Joker* had hit Bet Reef near Sue Island, but the helicopter crew could see no evidence of anyone on board the stricken yacht. By this time the mast had collapsed and a large hole was visible in the hull. Unfortunately the helicopter then had to make an emergency landing due to an electrical problem and was not operational again for another 24 hours.

Jolly Joker shows her potential at the start of the leg from Fiji.

With the helicopter out of action, the search was continued by *Elan Adventurer* and *Wachibou*. The area was thoroughly searched and an hour and a half later the liferaft was sighted at the western end of Bet Reef. The crew were safely picked up by *Elan Adventurer* who took them, and the liferaft, to Horn Island. Rather than dropping them off to face the authorities on their own, Julian Wilson decided to withdraw *Elan Adventurer* from the leg and accompany the Hungarian sailors to Thursday Island, the main centre in the area and a port of entry.

An operation was mounted the next day to try and salvage equipment from the wrecked yacht, but this proved very difficult as the yacht was full of water and fuel from the ruptured fuel tank. Some personal possessions were retrieved, including the crew's passports, but the yacht itself was not salvageable as it had completely lost its keel and was rapidly breaking up. After three days, *Elan Adventurer* set off for Darwin with two of the crew, leaving the skipper János Barzsantik on Thursday Island to finalise formalities.

When I met the crew later in Darwin, they described how earlier during the leg they had experienced problems with the steering cables, but had managed to sort them out. On the night of the accident, the helmsman on watch experienced some difficulty in steering. While sailing past Sue Island, the steering cables suddenly jammed and the wheel could no longer be turned to port. Unable to steer, the crew tried to lower the sails and start the engine but the strong wind and current pushed the yacht out of the channel where it struck a reef. The shock of the collision was so violent that the keel was broken off on impact. The skipper tried to activate their EPIRB while the crew launched the liferaft. Unable to activate the EPIRB, they tried to send a Mayday but by this time the cabin had filled with water and one of the crew had to dive for the radio and pass the microphone through an open porthole. Soon after the Mayday had been sent, the mast broke and collapsed on deck, so the crew decided to abandon the yacht and make for a navigation light they could see on the nearby island. As they cast off, the wind and current took hold of the liferaft, which started drifting rapidly away from the island. The small paddle provided with the raft then broke and it took some desperate efforts to reach shallower water and stop the liferaft. The crew made their way to the light where they remained until they were found at dawn by the crew of *Elan Adventurer*.

The loss of his yacht was particularly painful to András Jójárt who had been forced by family circumstances to return to Budapest and had left the others to cope in his absence as well as they could. He was profoundly distressed by the accident and felt guilty for not being on board when it happened. Undeterred by the tragedy, András agreed with Guy Libens to buy *Wachibou* and continue the rally with the boat renamed *Jolly Joker Again*. Although he managed to sail some of the remaining legs on *Wachibou*, the event came to an end before a payment from the insurance company allowed him to conclude the deal.

Meanwhile several yachts at the front of the fleet had already arrived in Darwin. The battle between *Gulliver* and *Gilma Express* continued right up to the finishing line, which *Gilma Express* crossed only 9 minutes ahead of *Gulliver* after 2500 miles of sailing. As *Who Dares Win* took nearly 10 more hours to finish, at least *Gulliver* had the satisfaction of winning the leg on corrected time, even if relinquishing line honours to Pasquale de Gregorio. Class II in the Racing Division was won by *Oingo*

Boingo, while the three classes in the Cruising Division were won by *Cheone*, *Libertad II* and *Tais*.

Australia's top end

Good winds from the ESE continued to speed the remainder of the fleet around the top of Australia, everyone reporting fast passage times. The winds dropped in the approaches to Darwin, and once the northwest corner of Bathurst Island had been rounded, light winds and strong tidal streams made everyone's life difficult. Such frustrating conditions nevertheless made for an interesting last 80 miles, many of the cruising boats succumbing to the temptation of using their engine for the first time on this leg. Not, however, *Octopus*, who was caught in the light airs created by a change in weather. Although becalmed for several days, Wilhelm still did not motor and was the last to finish almost three weeks after the start.

There were other hazards encountered *en route* including large banks of seaweed which caught both *Who Dares Wins* and *La Aventura* unaware, fouling their rudders and necessitating a diver to go overboard to clear them. *Eye of Ra* was even less fortunate when she came to a halt on a fishing net. The net had to be hauled up on either side of the yacht to cut a passage through, still leaving some six feet of netting entangled on the keel and only cleared when the yacht was hauled out in Darwin.

After six months in the South Seas, Darwin proved to be a very popular stop for all participants. Although the Darwin Sailing Club had generously offered its facilities to the visitors, the absence of adequate mooring facilities persuaded all skippers to dock their yachts in the marina type fishing boat basin, which had the added advantage of being closer to the city. The basin is surrounded by many workshops used to dealing with the large fishing fleet, which is based there. A welcoming committee, formed by local businesses under the chairmanship of Percy Mitchell, ensured that the visitors lacked nothing. Many skippers took advantage of the excellent repair facilities in Darwin and the boatyards were continuously busy with boats hauled out for antifouling or other routine maintenance work. Many postponed jobs and repairs were dealt with as skippers knew it would be a long time before they would see such repair facilities again.

The welcoming committee hosted one of the many informal parties that took place during the fleet's stay in Darwin. The Administrator of the Northern Territory, the Hon J Muirhead, invited all participants to a splendid reception at his official residence. Amidst this festive atmosphere, Hazel and John Smith, of *Eye of Ra*, decided to bring forward their planned wedding and, rather than wait until Bali, tied the knot in Darwin, Peter Bunting acting as best man and Jan Flowers as bridesmaid. After the wedding they invited everyone to join them for an informal party around the pool at the Beaufort Hotel. The hotel management generously gave them their luxurious bridal suite for the night.

Meanwhile, as Darwin was the only stop in Australia, other participants were busy travelling all over the country. While some made it as far as Melbourne, Sydney, Perth and even Tasmania, most agreed that few places matched the beauty and variety of the Northern Territory itself. One of the highlights for many was a trip to the Kakadu National Park, the unspoilt scenery and wildlife of this little known corner of Australia taking most people by surprise. Giovanna Caprini expressed the feelings of many when she told me later: 'We had not expected anything from Darwin and were truly impressed by everything we found there, the beauty of the country and the warmth of its people. A great place.'

Diesel engines

More than any other leg in the rally, the next leg to Bali was to show the yachts in the Cruising Division the importance of a dependable diesel engine, and a good supply of fuel. Every EUROPA yacht was equipped with a diesel engine and two yachts, *Cheone* and *La Aventura*, had twin engine installations. The skippers were asked to rate their engines both for performance and reliability and most makes were rated high on both counts. It was pointed out, however, that on the occasions when the engine was out of action it was rarely caused by a fault in the engine itself, but usually by some of the auxiliary equipment, particularly the starter motors. An even more common cause of engine failure was dirty fuel, the fuel sold in some of the countries along the EUROPA 92 route causing endless problems, either because it had been stored in rusty drums or because it had a high water content.

By far the most common engine make was Perkins, with half the fleet being equipped with one of its models. Reflecting this popularity, Perkins engines were rated high both for performance and reliability. Not all the engines were new and the oldest examples were two vintage 1967 Perkins 4236 M on *Cheone*. One of them had to be overhauled in Darwin as it was using too much oil and its lower reliability rating explains the lower average shown in Table 15, as without exception all the other Perkins owners gave their engines top ratings for reliability.

The skippers were also asked to comment on the rated power of their engines and to say whether they considered this to be adequate for their needs. Over three quarters of the skippers (28) considered their yachts to be adequately powered, five thought they were underpowered and three considered their yachts to be overpowered. Table 16 shows how engine power was divided among the 36 yachts as well as their average fuel consumption. The average engine power over the entire fleet came

Table 15 Diesel engines

Make	Number	Performance	Reliability
Perkins	20	9.9	9.6
Volvo	6	9.6	9.3
Ford	3	9	9
Yanmar	2	9.5	9.5
Fiat Aifo	2	10	6
Leyland	1	9	9
Westerbeke	1	9	9
Thorneycroft	1	8	9
Isuzu	1	9	9
IFA	1	8	7
Total:	38		

out at 84 hp. If one does not include the nine yachts equipped with engines over 100 hp, the average figure is reduced to 60 hp. This figure is closer to what would be considered adequate engine power bearing in mind that the average LOA of the yachts in the EUROPA 92 fleet was 49 ft.

One of the owners who was not happy with his engine power, nor with the fuel capacity of his yacht, was Pekka Hyryläinen. His *Soolo* was equipped with a Volvo MD31, rated at 62 hp, which he felt was too much for an easily driven yacht such as a Contest 43. At a cruising speed of 6.5 knots, at 2000 revs, the engine used 5 litres of fuel per hour, which Pekka considered unacceptably high, especially as his tankage only held 400 litres of fuel thus giving him a range of only 500 miles. Pekka was among those who used their main engine to charge the batteries for which the engine was run for four hours every day. Although fuel consumption was only 2 litres per hour while charging, he still felt that it did not make sense to run such a powerful engine just to turn an alternator.

Table 16 Engine power and fuel consumption

Number of yachts	hp	Average consumption litres/hour
2	under 40	3.2
10	40–60	3.5
9	60–80	5.2
6	80–100	5.5
9	over 100	9.4
Total: 36		

Cheone was one of the yachts equipped with two engines but its owner Marcello Murzilli felt that even the combined power of the two engines rated at 94 hp each was not adequate as he could not get the 72 ft heavy displacement boat to reach her maximum rated speed under power of 9 knots. As he could only reach 8 knots with his two three bladed Maxprops, Marcello suspected the pitch of the propellers to be wrong as he could not get the engines past 2500 revolutions.

La Aventura was also equipped with two Perkins engines driving two three bladed Maxprops. The two Perama engines, rated at 30 hp each, were only run together when more speed was needed. Usually only one was used, whether to drive the boat or charge the batteries. With this in mind, the starboard engine, which was more accessible, had been fitted with a larger alternator and was used as a generator. When more power was needed, the two engines were run in parallel, although on several occasions *La Aventura*'s displacement of 17 tons could have done with even more power.

Perkins engines were the most common make in EUROPA 92. On *Cacadu*, Arne Blässar is changing the oil filter as part of his regular maintenance routine.

Although not complaining about engine power on his Hallberg Rassy 45, Peter Bunting had another quibble. 'I cannot see the reason why one should have a turbo engine on a boat of this kind.' His Volvo MD31T used $\frac{3}{4}$ gallons (3.5 litres) per hour at 1700 revs at a cruising speed of 5.5 knots, but burnt over two gallons (9 litres) per hour to reach

8 knots at 2300 revs. Peter suspected that the engine was unable to deliver the power to the propeller, perhaps because the pitch on his three bladed Maxprop was incorrect. The skipper also blamed the propeller for *Gulkarna* hitting a dock on arrival in Panama. Although the engine had been shifted into reverse, the yacht continued moving forward and collided with the wooden dock. Some onlookers probably thought that the collision had been caused by a moment of inattention, which Peter insisted was not the case. He had to wait until Fiji to be vindicated when *Gulkarna* was hauled out and, on servicing the Maxprop, the propeller was found to be completely out of grease and the gears had almost seized up. This would have accounted for the accident in Panama when the propeller had presumambly remained in its forward mode and had not reversed its pitch when the engine was put in astern.

One of the owners who considered his engine to be underpowered for his yacht was Wes Harris. His steel hulled *Scorpio* was equipped with an 80 hp Ford Lees of 1979 vintage, which was still running well but was burning up too much fuel to drive the boat at a reasonable speed. Wes estimated that even at the most economical cruising speed of 5.5 knots, which was achieved at 1400 revs, the engine used at least 6 litres per hour. He felt that a more powerful engine would provide better speed for lower fuel consumption.

Fuel consumption and capacity

Table 16 also shows the average fuel consumption at cruising speed, as the skippers were asked to indicate their most economical speed and the engine revolutions at which this was achieved. On the basis of those figures fuel consumption and range under power could be assessed more accurately, and the majority felt that their yachts were well suited for a round the world voyage. Adequate fuel capacity was indeed an important consideration in a fleet where most yachts consumed a large amount of fuel every day, not necessarily for propulsion but to charge batteries, run freezers, watermakers, etc. Over half the yachts (19) ran their diesel generators on an average for $3\frac{1}{2}$ hours every day, while the main engines were run for an additional $2\frac{1}{2}$ hours daily to charge the batteries. This meant that the EUROPA 92 yachts burnt up a lot of fuel even while they were sailing. The first time I realised this was in the Galapagos Islands, where 14,000 litres of fuel mysteriously disappeared in their insatiable tanks not two weeks after the fleet had left Panama with full tanks, after having been warned that fuel may not be available until they reached Tahiti.

As seen in Table 17, most yachts had reasonable tankage, which was reflected in the overall average of 708 litres. Although 27 skippers

Table 17 Fuel capacity

Number of yachts	Litres
2	under 200
8	200–400
11	400–600
6	600–800
9	over 800
Total: 36	

regarded their fuel capacity to be adequate, seven thought it was insufficient and two considered it too much. Interestingly, it was not the owners of the yachts with the smallest tanks who complained that they had insufficient capacity. The boat with the smallest fuel capacity was *Elan Adventurer*, whose skipper Julian Wilson felt that his 35 gallons (160 litres) were sufficient for their needs. Indeed, as the Elan 43 was taking part in the Racing Division, the engine was used on passage for battery charging only and enough fuel was carried for that purpose. *Gilma Express* also had a small capacity (160 litres), with which Pasquale de Gregorio was nevertheless very happy. This was not surprising, as the yacht was sailed all the time, but even when running the engine, its fuel consumption was extremely low, the 28 hp Volvo engine pushing the ULDB at 7.5 knots using only 2.5 litres per hour at 2300 revs. The consumption rose to 4 litres per hour at 2700 revs, which gave the boat a speed under power of 9 knots.

John Smith, whose *Eye of Ra* was in the Cruising Division, was of a different opinion and pointed out that the 50 gallon (225 litres) tank on his Moody 419 was certainly too small for a cruising boat, especially on a voyage of this kind. Dutch Taylor, whose *Trillium* had a fuel capacity of 400 litres, felt the same. Indeed, while sailing from California to the Galapagos and on to the Marquesas to join the EUROPA 92 fleet, *Trillium* ran out of fuel. A rendezvous was arranged over the airwaves with *Sojourner* which gave *Trillium* sufficient fuel to enable them to charge the batteries.

Another yacht whose fuel capacity was considered too small was *Jolly Joker*, which could carry only 300 litres of diesel in its tank. This was equal to that of *Octopus*, whose owner considered it just right. Wilhelm Greiff had fitted out the aluminium Via 42 himself and had tried to optimise fuel consumption. With this in mind he chose a 17 in three bladed propeller on a saildrive, which would push the boat at the optimum cruising speed with the engine running at 1600 revs. The fuel consumption of the secondhand Perkins 4108 engine at a cruising speed of 5 knots was a remarkably low 1.6 litres per hour, which Wilhelm assured me was absolutely accurate as he had checked it during 1000 engine hours.

All of those who found their fuel capacity to be too low stressed that they considered it insufficient primarily for a voyage visiting places where fuel may not be easily available. Although this problem did not occur for participants in the rally, as the organisers managed to arrange fuel in all the more difficult places, the observation had some validity for others who might be sailing along the same route and could find that fuel was indeed unobtainable in some places. While some of the boats in the Cruising Division supplemented their capacity on the longer legs by carrying a few jerrycans on deck, Alessandro Mosconi never used the full capacity of *Gulliver's* tanks. Although the Swan 59 could carry as much as 1050 litres of diesel fuel, in order to save weight, they never took on more than 500 litres. Dave Sutherland, whose Rival 41 *Tais* had a fuel capacity of 150 gallons (680 litres), also considered it excessive, especially as he rarely used the engine on passage and preferred to sail whenever possible.

Table 18   Range under power

Number of yachts	Miles
3	under 400
12	400–600
10	600–800
11	over 800
Total: 36	

Range under power was also discussed and several skippers commented that even on the longest legs of the rally they had never felt the need for more fuel than what they carried. Among the three yachts which had a range under 400 miles, *Elan Adventurer*, *Orchidea* and *Eye of Ra*, only John Smith, the owner of the latter, felt that it was inadequate. The average range over the entire fleet worked out at 764 miles per yacht and, as Table 18 shows, the majority of yachts were indeed clustered around this figure.

Most sailors have a love-hate relationship with their engines and some talk about their engines quite affectionately, so during this section of the survey many other interesting matters were mentioned. For instance, Roger Gold was very pleased that *Rockhopper* had been fitted with a day tank with a 90 litres capacity, which he considered an excellent system. The only drawback was the fact that the day tank was topped up with a manual pump which meant that occasionally this could be forgotten.

'An electric pump activated electronically or by a float switch would make the system foolproof.'

A similar system was in use on *La Aventura*, on which the header tank had a capacity of 15 litres only and had to be refilled more frequently. This was done at two hour intervals by the crew coming off watch if the engine was in use. Having a separate header tank, which I also had on my previous boat, has several advantages, such as the fact that the fuel is gravity fed to the engine and any problems with the fuel lift pump are therefore eliminated. Also, if the fuel arrives at the injectors with air in it, the engine is less likely to stop. The most important advantage, however, is that the purity of the fuel is more easily controlled. On *La Aventura* any water or impurities are separated out before they can reach the engine. This is done either by a combined CAV filter and water trap connected to the electric pump transferring fuel from one of the two tanks, or by a similar filtering system installed between the header tank and the engine. The system also allows the exchange of filters while the engine is running. An even better system was in operation on *Oyinbo*, which had been fitted with a twin fuel filter system, so that one could switch over whenever the fuel filter pressure dropped. Such precautions should not be considered exaggerated as many of the engine failures experienced by the participants during the rally were caused by dirty fuel.

Propellers

Over half the yachts were equipped with Maxprop feathering propellers. Among the 20 propellers of this type, 18 were three bladed and two were two bladed. Fifteen yachts had fixed type propellers, of which 11 were three bladed and four were two bladed. One of the fixed three bladed propellers was fitted to a saildrive. Finally, two yachts had two bladed folding propellers and one had a saildrive fitted with a folding propeller.

Several yachts had acquired new propellers for the rally. *Oingo Boingo* had its fixed three bladed propeller replaced with a two bladed folding type which Roland Schlachter considered a very good idea as it reduced drag considerably. Most of the 20 Maxprop owners were pleased with them. 'My Maxprop is just wonderful' commented Paul Skilowitz of *Bluewater*. Although most Maxprop owners were pleased with their performance, for various reasons, Paul's enthusiasm was not shared by five of the skippers whose yachts were equipped with this type of propeller. Often at fault were boatyards which had either fitted the wrong sized propeller or had not been able to set the correct pitch. After having sailed *La Aventura* for two years with two bladed folding propellers, I decided to have them changed to three bladed Maxprops by a boatyard

A large proportion of the boats were equipped with Maxprop feathering type propellers.

in Florida. Unfortunately the propellers fitted by the yard proved to be too small and, even after altering their pitch three times, their performance still does not match that of the folding propellers which they had replaced.

Giovanna Caprini also thought that *Orchidea*'s two bladed Maxprop was too small and that a three bladed Maxprop of the same diameter would have performed much better. On *Ambler*, John Papp also felt the pitch of his three bladed Maxprop must be wrong because he could not get the boat to go faster than 6 knots under power. Correct pitch is essential for this type of propeller to perform well and, although altering the pitch of a Maxprop is a fairly simple operation, it does mean slipping the boat or drying out. From what I was told and found out from personal experience, boatyards which have not fitted this type of propeller before may not know how to choose the optimum pitch, so the owner ends up having the boat hauled and the pitch reset repeatedly until it is got right by trial and error.

11
LIGHT WINDS
AND CALM SEAS

Leg 10: Darwin to Bali

Light southwesterly winds made for a slow start to the next leg from
Darwin to Bali, but this was made up for by many of the yachts leaving
under spinnaker. This colourful spectacle was a suitable way to bid
farewell to the numerous spectators who had come out in their own
boats to see the EUROPA 92 fleet off on this beautiful Sunday. Unfortunately light airs prevailed for the whole of the 1000 miles to Bali, although
some yachts managed to find isolated pockets of wind. This meant that
it was a slow trip for the yachts in the Racing Division with most
recording average speeds below 4 knots. The course passed to the south
of the Indonesian archipelago, leaving all islands to starboard and, with
the exception of two offshore reefs and a few oil drilling platforms, it
proved to be one of the least challenging legs of the entire rally. The
lack of excitement was made up for in the flat calms by several encounters
between yachts. At one point, *Gulkarna*, *Pennypincher* and *Rockhopper*
stopped motoring for a few hours so that they could drift together and
enjoy each other's company for an offshore brunch. Other yachts also
arranged to rendezvous and visits were made by swimming from one
yacht to the other.

All the excitement was reserved for near the finishing line where
strong currents in the channel separating the islands of Bali and Lombok
caught a lot of yachts unaware, especially some of those in the Racing
Division. With only a few miles left to the small port of Benoa, on the
southeast coast of Bali, four of the yachts in Class I were approaching
the line close together when they were suddenly caught by the strong
current. *Gilma Express* managed to come out of it best and was the first
yacht to finish in the Racing Division. Half an hour later, the finishing
line was crossed by *Who Dares Wins*, followed nearly one hour later by
Gulliver and *Orchidea*. The latter two carried their fight right up to the
finishing line, which Alessandro Mosconi crossed less than two minutes
before Giovanna Caprini. Ian Kennedy's excellent performance assured
them of the overall victory and also consolidated *Who Dares Wins*' position at the top of the table.

This leg proved beyond any doubt the wisdom of allowing yachts in the Cruising Division to resort to their engines when there was no wind. To discourage unlimited motoring, every skipper was obliged to keep an accurate record of the hours the engine was used for propulsion, the details being recorded in an engine log, which had to be handed in to a rally official at the end of each leg. Also, the total motoring time had to be recorded on the Rally Declaration, which had to be signed by all adult crew members before it was also handed in. When results were calculated, the engine hours multiplied by a motoring factor were added to the elapsed time before being multiplied by the handicap of the yacht in question. The motoring factor was an additional penalty and depended on wind and other conditions encountered during that particular leg. This penalty factor was only declared at the end of the leg and varied between 1 and 2. This meant that even in legs with little wind, the winner was usually one of the yachts which had motored little or not at all. This concession did not apply to the yachts in the Racing Division where motoring was prohibited, and yachts which used their engines for propulsion were disqualified for that leg.

Balinese landfall

While *Gilma Express* and the other racing yachts were spreading every square inch of canvas to catch every puff of wind, John Rose turned on the iron staysail and thus *Midnight Stroller* was the first to reach Benoa. The local staff of the Bali International Yacht Club in Benoa gave them a tremendous welcome and treated them throughout their stay in Bali as the winners of the leg. Not only in Bali, but in most other places, the first yacht to arrive was considered the winner and it was no good trying to explain the intricacies of yacht racing, handicaps and motoring penalties, when to the locals it was obvious that if you are the first to arrive anywhere, you are the winner.

On this leg, the majority of the Cruising Division yachts motored for more than one third of the distance which meant that, although placed, they were not eligible for any prizes. This ruling had been introduced to avoid such windless legs being won, in the Cruising Division, by the yacht with the largest fuel tanks. In fact, only *Kite* and *Amadé* motored less than one third of the leg from Darwin.

Determined not to be disqualified, *Oingo Boingo* and *Dafne* spent a frustrating 48 hours battling it out within 15 miles of the finishing line. Eventually *Dafne* came in first and won Class II. In the same class, *Wachibou* gave up sailing and decided to reach port under power, but ran out of fuel near the finishing line and was towed the remaining five miles by *Eye of Ra*. By this time, *Octopus* might have given up as well, but they could not start their engine even if they had wanted to as their starter motor was yet again out of order. So Astrid and Wilhelm had no choice but to sail all the way and almost made it within the time limit, but were thwarted by the strong counter currents near the finish. While approaching Bali, Astrid saw a small boat in the distance which appeared to be moving in a very erratic fashion. As they got closer, they saw that it was a small outrigger sailing canoe with a young boy as sole crew, who had become separated from his companions for two days and had been drifting helplessly in the current. The boy was exhausted and severely dehydrated, and would have undoubtedly lost his life if he had not been discovered by *Octopus*. He climbed gratefully into a bunk on board *Octopus* and immediately fell asleep. A call on the radio brought *Oingo Boingo* out of Benoa to meet *Octopus*, who had been towing the outrigger for the last fifteen miles. Thus a strange procession entered the port of Benoa, with *Oingo Boingo* towing *Octopus*, who in turn was towing the outrigger, whose owner was fast asleep on board the German yacht. Later Astrid and Wilhelm had the satisfaction of returning the boy to a very grateful family.

The grandly named Bali International Yacht Club is neither international nor a yacht club in the strict sense of the word, although visiting sailors are welcome to use its few facilities. The new manager of the club, Mrs Greta Bär, had come from Jakarta especially to prepare the club for the arrival of the EUROPA 92 yachts. The wife of the President of the Indonesian Yachting Association, Greta had also arranged the Indonesian cruising permits for the EUROPA fleet, a difficult and time consuming formality which has discouraged many yachts from visiting this interesting country.

Greta was also instrumental in getting the local authorities to clean up the port area around the club and build a landing stage for dinghies. There was little else that could be done to improve the situation as the port was in the midst of a major redevelopment project and work was in hand turning it into a container terminal. A group of yachts such as the EUROPA 92 fleet was clearly a nuisance to everyone.

The unattractive state of the port persuaded most participants to use the opportunity to visit some of the unspoilt parts in the interior of Bali, while some of the more ambitious made it to Java or across to Lombok. The most exciting excursion, which was enjoyed by almost everyone, was a white water rafting expedition in the centre of Bali. Back in Benoa, the EUROPA fleet fielded a football team and challenged the local officials to a friendly game, while the American contingent decided it was their turn to liven up the social scene and hosted a hamburger party for the rest of the fleet. The stay in Bali was brought to a close by a prize giving and presentation dinner in the Bali Hyatt Hotel.

Leg 11: Bali to Singapore

Like a good book, each leg of EUROPA 92 unfolded another chapter adding a twist to the tale. Not that the fleet of 33 yachts were particularly looking forward to turning the page on to Leg 11, the 1000 mile passage from Bali to Singapore. This lay across the South China Sea, a stretch of water whose infamy is well known to sailors, with frequent incidents in recent years involving Vietnamese boat people, as well as rumours of occasional pirate activity. The anxiety voiced by many, as well as the light wind conditions expected, led to the decision to declare this leg non-competitive for yachts in the Cruising Division. This enabled the yachts to sail together during the passage and keep within sight of each other if they so wished. As an added precaution, a 24 hour listening watch was also maintained by all yachts on the SSB working channel.

The starts of the various legs of the rally had been given from a variety of vessels, from large Naval ships to small fishing boats. In Bali a 63 ft game fishing boat, the *Osprey O*, was used, which provided the starting committee with a challenge as in the five foot swell and little wind, all the journalists and most of the spectators aboard succumbed to the rolling. The start line had been set off the Bali Hyatt Hotel with the inner end as close to the reef as possible to give a good view to spectators. They were rewarded by a colourful start by the yachts in the Racing Division with the majority starting under spinnaker. First across the line was *Elan Adventurer* followed closely by *Gulliver* and *Who Dares Wins*. The Cruising Division started ten minutes later, and even though this was a non-competitive leg, many of the cruising boats still started under spinnaker and could not resist trying to outpace each other.

The start had been timed so as to use the current to advantage and allow the boats to sail through the Lombok Channel and clear the NE corner of Bali in one tide. The effect of the current became obvious as *Wachibou*, which was not flying a spinnaker, kept pace with some of those who were by making better use of the current. Trying to gain an advantage, *Gilma Express* tacked downwind, but this did not appear to give them any help, as it ended up taking them into an area of adverse current.

After their excellent start, *Elan Adventurer* ran into trouble when Julia Woodham was knocked out by the boom. Only 24 hours out of Bali, acting skipper John Driscoll had to decide whether to return to Bali or carry on to Singapore. *Elan Adventurer* seemed fated as Julian Wilson had already had to fly earlier from Bali to Singapore for a minor operation and John Driscoll had taken over. Keeping Julia under close observation for the next 24 hours, they decided to continue to Singapore with its better medical facilities, but to motor whenever the wind dropped.

Crossing the South China Sea

Apart from this incident the passage to Singapore was without problems except for the lack of wind. These conditions were expected at that time of the year as they were typical of the changeover between the two monsoons. For much of the time the sea was as flat as a mill pond and the winds were unpredictable, either very light or gusting to 25 knots. Several times there was the strange situation of boats, within half a mile of each other, either one with wind and one without, or both with winds from completely different directions. Earlier apprehensions proved unfounded and all the boats sailed through the South China Sea safely. Although relieved to have made the passage without misadventure, participants in both divisions found it to be the most frustrating leg of the entire event.

Several crews celebrated the re-crossing of the equator in different ways, while a big party was held on board *Brydie* as the equator crossing coincided with crew member Enroy's birthday. The first boat to arrive in Singapore was *Locura*, whose skipper Leo Birkby had again given up and started motoring, preferring to face disqualification in the Racing Division rather than sit it out waiting for wind. Not wanting to arrive in Singapore in the middle of the night, *Cheone*, *Twilight* and *Libertad II* decided to slow down and have a lunch time party. They all rafted up, the two Italian yachts providing the inevitable pasta, while the French crew contributed a flambé dessert. The three boats then arrived in Singapore together the following morning.

Despite the uncooperative nature of the elements, the racing spirit remained unquenched for some. *Gulliver* and *Who Dares Wins* continued to battle it out for the overall lead in the Racing Division. The Italian yacht was the first arrival in Singapore to have sailed all the way, yet *Who Dares Wins* narrowly won the leg on corrected time, thus continuing to hold on to the overall lead. *Oingo Boingo* was the only Class II yacht to stick it out and not motor, so winning their class and reducing *Soolo*'s lead in Class II to 0.75.

A delay in the building of Raffles Marina, in the west of Singapore island, which had been scheduled to host the fleet, meant that an alternative place had to be found to moor the fleet together. An excellent solution was found by anchoring the entire fleet off the East Coast Sailing Centre, which is normally a windsurfing and sailing dinghy centre. It was conveniently situated with frequent buses to the city centre and also had good facilities, the restaurant opening for breakfast and a chandlery operating especially for the duration of the fleet's stay.

Every leg had its share of drama and Leg 11 was no exception. Very early on the morning of 30 October, the watchkeeper on *Pennypincher* heard a Mayday from the *Kinryu*, a Honduran cargo ship which had run aground on some rocks east of Singapore. As the only vessel to respond to the Mayday call, skipper Alan Spriggs made for the stricken vessel and agreed to pick up seven of the Indonesian crew, who had spent the night in their liferaft. The other five crew had remained on board to man the pumps of the ship. The *Kinryu* had been returning from Vietnam with a cargo of pottery, some of which the shipwrecked seamen insisted on bringing with them. Having embarked the seven sailors, *Pennypincher* continued to Singapore and the East Coast Sailing Centre, as advised in the Sailing Instructions, hoping to offload her shipment of grateful mariners there. It was then that serious problems began for Alan Spriggs as the authorities refused to give permission for the rescued crew to disembark. The tense situation was only resolved when the British High Commission finally persuaded the Singapore Authorities to allow the shipwrecked sailors to leave the British yacht. Although aware of the risks involved in picking up the seamen, Alan observed that as he had been the only vessel to answer the distress call, the law of the sea did not allow him to act in any other way.

The Singapore Tourist Promotion Board, who had done everything possible to ensure the success of the Singapore stopover, hosted a beach party at the Sailing Centre, during which the prizes for the Racing Division, as well as many fun prizes were presented. On arriving at the party every participant was garlanded with a silk flower necklace and each skipper received a special plaque commemorating their visit to Singapore. After the prize giving, the party continued with dancing and a limbo competition and was wound up by most of the English and Australian crews converging on the television, which had been especially set up to watch the Rugby World Cup final relayed from England, the three Australians in the audience being delighted at their team's success in beating their English hosts. Magnus McGlashan, who had recently left *Who Dares Wins* to sail on *Locura*, summed up the feelings of the outnumbered Australians, 'If you can't join them, beat them!'

Refrigeration

Watermakers and freezers have profoundly influenced the style of offshore sailing, just as GPS has changed that of navigation. Although not yet as widespread as GPS, which almost all the yachts had, the time cannot be far off when every long distance cruising boat will be equipped with watermaker, refrigerator and freezer as a matter of routine. Hopefully they will choose their equipment carefully as not all freezer or watermaker brands passed the EUROPA 92 test with flying colours.

There were 20 different makes among the 30 refrigerators, and almost as many makes of freezers, so a comparison of their individual performances was almost impossible. One of the happiest customers was Peter Bunting. 'I am very impressed with the performance of our Frigoboat. It is really excellent.' Frigoboat was the most common make, with six yachts being equipped with Frigoboat freezers and refrigerators, and while most owners were content with it, two low ratings brought down their average performance rating considerably. Frigomar and Isotherm were rated higher as were the later models of Grunnert. Top ratings were also given to in-house models of such yachts as Swan and Nordia.

Table 19   Refrigeration

Make	Number	Performance	Number	Performance
	Refrigerators		**Freezers**	
Frigoboat	6	7.3	6	6.8
Grunnert	3	9.3	3	8.7
Isotherm	2	9.5	2	9.5
Swan	2	10	2	10
Frigomar	2	10	2	10
Elan	1	10	1	10
Amel	1	8	1	9
Nordia	1	10	1	10
Techmatics	1	5	1	5
Electrolux	1	10		
Philips	1	10		
ITT	1	7		
Aquair	1	8	1	10
Danfoss	1	4		
Engel			1	10
Unknown	9	7.8	4	6.7
Total:	33		25	

There were a few common complaints, some of which were not so much the fault of the manufacturer but rather that of the boatbuilder or whoever had installed the appliance, such as not providing adequate insulation. The performance of freezers was particularly affected by the quality and amount of insulation and some of the freezers, which had performed satisfactorily in the cooler conditions of higher latitudes, were unable to cope with the heat of the tropics. Some owners managed to put this right *en route*, such as *Amadé* in Tahiti, while on *Lady Samantha*, Enio Nardi gave up trying and used a six year old Frigoboat freezer as a fridge, so ending up with two refrigerators. In fact this solution became the fate of several freezers unable to cope in the tropics. The installation on *Oyinbo*, a Nordia 61, was excellent as both fridge and freezer had their own thermostat. Each unit ran for approximately $3\frac{1}{2}$ hours daily, although this was increased by one hour in hot climates.

A frequent complaint was the higher than expected power consumption of electrically operated units, either refrigerators or freezers. Coupled with poor insulation, this led some of the skippers either to stop their freezers altogether or use them as fridges. Even so, of the 25 freezers, 20 were more or less in permanent use. The majority (15) were equipped with electrical compressors, six had mechanical, engine driven compressors, while four units had both. Of the electrical compressors, six used either 110 or 240 V and therefore could only be run in conjunction with a generator, or on shore power. The normal routine was for the compressor to be switched on at the same time as the generator charged the batteries. This practice was also followed on most of the yachts with 12 or 24 V compressors.

On *Cacadu*, a mechanical compressor operated by the main engine served both the refrigerator and freezer, the engine being run on average 45 minutes every day for this purpose, charging the batteries at the same time. There was an additional 12 V compressor which could be used if the mechanical compressor broke down. According to Arne, the people at Bénéteau laughed when he insisted on having the two compressors and asked him why. 'Because they always break down', was Arne's answer. 'And indeed they do', he told me. 'At least when it happens, I have a spare!'

A belt and braces approach was also Enio Nardi's on *Lady Samantha* where the Frigoboat fridge had been converted to run off two compressors. One was mechanical and was mounted on the main engine, while the other was electric. The latter was capable of running both on 24 V from the batteries, or on 240 V from the generator. There was a similar installation on *Locura* where the Aquair fridge and freezer were hooked up to both electric and mechanical compressors. The compressors operated two separate sets of cold plates in both freezer and fridge.

In most cases, the fridges which ran independently of the freezers were left on all the time and the high electricity consumption took most skippers by surprise. Consumption estimates over a 24 hour period varied widely, the only consensus being the fact that consumption was much higher than anyone had expected. In order to cut down on power consumption, on *Twilight* the fridge was turned off at night; a number of ice bags kept the temperature down if the door was not opened too often. However, Brad Bernardo found on *Brydie* that his previous practice of switching the fridge off when the engine was not running and on again when the engine was running consumed more electricity, so he ended up leaving the fridge on all the time, which showed an overall reduction in electricity consumption.

There were only three boats without a fridge among the 36 yachts. In spite of frequent complaints about high consumption, almost all fridges were in constant use on the remaining 33 yachts, with only three skippers stating that they never used their fridges at sea only in port. Although he gave his fridge top marks for its performance, Ian Kennedy wasn't happy with its location on his Swan 53. He particularly criticised the fact that the fridge was of the front opening type, which meant that every time it was opened, it lost all the cold air inside. Also, as the fridge faced inboard, one had to be very careful when opening it while the boat was on port tack. He suggested that fridges should also be of the chest type like freezers, or at least should open either fore or aft. A problem of a different kind occurred on *Soolo*, a Contest 43, where the water cooled fridge could not be used when the boat was heeling on one tack as the cooling water inlet was too high.

On several yachts the existing refrigeration system had been either upgraded or supplemented especially for the rally. On *Kite*, the ten year old fridge-freezer unit, run by a mechanical compressor driven by the main engine, was supplemented by a separate 12 V freezer. However, the latter proved to be too small, so it ended up being used as a fridge. On *Elan Adventurer*, a portable Engel freezer worked perfectly and was rated by skipper Julian Wilson a top 10. The 12 V unit, with a capacity of 35 litres, could run off the batteries, or on 240 V, either from shore power or a portable generator.

Food on passage

An interesting observation was that freezers were much more popular among Anglo-Saxon sailors. With only one exception, all US yachts had freezers and used them permanently, whereas among the eight Italian yachts, five did not have freezers and two did not even have a fridge. 'Whenever possible, we prefer fresh food', explained Marcello Murzilli who had left Italy with enough spaghetti on board *Cheone* to last several circumnavigations. The Italians obviously knew how to get their priorities right. 'They eat too well on *Lady Samantha*, Enio has put on weight on every leg' complained Ksenjia Nardi.

Indeed, provisioning with fresh produce was rarely a problem as there were excellent markets in most ports along the EUROPA 92 route. Fresh fruit was usually stored in hanging nets, while vegetables were kept on open shelves, well ventilated racks or in plastic boxes with holes drilled in the sides. The swinging nets did not necessarily provide the perfect solution for storing fruit. 'Because the boat is being raced hard, fruit is getting badly damaged so we end up throwing out more than we consume' remarked Ian Kennedy.

Who Dares Wins was one of the few yachts with a full time cook among the crew, so the question as to whether any meals were cooked before a long passage did not apply. This practice was followed on seven of the yachts, mainly those where the usual cook had the misfortune of feeling sick at the start of a passage. On an additional six yachts, the practice of pre-cooking meals was only followed if rough weather was expected. 'We always prepare a few meals and put them in the fridge. It is definitely a good idea as for the first few days the crew is often more tired, seasick or both', explained Arne Blässar. Meals for the first four days were prepared and frozen on the eve of each passage on *Sojourner*, while on *Locura* Kathy Birkby cooked three casseroles before a long passage and put them in the freezer to be heated up when needed.

Fresh produce on sale on the dock in Malta.

On *Oyinbo*, Richard Goord tried to alternate fresh with tinned food, with the occasional pre-cooked frozen lasagne giving the cook a break. Such niceties were unknown on *Jolly Joker*, whose support team had arrived in Gibraltar on the eve of the start with a large van loaded with tinned food. The performance of the Admiral's Cup inspired design visibly suffered as its waterline sank under the weight of one ton of goulash, smoked sausages and other Hungarian goodies.

In order to save weight, but also to get rid of unwanted stowaways, on *Kite*, *Locura* and *Rockhopper* all dry goods, such as pasta, cereals, rice and flour, were vacuum sealed. 'This not only helps preservation, but eliminates a lot of bulky packaging and also suffocates weevils and other unsavoury creepy crawlies' explained Moira Gold.

The diet of most crews was supplemented considerably on long passages by fishing. Almost all yachts had fishing gear, although the rate of success across the fleet was quite uneven. 'We are not exactly kingfishers' admitted *Amadé*'s Walter Gollhofer, while Mario Filipponi's uncanny success on *Laura* earned him the nickname 'Pescareccio Azzuro'. Not being one of nature's most gifted fishermen, I tried to pick up some tips myself and so I enquired about the lures used by some of the self-confessed champions. Alan Spriggs dismissed any scientific approach to the subject. 'On *Pennypincher* we use any old lure, cut up sandals, rubber gloves, sunglass cases, anything!'

The unchallenged EUROPA 92 champion was Frank Wilson on *Midnight Stroller* who managed to catch and land a 120 pound wahoo while cruising in the Marquesas, most of which was donated to a school canteen on Nuku Hiva. Apparently speed is more essential to success than the gear used and as Pasquale de Gregorio explained '*Gilma Express* is usually sailing too fast to catch anything'. At least he had the compensation of arriving first in most legs.

Water and watermakers

With one third of the boats in the EUROPA fleet having a watermaker, this aspect of offshore sailing produced very different results to similar surveys conducted in the past. There was a marked difference between the yachts with watermakers and those without, although there were some notable exceptions too. Especially among the serious racers (*Dafne*, *Gilma Express*, *Orchidea*), water was strictly rationed and only the minimum was carried so as to save weight. On *Orchidea* the fresh water allowance only covered enough for drinking and brushing one's teeth. 'Water is like gold to us, so we use it very sparingly', explained Nicola Borsó.

On *Lady Samantha*, the tanks were turned off at sea and every person received each morning one bottle of 1.5 litres of water for washing. Drinking water was not rationed and was available from the galley. This strictness was not dictated by shortage of water, as the boat was equipped with a watermaker, but formed part of the offshore training course which Enio Nardi has been running successfully for the last 15 years.

'I wish we had the means to measure water consumption accurately' complained Peter Bunting. This is indeed what happened on *Oyinbo*, where water consumption was recorded daily, another aspect of this tightly run ship. A very generous allowance was made on *Gulkarna*, where water consumption was virtually unrestricted. The skipper reckoned that the consumption averaged about 15 gallons (70 litres) per person per day. However, he quickly pointed out that he only allowed his crew to be profligate with water when he was confident that the watermaker was working. Consumption was even higher on *Twilight*, where the skipper estimated that the crew got through an amazing amount totalling 600 litres of water every day. 'I like having a lot of water and this is one aspect where I don't want to be hard on my crew', explained Dino Blancodini. To supply this amount he ran his watermaker between 5 and 6 hours every day.

Although there were one or two cases of boats running short of water on longer passages, no one actually arrived in port completely out of water, as has happened in the ARC every year. The average water capacity worked out at 868 litres per yacht, which is substantially more than one would have expected from a group of yachts with an average length of 49 feet. In fact, the figure should be somewhat lower as three of the largest yachts had considerably higher than average tankage. Among those larger yachts, the owners of *Midnight Stroller* and *Twilight* were not happy about having all their water in only one tank, or, as Roger Gold put it, 'Having all water in only one tank is daft.' Therefore on *Rockhopper*, the water produced by the watermaker was stored in bottles, so as not to spoil its taste by mixing it with the water in the one and only tank, which had been chlorinated and was used mainly for washing.

Table 20   Water capacity

Number of yachts	Water capacity (litres)
1	under 400
8	400–600
9	600–800
12	800–1200
3	1200–1500
3	over 1500
Total: 36	

As shown in Table 20, the majority of yachts were endowed with ample tankage, with only one yacht, the ULDB *Orchidea*, having two small tanks of 100 litres each, while at the other extremity, *Oyinbo* carried no less than 3000 litres, also in two tanks. The two tank configuration was most common, with nearly half the yachts (16) having two tanks, the rest of the fleet having anything from one to six tanks, as seen in Table 21.

Table 21   Water tanks

Number of yachts	Number of tanks
4	1
16	2
9	3
5	4
1	5
1	6
Total: 36	

With a fleet average of 5 crew per yacht, the average water consumption per person worked out at 14 litres per day. However, the average personal consumption was only half that on the 13 yachts without a watermaker, or a daily average of 7 litres per person, which is still rather high.

The proliferation of watermakers has certainly affected water management, with average consumptions being on the whole much higher than in the past. The use of showers most certainly had something to do with this as on almost half the yachts (14), the crew showered with fresh water daily. On another nine yachts, the shower was used occasionally, the use being controlled or rationed, while on a similar number of yachts, the shower was not used on passage. On one of the yachts only the skipper could have a fresh water shower at sea, while the rest of the crew had to make do with sea water showers on deck. Many other crews also washed in sea water while on passage, although there were variations. On *Oingo Boingo*, the crew could rinse off afterwards with fresh water and there was a shower for this on deck. Finally, four of the yachts did not have showers and so their crew had little choice.

Of the 23 yachts which had watermakers, two thirds (15) used them daily, and four every other day. On two more yachts, the watermaker was only used when needed, while on another two, the watermaker was kept for emergencies only. The most watermakers were on board *Locura*, which had three separate units, two Power Survivors for alternate daily use, and a third hand operated set, which was kept in the panic bag.

Table 22   Water consumption

Number of yachts	Daily water consumption (litres)
4	under 20
16	20–50
12	50–100
3	100–200
1	over 200
Total: 36	

One of the makes bought primarily with an emergency in mind was the Power Survivor, although people soon got used to the convenience of a watermaker and most ended up using it daily. There were six Power Survivors installed and in normal use, while several more were kept in the panic bag. This model has the advantage of being able to be operated both manually and electrically. The watermakers output varied from 5 litres per hour for the Power Survivor, to as much as 130 litres per hour for the Hydromar on *Twilight*.

Watermakers were used between one and 5 hours per day, with an average of $2\frac{1}{2}$ hours daily use. Usually watermakers were switched on at

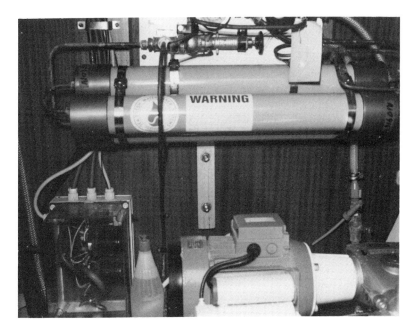

The watermaker was installed in an easily accessible place in *Gulkarna*'s forward cabin.

the same time as the generator, or the main engine, if the latter was used to charge the batteries. There were several complaints about watermaker reliability. On *Who Dares Wins*, the older Seafresh unit, which came with the boat, gave so much trouble that it had to be replaced with a new HEM unit, while on *Sojourner*, the one year old Sea Recovery unit was described as the worst system on the boat as it had broken down on several occasions. Similarly on *Cheone*, a newly installed Marenco broke down several times, being described as too delicate by Marcello Murzilli. On the other hand, Julian Wilson, whose Aquafresh watermaker ran directly off *Elan Adventurer*'s engine, described is as 'Excellent. It's wonderful.'

Not wishing to be totally dependent on their watermaker, the skipper of every yacht equipped with one made the point that, as a matter of principle, they always left port with full tanks and normally used the watermaker to top them up. On *Jakes Fantasia*, only one tank was in use and was refilled by the watermaker while the other two tanks were kept full.

There were almost as many different routines as there were water-makers, just as there were different reasons why people acquired water-makers. Ian Kennedy had no doubts about its usefulness. 'A watermaker is invaluable. It gives a lot of freedom of action and is also very good for crew morale.'

'One of the nice things on passage is to have a fresh water shower in the afternoon and relax. That's the main reason why we have a water-maker on *Sojourner*. Cruising is not camping, certainly not if the boat is your home for one or two years', commented Rick Palm.

12
WINTER MONSOON

A change of seasons and switch of hemispheres in Singapore gave partici-pants the opportunity to see more of South East Asia before embarking on the last stage of their odyssey. After one year of almost uninterrupted sailing, it was felt that both participants and their yachts needed a longer break before the start of the leg from Phuket to Sri Lanka at the beginning of 1992. The facilities in Singapore as well as its excellent flight connec-tions to all parts of the world made it the ideal place for starting this two month break.

After enjoying the vibrant atmosphere of this cosmopolitan metro-polis, the fleet started splitting up. Some took advantage of the long break to fly home to Europe or the USA, while others made their way slowly along the west coast of the Malay peninsula, from the Malacca Straits to the Langkawi Islands, on the Thai border. Many decided to join the Raja Muda Cup, a series of rallies along the Malaysian coast organised by the Royal Selangor Yacht Club. After sailing in a group for a year, it was not surprising that some were reluctant to set off on their own and the Raja Muda Cup provided an ideal opportunity to see some of Malaysia, without having to worry about formalities or suitable anchorages.

Although competition was not the reason why most joined the event, the EUROPA 92 yachts came through with flying colours. The first race from Port Klang to Pangkor was rather disappointing, as the winds were so light that only two boats finished in the required time, *Gilma Express* and the Singapore based *Wet Express*. A Malaysian buffet dinner was held that night at Pansea Pangor Laut, to which everyone was requested to come in sarong and straw hat. EUROPA participants took all the prizes for the best outfits. Success also smiled upon the EUROPA yachts in a triangle race held further along the coast, in which *Gulkarna*, *Bluewater* and *Pennypincher* won the first three places in the Cruising Division. Local yachts continued to dominate the Racing Divi-sion, although the EUROPA yachts held their own in the Cruising Divi-sion and in the the the race from Penang to Langkawi, *Trillium* placed first and *Bluewater* second. The race was marred by an accident when Leo Birkby sliced off the top of his thumb with a sheet while handling the spinnaker on *Locura*. He received emergency first aid on board and in Langkawi, but had to go to Kuala Lumpur for surgery. Fortunately he was soon back on board and *Locura* rejoined the fleet.

The last race of the event, the Langkawi Triangle, was a clean up for EUROPA yachts with *Who Dares Wins* taking line honours and second place in the Racing Division, while in the Cruising Division *Bluewater* came first, *Amadé* second and *Gulkarna* third. Overall, the Raja Muda Cup was won by *Wet Express*, followed by *Gilma Express* and *Trillium*.

Raja Muda was a good introduction to the next event, the King's Cup Regatta held in Phuket at the beginning of December. At the request of the King's Cup organisers, the arrival of EUROPA 92 in Thailand had been planned to coincide with this annual event. Many EUROPA yachts joined the event bringing the total entries to an unprecedented 77 yachts representing twenty countries. The local Thai yacht *Buzzard*, skippered by Bill Gasson, took the Cup for the third successive year. In the Racing Division, *Who Dares Wins* was the highest placed EUROPA boat coming fourth in Racing Division A, while in the Cruising Division *Oingo Boingo* was placed second in Class A, *Kite* fourth and *Bluewater* fifth. In the Thai Handicap Category, *Elan Adventurer*, skippered by John Driscoll, ran away with the trophy with five straight wins in as many races.

Thai break

The long break offered all participants the opportunity to explore the many anchorages and quiet spots around Phuket and surrounding islands. As 1992 dawned the fleet started reassembling for the start of the next leg, the fleet splitting between Phuket's Nai Harn and Ao Chalong Bays. Most preferred the anchorage at Ao Chalong, although it had a serious drawback as the knee deep mud made for squelchy landings from the dinghy when the tide was out. This was more than made up for by the hospitality offered by local businesses and there were many good parties at the newly opened restaurant Latitude Eight, whose management and staff made all participants extremely welcome. Two nights before the start of Leg 12, the Ao Chalong Cruising Yacht Club organised a big farewell party at Latitude Eight, attended by all the EUROPA participants and many of the expatriate sailors who had settled in Phuket and are now running various businesses associated with yachting. The beer for the party was donated by John Batt, a New Zealand sailor based in Phuket, where he operates Quantum Marine, a sail loft which also offers various other services to visiting sailors. The restaurant management took everyone by surprise when they produced a Thai buffet supper, which was followed by an excellent programme of classic Thai dancing.

After the skippers briefing on the eve of the start, the official farewell party was held at the Phuket Yacht Club Hotel. The hotel had been taken over recently by a Hong Kong based company and Jeff Yorke, its General Manager, had flown in especially to bid the EUROPA sailors goodbye and make sure that they left Phuket with a better impression than the one gained from their dealings with this hotel in the past. He assured participants that the hotel would live up to its name in the future and offer visiting sailors the kind of welcome they expected. The members of the King's Cup Committee, Peter Herning, Peter Cummins, Sam Cohen, David Wales, Pornchai Potikanon, Jens Overgaard and Bill Gasson, had also come from Bangkok to see the EUROPA yachts off and organise the start. The Phuket Yacht Club Hotel put on a magnificent display of canapés, while the beer and soft drinks were supplied by a number of generous individuals, 150 bottles of beer apiece being donated by Jeff Yorke, Peter Herning, Bill Gasson and Sam Cohen, while Leo Birkby donated 100 bottles of beer as an early birthday celebration for his wife Kathy, who would be spending her birthday at sea.

Leg 12: Phuket to Sri Lanka

On Sunday 5 January a favourable wind set in, making for a downwind start. The Committee vessel was the 220 ft motor yacht *Rosenkavalier*, built in 1926 and looking resplendent after recently having an extensive refit. The Governor of Phuket, HE Dr Yuwat Vuthimedhi, was due to officiate at the start, but arrived on board *Rosenkavalier* two minutes too late to fire the starting cannon. Nevertheless, he was still rewarded with the magnificant spectacle of the yachts setting course for Galle under spinnaker.

Unfortunately the perfect conditions at the start did not last long and as the yachts proceeded offshore they encountered lighter airs, gradually the wind backing to the west. The wind then veered to NE, but remained light for two more days before settling in the NNE and blowing at 15 to 20 knots. These were the kind of conditions everyone had expected during the NE monsoon of winter.

While the monsoon blew *Orchidea* along, a new crew member Simon Alltree asked Giovanna whether *Dafne* usually kept up with them. Not since being beaten to the mark by *Dafne* at the start in St Lucia did Giovanna allow Nicola's yacht to come anywhere close to challenging *Orchidea*, so it was not surprising that Simon's question caused her some concern. The crew had to wait for first light before someone could dive under the boat, where a large palm frond was discovered stuck on the leading edge of the keel; once it was removed they made much better speed and quickly left *Dafne* behind. Another yacht to be slowed down by foreign matters was *Rockhopper* when it became entangled in a fishing net. The crew were relieved to be given assistance by *Pennypincher*'s diving team who happened to be close by. *Kite* also sailed over to help, but the net had been cleared by the time they arrived.

The excellent winds during the latter part of the passage made for ideal sailing conditions with many yachts recording their personal best 24 hour runs. *Rockhopper* averaged 7.5 knots over one 24 hour period, while *Orchidea* reported a 24 hour run of 266 miles. This was not enough, however, especially after the palm frond incident, and so once again *Orchidea* was beaten for line honours by her sister ship, *Gilma Express*, who completed the 1200 miles in 5 days and 20 hours. Although *Gulliver* finished next, with *Who Dares Wins* astern of them, it was Ian Kennedy who won the leg on corrected time.

Ceylon tea party

The perfect sailing conditions meant that the majority of yachts finished within 48 hours of the first arrival. The Galle Port Authority had made great efforts to prepare the port for the arrival of the EUROPA fleet, laying down moorings, cleaning up the entire area and making sure that the normally lengthy formalities were dealt with speedily. At an official welcoming ceremony, traditional dances were performed and local dignitaries made speeches, with Ceylon tea being served.

Sri Lanka was one of the countries on the EUROPA 92 route which had caused organisers and participants alike serious concern. The fighting against the Tamil rebels in the north of the island, which had been going on for a long time, filled most participants with apprehension as they felt that they would not be able to see much of this fascinating country. These worries proved unfounded and, as most of the troubles were confined to the north, travel in other parts was almost unrestricted. The most popular destinations were Kandy and Nuwara Eliya, also known as Little England, due to its golf course, English-style church and Post Office. The scenery along the route leading into the hilly interior through countless tea plantations was spectacular, whether going by road or train. The British influence was evident in all walks of life, but nowhere more than in sports, cricket being a national institution. Not wanting to pass up the opportunity of a good game of cricket, Gordon Kay challenged a local team to a match. In the historic setting of Galle, on one of the oldest pitches in Asia, the EUROPA team put in a creditable performance considering that not only was it the first time they had played as a team, but for many of them it was the first time they had played for many years.

Having been under Portuguese, Dutch and British rule, the walled town of Galle has many attractive old buildings, particularly from the Dutch era. The prize giving for the leg from Phuket was held in the splendid Town Hall and was hosted by the Galle Municipality with the Chief Minister of the Southern Province, the Hon M S Amarasiri, the guest of honour. The Mayor of Galle, Mr Vijaya Dahanayake, greeted every participant personally and each crew member received a small memento. To open the ceremony, the distinguished guests were invited to light the traditional oil lamp. Every skipper was presented with a carved wooden plaque to commemorate their stay in Galle.

After an enjoyable stay in Sri Lanka, the yachts headed out of the harbour on 23 January for the start of the leg to Djibouti. A light westerly wind made for a windward start, but despite this, the yachts made an impressive sight as they jostled for prime starting positions. Across 2300 miles of North Indian Ocean lay the last continent on their circumnavigation – Africa.

Life on board

As Rick Palm rightly pointed out, cruising is not camping, and indeed more and more yachts are fitted out to high degrees of comfort, as owners demand that their yachts are at least as comfortable, if not more comfortable, than their homes. Before the start of one of the ARC rallies in Las Palmas, an over zealous landlubber journalist tried to shock the readers of a local newspaper by writing that while the organisers of the ARC resided in a five star hotel, the poor participants in the event were forced to sleep on their boats. Among the yachts of some of those poor sailors were a Jongert 22, two Swan 65s, a Dynamique 80, a bevy of Oysters and many other, admittedly less luxurious yachts. But even at the more modest end of the fleet, no one merited the pity of that naive journalist. Gone are the days of wet bunks and food eaten straight out of cans as more and more shore comforts make their way afloat.

Personal comfort had been an even more important factor among participants in EUROPA 92, most of whom had obviously paid close attention to this aspect. Among the new yachts, *Gulliver*, *Amadé* and *Gulkarna* had some of the best appointed interiors, while the venerable *Cheone* had been restored to a standard of luxury only to be expected from her fashion designer owner. The two Tayanas, *Sojourner* and *Bluewater*, were good examples of production boats built with comfortable living in mind. Even one of the smallest boats, such as *Octopus*, had been purposely designed to carry Astrid and Wilhelm in comfort around the world. This was also the reason why Penny and Alan Spriggs chose an Oyster 46 rather than a more sporty model, *Pennypincher*'s pilot house proving an excellent feature in which to while away the time at sea or entertain in port. The same purpose was served by *Twilight*'s stern cabin, an ideal arrangement which was also much appreciated on *La Aventura*. The Dutch built *Oyinbo* and *Midnight Stroller* were probably the most comfortable yachts in the rally, their range of modern conveniences being equal if not superior to many a shore based apartment.

The above yachts were not necessarily the exception, as most owners had made preparations to cater for the comfort and leisure of their crew.

Those who had not were soon to pay the price as some of their crew moved to yachts with a higher degree of comfort or better quality of cooking. As Francesco Casoli commented at the end of the rally, 'Keeping a crew together was by far the most difficult part of the event and my skipper Alessandro displayed great tact and talent in maintaining a happy atmosphere on *Gulliver* from beginning to end.'

Although the relationship between skipper and crew is of utmost importance, there are many other factors that can contribute to creating a pleasant atmosphere on board a yacht undertaking a long voyage, especially in such a sustained rhythm as EUROPA 92.

Either for their own comfort and leisure, or for that of their crew, the owners had equipped their yachts with various appliances. With only two exceptions, *Dafne* and *Ambler*, every yacht had at least a stereo system, either on cassette, or, on five yachts, the better quality compact disc system. Most of the cassette recorders were of the kind used in cars. 'Lo-fi rather than hi-fi, I would say', quipped Alan Spriggs.

Altogether 20 yachts had television sets, of which 18 also had a video tape recorder. *Daughter of Baltic* was one of the boats without television or similar equipment, except a stereo. 'There is no leisure on DOB!' commented Ismo Nikola half seriously. A very different answer met me on *Kite* when I asked Lona Wilson the same question. 'Of course, we have a television!' she exclaimed, evidently surprised at such a naive question. 'And also two video recorders' she added. Their VTRs were of the domestic type and were connected to a 110 V inverter. As part of *Kite*'s long term preparations, Lona and Dick had recorded 176 movies on video 8 tapes before leaving, two films being recorded on each tape to be watched during their voyage.

Not many people had had such foresight and, with the availability of new videos severely limited, the video fare had to be rationed, as on *Scorpio* where videos were watched twice a week. Video swapping became a regular feature of the rally and in many a port and anchorage, deals were struck over the VHF. Some were so desperate for new material that rendezvous were even arranged at sea to swap tapes. Some of the keenest film watchers were on *Midnight Stroller*, whose owner John Rose had had the foresight to provide his yacht with two video recorders, one PAL and one NTSC set, the latter system being used in the USA, Caribbean and much of South and Central America. As the PAL system, used in most European countries, except France, is not compatible with the US system, owners of television sets and video recorders found that they could not use their PAL sets outside of Europe. This problem did not occur on yachts equipped with sets capable of operating in all systems, such as the Grundig Multisystem sets on *Gulliver*, *Gulkarna* and *Lady Samantha*.

Video games and an electronic keyboard were greatly appreciated by the young members of *Locura*'s crew, who also had a good selection of pre-recorded movies which were watched by the crew every afternoon. *Who Dares Wins* also had a selection of video games and Ian Kennedy considered these, as well as the television set, as very useful for entertaining his children when they joined the cruising legs, but as they consumed too much battery power they were never used at sea. Ian also stressed the importance of having a good quality aerial so as to be able to pick up local television broadcasts, provided one had the right system.

The most outspoken criticism of television in any form came from Dino Blancodini. 'Why have it on a boat when it is such a nuisance ashore and kills any attempts at conversation in the family?' Roger Gold disagreed and asked every new crew joining *Rockhopper* to bring out two video tapes, on which they had recorded films, sports or interesting television programmes. The crew were also told to bring a selection of paperbacks as well as music on compact disc or cassette. In this way, an excellent library was gradually built up on *Rockhopper*.

Anne and Peter Bunting in *Gulkarna*'s comfortable saloon.

Rockhopper was also one of ten yachts which had a personal computer on board. It was interesting to note that hardly any of these were used for navigation, but mainly as wordprocessors. On a few yachts, a record of the stores was kept on the computer, while Peter Bunting used his to keep track of the various watch systems.

Also with leisure in mind, seven yachts had diving compressors and one, *Gilma Express*, a hookah gear, which was used mainly to clean the hull. On 17 yachts, one or more diving tanks were kept full to be used in emergencies. Diving expeditions were organised in many places along the EUROPA 92 route and were joined by those who had their own diving equipment.

The crew factor

The comparison of the EUROPA 92 fleet to a floating village was no exaggeration as it had all the characteristics of a small village community. The ages of the participants spanned the entire range, from 10 year old Scott on *Locura* to several participants over 70 years old. There was also a much higher proportion of women than is normal in yacht racing, and this factor contributed more than any other to the excellent atmosphere in the places where the fleet was docked together. It undoubtedly accounted for the total absence of the raucous behaviour normally encountered in male dominated yachting events. This female factor also brought a welcome dimension to the social side of the event which became a fertile ground for countless relationships with many idylls blossoming during the 15 month long voyage, some proving to be more lasting than others. Hazel and John's wedding in Darwin was the first of several marriages resulting from the round the world rally, while for others it was the perfect setting for an extended honeymoon, such as Paul and Karen on *Bluewater* who got married shortly before setting off from the USA to join the start in Gibraltar. Similarly, Annie and Trevor Parkes, who also had their wedding on the eve of the start, considered sailing in the rally on *Elan Adventurer* as their honeymoon.

The professional background of the participants was as diverse as the people themselves and there were few professions which were not represented in the fleet. Among the owners of the yachts there was a high proportion of successful businessmen who had either retired early or could arrange to take a long break from their activities to join the event. Some of those whose businesses were still active were fortunate in being able to persuade someone in the family to look after their affairs while they fulfilled their dream of sailing around the world. The Gollhofer children made such a success of running the family business in Salzburg that Walter and Brunhilde decided to let them carry on permanently. Occasionally, business affairs were run by a wife not keen on sailing, although this sacrifice was too much for some wives who preferred to sail around the world as well. Apart from the Birkby family on *Locura*, several yachts had a couple on board, sailing with the help of additional crew such as *Bluewater*, *Sojourner*, *Pennypincher*, *Amadé*, *Jakes Fantasia*, *Kite* and *Eye of Ra*, or just the two of them, as on *Octopus* and, towards the end of the rally, *Trillium*. Some fathers were joined for the rally by their older children, such as Mario Filipponi by his son Carlo, or Christian Philibert by daughter Christine and son Richard. The above examples refer to the entire rally, although there were many more examples of wives or children joining yachts for one or more legs, usually during the holiday seasons.

With the notable exception of a few yachts which completed the rally with minimal crew changes, the number of crew fluctuated widely, with the numbers declining as the fleet reached the South Pacific where the cost of flights proved too high for anyone wishing to join a yacht from Europe for a short time. As a result, some skippers found it difficult to persuade friends to join them and were forced to sail with less crew than they would have preferred.

The most remarkable aspect of the event, and for the organisers the most satisfying, was the warm feeling of camaraderie which developed soon after the start and prevailed throughout the event. Many friendships were forged among participants, regardless of age or nationality, and even language proved to be no barrier. In this linguistic Babylon, in which English was the mother tongue on exactly half the yachts, the English language became the lingua franca mainly because of convenience rather than by force. This had welcome results as even some of the Italian participants, who spoke little or no English at the start, were fluent 15 months later. By the same token, English speaking participants who joined Italian yachts as crew learned Italian. Not surprisingly, the German speaking yachts, the Austrian *Amadé*, Swiss *Oingo Boingo* and German *Octopus*, tended to gravitate together, just as did the Finnish speakers. Although outnumbered in most places, French speaking *Libertad* and *Wachibou* had the satisfaction of being treated as guests of honour when the fleet arrived in French speaking Polynesia and Djibouti.

Table 23 shows the usual number of crew on the EUROPA 92 yachts, although in many places, especially when cruising between two competitive legs, the crew was often supplemented by family and friends.

Table 23   Average number of crew

Number of yachts	Number of crew
1	2
7	3
11	4
8	5
6	6
3	8
Total: 36	

The skippers were asked if they considered the number of crew to be sufficient and over three quarters (29) declared themselves satisfied with their crew complement. The only skipper who considered his crew of five to be too large was Wes Harris, who felt that four persons would have been ideal on *Scorpio*. Among the six skippers who considered their

crew to be too few was Walter Gollhofer, whose *Amadé* sailed most of
the first half of the rally with only three persons on board, which Walter
did not consider enough. Depending on weather conditions, and if
Amadé's autopilot was coping, the crew took four hour watches, but in
the more boisterous conditions encountered in the Atlantic, the watches
were reduced to two or three hours. Walter considered that a crew of
four would have been ideally suited to sail the 53 footer to its full
potential and later in the rally *Amadé* was indeed sailed with such an
optimum crew. Also initially crewed by three persons was *Trillium*,
whose skipper Dutch Taylor considered an insufficient number. He
found the boat even more difficult to manage later in the rally, when
occasionally there were only the two of them on board.

Three of the yachts whose skippers considered the crew too small
were in the Racing Division, such as *Oingo Boingo*, where every person
took three hour watches, with a change of watch at $1\frac{1}{2}$ hour intervals,
so that there were always two people in the cockpit. Although this
system worked well most of the time, Roland Schlachter felt that his
crew of five was too small to sail the yacht to its full potential. Two
other skippers in the Racing Division, Guy Libens and Ian Kennedy,
agreed for the same reasons. As Guy pointed out, his crew of five would
have been perfect while *Wachibou* was cruising, but was totally inadequate
for racing. Ian Kennedy, who started the rally with a crew of five on
Who Dares Wins, realised in the Pacific that his chances of doing well
were severely restricted by this fact and decided to increase his crew to
eight. In Fiji, the yacht was joined by Phil Barrett and Stephen Dodd,

The Swan 53 *Who Dares Wins* could only be sailed efficiently with a large crew.

both of whom had raced in the Whitbread and brought with them a considerable amount of offshore racing experience. There is little doubt that if *Who Dares Wins* had started off with a full crew from the beginning of the rally, the final result might have been different.

The majority of skippers considered the number of crew to be right for their boats and even Wilhelm Greiff did not consider a crew of two to be insufficient on *Octopus*, the only yacht to be sailed by a couple alone throughout the rally. However, his other half disagreed. 'Sometimes it is rather tiring' admitted Astrid. Normally they took four hour watches each, both by day and night, but if the weather was settled the night watch was extended to six hours. They tried to give the other partner a minimum of four hours of uninterrupted sleep and, whenever possible, the person on watch tried to deal with everything alone.

Brad Bernardo considered his crew of three to be the perfect number for *Brydie*. When the autopilot was working, everyone took three hour watches and was off for six. 'But when the pilot is not working, you steer until you drop – in other words, you do as much as you can. We have an alarm in the cockpit to call the next watch if help is necessary.'

Leo Birkby, who started off with only one extra crew besides his family on *Locura*, considered three adults to be sufficient on a boat the size of *Locura*. Although his children Stacey and Scott helped with sail changes and domestic chores, they did not take watches, so the nights had to be split up between Leo, Kathy and whoever happened to be crew at the time. However, when I sailed on *Locura* myself from Djibouti to Port Sudan, Leo agreed that having sailed with two additional crew members for the last few legs had shown him the merits of a larger crew. Although the Deerfoot 72 was a boat designed to be handled easily by a small crew, *Locura* itself had not been set up to be sailed shorthanded. For this reason the entire crew had to be called on deck for any sail change. Earlier in the rally, when *Locura* had been sailed with a smaller crew, Leo had tried to set up the boat for the whole night so that sail changes were avoided, which meant that often the boat ended up being sailed below her potential. On *Tais*, which had a crew of three for most of the rally, Dave Sutherland also tried to keep the same sails throughout the night and avoid sail changes. However, the entire crew were called if a sail change became necessary. On *Sojourner*, where night watches started at 2000 with one person on watch for three hours, the watch would call as many of the others as were needed for sail changes, although the entire crew were needed to douse the spinnaker.

Watch systems

Several skippers in the Cruising Division pointed out that strict watches were only kept at night. Table 24 shows the length of the watch periods and also how many crew were doing watches at the same time. On more than half the yachts (20) there was normally only one person on watch and, as expected, these were almost all yachts in the Cruising Division. The only Racing Division yachts to have only one person on watch were *Octopus*, which was unavoidable, and *Soolo*, whose skipper explained that as the boat was most of the time on automatic pilot, there was no need for a second person to stay awake as well.

Table 24   Watch systems

Number of yachts	Crew on watch	Watch period (hours)
5	1	2
1	1	$2\frac{1}{2}$
10	1	3
4	1	4
6	2	3
6	2	4
1	3	4
3	4	4
Total: 36		

On the yachts with only one person on watch various arrangements had been made if help was needed. On *Bluewater*, the next person due to come on watch would be called, with the entire crew being called if there was a spinnaker change, or any work on the spinnaker. On *Twilight*, the skipper was to be called for any sail change or work on deck. Dino Blancodini was one of those who considered his usual crew of five to be too small to handle a yacht the size of 55 ft *Twilight* efficiently and he blamed their disappointing performance on some legs on this shortage. On *Jakes Fantasia*, one of the yachts on which watches were only kept at night, skipper Jake also had to be called for any sail change. This was easiest on *Gilma Express*, where Pasquale de Gregorio slept in the cockpit. At night, the rest of the crew would take three hour watches and wake Pasquale if he was needed. Only in daytime would Pasquale go below to rest, and even then he would only allow himself one hour. This punishing regime had a visible effect on him and when I met him in Darwin, after the 2500 mile leg from Vanuatu through the Torres Strait, he looked completely exhausted. This fact undoubtedly accounted for *Gilma*'s rather disappointing performance during Leg 9, when the ULDB was only able to beat *Gulliver* by 9 minutes over the line.

In case help was needed by the crew on watch, on some boats a second person was on standby below, while on *Cheone*, the second crew on watch was allowed to sleep in the cockpit, but fully dressed. This meant that although one was on watch for four hours, only two hours of the watch were actually spent awake. On *Jolly Joker*, where every crew had a three hour stint at the wheel, the person coming off watch remained on standby to help if necessary.

Several skippers specified that the normal watch system was altered under certain conditions. In bad weather the watches were usually shortened and perhaps the number of crew on watch also increased. On *Gulliver*, where four crew were always on watch in the cockpit regardless of weather conditions, four hour watches were taken on the shorter legs and five hour watches on the longer ones, the cook rotating and taking watches like everyone else. On *Pennypincher*, the watches were shortened to one hour in daytime. 'It's too hot and after one hour you want to get out of the sun' explained Alan Spriggs.

Marcello Murzilli, who normally had six people in his crew, said that the number was right, providing they were six good people. This point was made by several skippers who felt that the quality of the crew was as important, if not more important, than quantity. Peter Bunting, who considered five to be the perfect crew on his Hallberg Rassy 45, did not operate a set system of watches and varied it on every leg depending on the experience of his crew. 'Rather than have a novice at the helm, I prefer to have the boat on autopilot. The other person on watch can then trim the sails and take over the helm if necessary.' As former Commodore of the Irish Cruising Club, Peter used *Gulkarna's* circumnavigation to invite many of his sailing friends from both sides of the Irish border to join him on one or more legs of the rally.

On *Rockhopper*, the boat with most crew changes, teams of two would take four hour watches at night and six hour watches in daytime. These five watches in every 24 hour period meant that the actual time when one came on watch changed every day. Every third day, one of the teams was on galley and cleaning duty. A watch leader system also operated on *Oyinbo*, where four hour watches were taken at night, the watch leaders changing in the middle of the watch, so that the other crew would spend two hours with either of them.

On *Lady Samantha*, which normally sailed with eight people, neither the skipper nor the duty cook took watches. The remaining six members of the crew took four hour watches, of which two were spent at the wheel and two on deck watch, two persons being in the cockpit at the same time. A change of watch occurred every two hours, when the person coming on watch took over from the one at the helm, who would brief the new watch on the state of the sea and weather. For the next two hours, the person who had been at the helm remained on deck watch, relieving the person who had completed a four hour stint. Fifteen minutes before the deck watch was due to go off watch, he woke up the new watch, so that at changeover time there were three persons available should there be any need for sail changes. Enio did not take watches himself, although as skipper he was on call 24 hours. He usually got up every two hours to check the position, plot it on the chart and, if necessary, give the helmsman a new course. During the day, the individual watch period was extended to $2\frac{1}{2}$ hours so as to alter the individual watch times. The system had been perfected during many Atlantic crossings and Enio found it best suited the needs of a yacht usually being sailed by a mixture of experienced and inexperienced crew.

There were almost as many arrangements for the cook as there were yachts in the rally. On *Cacadu*, everyone had to be cook for one day and also do the washing up, without being taken off watch duty. *Cacadu* was one of the six yachts with two crew on four hour watches, with an overlapping watch in the middle, which meant that everyone was off for six hours. On *Dafne*, where two persons were on watch together for four hours, then off for the next four hours, the cook on duty was only excused his watch duties if a meal had to be prepared while he was on watch. Washing up was also done in rotation, so that the person who did the cooking did not have to wash up as well. On *Elan Adventurer*, where the crew of six took three hour watches in teams of two, one of the persons who was on the 1200 to 1500 watch would cook the evening meal. On *Kite*, one person was designated cook and took no watches, while the other four split up the watches among themselves, with teams of two taking three hour watches at night and four hour watches in daytime. On *Eye of Ra*, the crew on galley duty was excused day watches, although everyone was supposed to take their turn at night watches.

While sailing with a crew of five, on *Who Dares Wins* the crew on watch had to cover for the person on galley duty and therefore had to stay longer on watch. The cook served the two crew going on watch first and then the two coming off. The system worked, but wasn't perfect, and Ian Kennedy decided to employ a full time cook shortly after the start of the rally. 'It is essential to have someone designated as cook, especially if one is racing. That person is then in charge not only of cooking meals but also provisioning and storage.'

On almost all yachts, dinner was the main meal. It was usually preceded by a sundowner and, judging by the amount of duty free spirits, cases of wine and truckloads of beer that were loaded on the EUROPA boats at various ports along the route, this was one custom that even some of those in the Racing Division were not prepared to relinquish. When Customs came on board *Cheone* in Port Sudan to seal any alcoholic drinks, Marcello protested, 'This is a dry ship. It doesn't leak a drop.' Indeed, the battery of wine bottles stored in *Cheone*'s spacious bilges were bone dry and in perfect condition.

13
PASSAGE TO AFRICA

Leg 13: Sri Lanka to Djibouti

The thirteenth leg lived up to its superstitious reputation with almost as many problems in this one leg as in all the previous ones put together. Everyone had left Sri Lanka looking forward to a fast and pleasant passage to Djibouti. However, it soon became apparent that the hoped for constant northeast winds, a hallmark of the winter monsoon, were not going to materialise. Instead, much of the passage was bedevilled by light winds and calms, with most boats taking longer to arrive in Djibouti than anticipated. The best winds, at least for some boats, were right at the start when most yachts experienced 30 knots or more from the northeast. The winds were strongest as the yachts passed between the small islands which form a chain between the Maldives and India.

Only a short time after the start from Galle, the first incident occurred. While sailing fast in the strong following wind and buffeted by a violent cross swell, the ULDB *Orchidea* lost her rudder. The crew immediately contacted other yachts in the vicinity by radio. *Cacadu* answered the call first and stood by to help. *Libertad*, who was some 35 miles behind *Orchidea*, immediately offered to catch up to give assistance. After the crew had established that the entire rudder had been lost, skipper Giovanna considered it too risky to carry on the remaining 2000 miles to Djibouti. She asked Christian Philibert if he would attempt to tow *Orchidea* to the nearest port, Malé atoll in the Maldives. Christian agreed, caught up with *Orchidea* and started what turned out to be a much more difficult operation than either of them had imagined. Towing another yacht for 300 miles in headwinds of around 30 knots was a tremendous test of endurance and seamanship for Christian and his crew. On several occasions, the faster *Orchidea* surged forward and overtook *Libertad*, whose crew were forced to cast off the tow line instantly. Twice the rope had to be cut, but eventually the two boats reached the protection of Malé. Alerted by radio, the crew of *Twilight*, who had made a previously planned detour to the Maldives and were in Malé, came out in their inflatable to help. As the two yachts were manoeuvring with great difficulty against the strong wind and 5 knot current in the lagoon entrance, *Orchidea* was pushed onto a reef, where she sustained additional damage to her keel and external ballast. While *Libertad* was forced to cast off the towing line and seek deeper water to avoid also being pushed on to the reef, *Twilight*'s crew in the dinghy tried to push *Orchidea* off the reef, but to no avail. Several other yachts in Malé supplied dinghies and the crews of *Orchidea*, *Libertad* and *Twilight* worked all night to lighten the stranded yacht. The conditions were awful and it was the help given by these crews which helped prevent the total loss of the yacht. The following morning, at high tide, *Orchidea* was pulled off the reef by a local fishing vessel.

Although it was ascertained that the damage sustained on the reef was not as serious as had been first feared, the yacht could not continue without a new rudder, as the old blade had fallen off completely after the stainless steel tubular rudder stock had sheared. A replacement rudder blade was ordered from the Italian builders and arrangements were made to have it airfreighted to the Maldives. *Orchidea* was hauled out on a local slipway so that the necessary repairs could be carried out. Adamo Ricci, the co-owner of *Orchidea*, also arranged for two specialists to fly out from Italy to supervise the work. Unfortunately as a result of a dispute among the owners of the yacht, Giovanna Caprini, who only had a minority share in the venture, was relieved of her duties and asked to hand over to Luca Repeto as skipper.

While *Orchidea*'s drama unfolded in Malé, another incident involved *Eye of Ra* when she was visited by a large whale. After observing the boat and swimming alongside for a while, the whale dived and tried to scratch its back on the keel. Unfortunately the friendly nudge resulted in a bent propeller shaft and the bracket supporting it. No longer able to use the engine, the crew of *Eye of Ra* were forcefully transferred into the Sailing Division, which by now had shrunk considerably in the light winds as *Cacadu*, *Locura*, *Sojourner* and *Octopus* tried to make up for the lack of wind by diesel power. The unexpectedly high fuel consumption on this leg also forced *Brydie* and *Jakes Fantasia* to stop in Aden for refuelling. *Rockhopper* thought they had discovered a more effortless way of refilling their tanks by stopping a passing ship. The captain responded to their request, but gave them second thoughts by dropping two drums of diesel rather too close to the yacht.

The lack of wind forced several skippers into feats of ingenuity. Close to Djibouti, *Amadé* trailed a jerrycan of fuel on a long line to be picked up by *Midnight Stroller*. Approaching Djibouti and short of fuel, but with no one to call on for help in the vicinity and three crew members due to catch a flight out the same evening, *Lady Samantha* lowered her dinghy in the water, which towed the yacht through the glassy sea at 3 knots with the outboard engine. An engine out of action due to dirty fuel forced *Trillium* to request a tow from *Octopus*, while further back *Eye of Ra* got the same help from *Jolly Joker Again*. In Phuket, Guy Libens and András Jójárt had agreed on the sale of the yacht and although the sale had not been formalised, Guy agreed to allow *Wachibou*'s name to be changed to *Jolly Joker Again*.

Problems of a very different nature befell *Gulkarna* where a crew member became so seriously ill as to require the intervention of a specialist from the French Navy based in Djibouti. The consultation was carried out over the airwaves with several boats relaying information to and fro. Eventually the nature of the disease was diagnosed and the necessary medication prescribed. The patient showed an immediate improvement and as soon as *Gulkarna* reached Djibouti, he flew home to rejoin his family in Ireland.

African Landfall

The French Navy, who have a large base in Djibouti, were of great help both during and after the finish of this leg. Their Communications Centre was put at the disposal of EUROPA 92 where a special frequency was kept on 24 hour listening watch in case any yacht needed assistance. Rally Control ran the daily net from this centre and the French Navy also agreed to maintain a 24 hour listening watch during *Orchidea*'s passage from the Maldives when the Italian yacht tried to catch up with the rest of the fleet.

The Djibouti Yacht Club was just as helpful and its Commodore, Guy Maurice, had worked for three years to ensure the success of EUROPA 92's stay in Djibouti. The club, whose members were mostly expatriate French, had made wide-ranging preparations to welcome the EUROPA yachts, installing an international telephone, fax and telex for the use of participants, as well as taking care of all the entry formalities. Every yacht was met by the club launch on the finishing line, with a cold drink for each crew member and a welcome pack with information on Djibouti.

The original intention had been to use Aden as a port of call, but as soon as the round the world rally route became known, the Djibouti authorities contacted the organisers and promised their full support if the rally stopped in Djibouti. The matter was discussed when the Prime Minister of Djibouti visited London and the decision was taken to drop Aden in favour of Djibouti. The move was well justified as repair facilities as well as provisioning are incomparably better in Djibouti than in Aden.

Unfortunately civil disturbances in the north of Djibouti had forced the cancellation of a proposed visit into the interior of this small country, so participants had to restrict their movement to the capital itself, which was a disappointment for those for whom this was their first African landfall. However, an excursion was organised into the hills of the interior in an area unaffected by the troubles. To make up for not being able to visit more of the interior, the yacht club organised various activities, such as a triangular race in Tadjoura Bay in which several local yachts as well as EUROPA yachts took part. The crew of the latter were augmented by members of the Djibouti Yacht Club as well as the French Navy. The Commodore was invited to sail on *Gulliver*, as the yacht had won the Commodore's Cup awarded to the first yacht to sail across the finishing line. The following day 225 Djiboutian children answered an invitation by the EUROPA 92 organisers to visit the yachts and go for a sail around the harbour. Most Djiboutians have little or no knowledge of the sea and hardly any of the children had ever set foot on a boat before. Eight yachts, *Kite*, *Gulkarna*, *Twilight*, *Libertad*, *Elan Adventurer*, *Midnight Stroller*, *Oingo Boingo* and *Amadé* took children out for a trip around the bay and the outing was a great success with both the hosts and their young guests.

Following this, the crew of *Amadé* were invited to visit the class whose pupils they had taken out sailing. The children seemed very interested in life on board a sailing boat and asked Brunhilde and Walter many questions. Towards the end of the visit, a small girl got up and asked Brunhilde 'From what you say it seems that sailing is dangerous, it is uncomfortable and it is also expensive. Please tell me then, why do you do it?' It is a question that neither quick witted Brunhilde nor many a sailor could probably answer.

The activities in Djibouti were rounded off by a party and presentation at the Sheraton Hotel, when the Prime Minister of Djibouti, Mr Barkat Gourad Hamadou, presented some beautiful trophies donated by the Djibouti Yacht Club to the winners of the five classes. As well as taking line honours *Gulliver* also won the Racing Division on corrected time, while once again *Bluewater* won the Cruising Division.

Breakages

A few days earlier, I had been sitting on the terrace of the Djibouti Yacht Club waiting for the EUROPA yachts to come into their first African landfall. The daily SSB radio schedule had just finished and the first yacht was expected to arrive after midnight. Light winds and a host of other problems had caused the fleet to fan out right across the Indian Ocean. The 13th leg of the round the world rally had certainly lived up to its reputation and almost every day on the radio net there was a tale of yet another breakage. Of course, the mileage sailed by the boats in over one year was beginning to take its toll and conditions in the Red Sea were to add to the catalogue of problems.

The damage sustained by *Orchidea* and *Eye of Ra* had been the latest in a long list of breakages which had bedevilled some yachts almost from the beginning. Many breakages were caused by faulty equipment or materials, with almost as many by chafe or continuous use. Bad luck, as in the case of *Eye of Ra*'s encounter with a whale, had played its part too, while human error was also to blame in some cases. Among the latter, *Amadé*'s Tongan incident resulted in a rudder which had to be completely rebuilt when the yacht was hauled out shortly afterwards in Fiji. The rest of the damage was mostly superficial, although some dents had to wait until the yacht was returned to its builders for the aluminium hull to be properly faired. *Elan Adventurer* was hauled out at the same Fijian yard to be antifouled and, while inspecting the keel, skipper Julian Wilson was surprised to see that it had moved slightly and there was a narrow gap showing where the keel plate joined the hull. With the keel removed it became evident that the Yugoslav manufacturer had not applied sufficient sealant to the area where the keel plate rested on the hull. This explained a consistent and mysterious leak which the crew had been unable to trace.

Julian Wilson points to the source of a chronic leak on *Elan Adventurer*.

In spite of the spate of problems experienced on Leg 13, if the list of breakages is looked at in perspective, the situation does not appear so bad. After all, every one of the boats had sailed in the previous year more miles than the vast majority of yachts would equal in their lifetime. As Leo Birkby of *Locura* observed, 'I am amazed how *few* breakages we have all suffered. I put this down to rigorous maintenance. At every stop I notice how everyone deals with problems as they occur – most boats are probably in better shape than when they left Gibraltar.' Indeed, considering that by the time they reached Djibouti the yachts had sailed between them well over 600,000 miles in the previous twelve months, the list of breakages suddenly seemed less dramatic.

One of the first major breakages occurred on *Jolly Joker* shortly after the start of the transatlantic leg from Las Palmas when the boat went into an uncontrolled gybe and the boom, which was not prevented from the end but from the vang point, broke in the middle. The weakness of a boom at this point was experienced by both *Soolo* and *Oyinbo*, while *Orchidea*'s boom cracked at the same point during the Atlantic crossing. This persuaded Giovanna Caprini that some of the equipment on her ULDB was not up to the job, especially after she also lost a lower shroud while closing with St Lucia. The stemball fitting attaching the stay to the mast sheared due to metal fatigue. During the stop in St Lucia, Giovanna not only strengthened *Orchidea*'s boom, but also changed the system of attachment of the rigging to the mast, from stemball fittings to bolted plates. Similar modifications to their rigging were made before the rally by the owners of *Rockhopper* and *Gulkarna*. These modifications did not solve *Gulkarna*'s problems, but on the contrary, might have contributed to them.

Spars and rigging

Rigging failures were quite common on the EUROPA 92 yachts. *Eye of Ra* nearly lost its mast on the leg from Bora Bora to Tonga when a cotter pin securing the jib furling gear sheared and took the forestay with it. It was only quick action by the crew that prevented the entire rig going over the side. *Gilma Express* also nearly lost its furling gear when the whole assembly collapsed on deck because of one loose screw. Also during the Atlantic crossing, the spinnaker track on the mast pulled away due to the continuous filling and stalling of the spinnaker as the ULDB accelerated down the waves. In St Lucia, Pasquale de Gregorio removed the track and mounted the spinnaker cups permanently on to the mast thus solving the problem once and for all.

Both the mainsail track and one of the genoa tracks came adrift on *Libertad* during the Atlantic crossing, a passage on which participants realised the kind of damage that can be sustained by a boat which covers in one single passage more miles than many cruising boats sail in a year. *Rockhopper*'s genoa car virtually disintegrated as they were sailing under spinnaker, causing Roger Gold to comment 'This Shaefer equipment is supposed to be heavy duty but I'm not at all impressed with it.'

Metal fatigue or faulty material caused a number of breakages. Also during the Atlantic crossing, *Lady Samantha*'s forestay broke at the point of entry into the upper swaged terminal. The forestay fell down and the mast had to be stayed with two halyards for the rest of the crossing. Halfway across the Atlantic, *Pennypincher*'s inner forestay broke at the bottom swage and the mast had to be steadied with a topping lift for the remainder of the passage. On *Gulliver*, the inner forestay rod sheared in the middle during the leg from Bora Bora to Tonga, although this did not put the mast in danger. The inner forestay also had to be replaced on *Who Dares Wins* as the wire had been damaged by chafing while strapped against the mast when running.

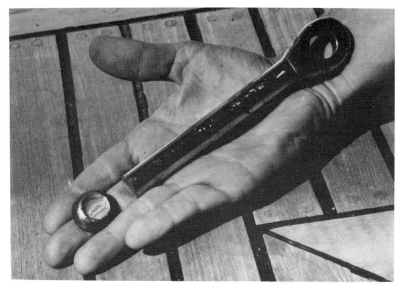

A broken forestay fitting almost resulted in *Elan Adventurer* being dismasted in the Red Sea.

Broken strands at the swaged terminal were the first indication of *Gulkarna*'s weakening rigging.

On the leg from Djibouti to Port Sudan, *Elan Adventurer* nearly lost its mast when the forestay masthead fitting broke. 'Thank God, the mast was held up by the two spinnaker halyards which are always clipped on the pulpit, or we would have lost the mast', commented a very relieved Julian Wilson. Fortunately he could effect provisional repairs in Port Sudan which allowed him to continue the rally. On the same leg, the crew of *Gulkarna* discovered that both cap shrouds and one lower stay had started parting at the swage fitting with several cable strands already broken. 'The problem was probably caused by the fact that the turnbuckles had not been fitted with toggles. This made the rigging very rigid with no allowance for fore and aft movement', explained Peter Bunting. The boatbuilders Hallberg Rassy were contacted and they immediately sent out replacement cables cut to the correct length as well as the necessary fittings. Miraculously, the consignment arrived one week later in Port Sudan and *Gulkarna* was also able to join the rest of the fleet on its way to Suez. Later in Malta, Hallberg Rassy decided to play it safe and arranged for *Gulkarna*'s entire rigging to be replaced.

Chafe

As can be expected, chafe was at the root of many breakages. Both *Elan Adventurer* and *Oingo Boingo* lost several halyards chafed on the masthead sheaves. On *Elan Adventurer* the original halyards had been rope and wire, but it was found that the wire chafed through the metal sheave, so all halyards were replaced with rope. On *Oingo Boingo* wrongly designed sheaves caused similar problems, so new sheaves were fitted in St Lucia and again in Fiji where the mast had to be taken off to fit the sheaves. By Sri Lanka, the mast had to be taken off and dealt with once again. Jammed halyards also persuaded Wilhelm Greiff of *Octopus* to replace his masthead sheaves with a better design, especially after having to climb to the top of the mast at sea twice to free a jammed halyard.

After losing several spinnaker halyards due to chafe at the masthead block, Richard Goord of *Oyinbo* adapted a method used by yachts taking part in the Whitbread Round the World Race. A wire strop is permanently fixed at the top of the mast and, after the spinnaker is hoisted, a man goes up on another halyard, shackles the spinnaker to the strop and the spinnaker halyard is slackened off. When the spinnaker needs to be lowered, a trip line opens the shackle and the halyard takes over. It is a method worth adopting, especially on a long spinnaker run.

There were a few autopilot breakages which forced the crew to steer by hand, but in most cases the fault was put right, usually by the defective part being replaced by the manufacturer. There were almost as many steering failures, mostly caused by slipped or broken cables. The loss of *Jolly Joker* in the Torres Strait was caused by a jammed cable, the helmsman not being able to turn the boat to port. Being close to the edge of the navigable channel, the crew was forced to turn to starboard and gybe. While trying to bring the boat under control, the strong wind and current pushed them on to a reef where the boat was wrecked. The crew had reported a similar problem earlier in the same leg when a jammed cable had rendered the steering inoperable although they managed to put it right.

Steering failure also put *Eye of Ra* out of action during a blow in the Atlantic when the steering chain jumped off a sprocket rendering it inoperable. John Smith had to smash the steering column and binnacle to reach the cables to slacken them off and reset the chain. It was a particularly difficult operation at night with the boat hove to. Paul Skilowitz also suffered a broken steering cable on *Bluewater* during the Atlantic crossing. This was particularly annoying as he had fitted new steering cables in Gibraltar. Paul suspected that the new cable had probably stretched and come off the quadrant, but as the boat was on autopilot, this had not been noticed. The cable eventually chafed through and broke, but was replaced fairly easily as the crew had had the experience of doing the same job only weeks before. Paul's experience and spare cables came into good use in the Marquesas when he helped repair *Rockhopper*'s steering which had jammed solid. As the steering had not been provided with proper greasing points, over the years there had been a gradual build-up of grease inside the conduit holding the cables which caused the cables to jam.

Bluewater was one of the boats which experienced the least problems and breakages during the rally. According to Paul, the main reason for this was that he had lived on board *Bluewater* since 1985 and on previous boats for the last 22 years. 'As I am a compulsive tinkerer, everything was put right long before leaving on the present voyage.' Also, as a Tayana dealer, Paul had had the opportunity to learn from other owners' complaints. After any complaint had been put right, Paul would look carefully at his own boat and often discover the same problem.

Essential spares

A Morse control cable broke on *Cacadu*'s engine and, as there was no spare available, a temporary arrangement had to be improvised with a rope and tackle to be able to put the engine in gear. Arne's advice was that everyone should carry a replacement for their engine control cables, or at least for the longest cable used on the boat. Also on *Cacadu*, the Lewmar electric windlass had been improperly sealed and rusted through in less than six months of service, but was replaced under guarantee by Bénéteau. On *Octopus*, a faulty Simpson & Lawrence vertical anchor winch caused the loss of a CQR anchor and chain off the Pitons in St Lucia. A broken shaft put *Wachibou*'s Lofran windlass out of action, but the skipper accepted the blame as the crew had overloaded the windlass to the point where it broke.

Marcello Murzilli also had problems with *Cheone*'s electrical equipment, a burnt out Bosch electric motor on his Reckmann jib furling gear and three failed voltage regulators. The most bitter complaints about quality came from the owner of this 1937 built yacht on which no expense had been spared to restore her to her original beauty. Before leaving in the rally, *Cheone* had undergone an extensive refit and although Marcello had acquired expensive equipment, this had been no guarantee of quality compared to cheaper makes.

There were problems with starter motors on several boats and, as mentioned when dealing with diesel engines, altogether starter motors gave more trouble than the engines themselves. Nicola Borsó had to replace the starter motor on *Dafne*'s ten year old engine and later on experienced problems with the new motor too. *Octopus* could not get their starter motor repaired in the Galapagos. Undaunted by this, Wilhelm Greiff decided to sail to the Marquesas, although to be on the safe side he borrowed *Oingo Boingo*'s spare starter motor which could have been pressed into service in an emergency.

The most common problems were electrical and at the end of almost every leg there was at least one alternator that had to be repaired. Fortunately such relatively simple repairs could be carried out by car electricians even in the remotest places, such as the Galapagos or Marquesas.

Engine problems occurred on several boats. *Tais* had to wait six weeks to get a replacement for the fresh water pump on an older model engine. Dino Blancodini overhauled *Twilight*'s engine himself by replacing pistons and cylinders after being forced to sail from Gibraltar to St Lucia with a broken engine. Dino's experience came in handy and he was often seen helping out his fellow sailors with mechanical problems, just as Wilhelm Greiff of *Octopus* stepped in when there was an electrical problem or Dave Sutherland of *Tais* when electronics failed.

Refrigerators and freezers broke down for a variety of reasons. On *Gulliver* the failure was caused by a faulty cooling water pump, while on *Kite* a burnt out compressor clutch put both fridge and freezer out of action. On *Oyinbo*, both the freon gas and condensor got overheated causing the high pressure switch to continuously cut out the system. The overheating was caused by scaling in the 90° bends of the raw water cooling system. Loss of freon also stopped the freezer working on *Cacadu*, but this was promptly dealt with on arrival in St Lucia.

Undoubtedly the most frustrating breakages were those which could have been avoided, such as the incident on *Libertad* when Christian Philibert was called away while changing the oil on the engine. He forgot to screw on the filler cap and when the engine was turned on, everything was sprayed in oil. Even more annoying was a fire in *Rockhopper*'s generator room. While servicing the generator, skipper Roger Gold was also called away. He later returned and switched on the generator having forgotten that he had turned off the seacock on the seawater inlet. Overheating caused the generator exhaust to catch fire. Roger had a whole catalogue of problems, very few of them of his own making. One of the most frustrating happened at Neisau Marina, in Fiji, where the travelift operator ignored his advice and positioned the lifting straps in the wrong place with the result that the propeller shaft was bent and the cutlass bearing damaged. The yacht had to return to the yard to be lifted out again thus missing the start from Musket Cove.

Rockhopper seemed to be pursued by bad luck, especially towards the end of the rally. After blowing out two sails in the Red Sea, they valiantly pushed on and made it to Malta. Repairs were carried out once again on their chronically troublesome transmission. On the eve of the start of the last leg, while going for a spin in the harbour to test the transmission, it seized up again and was pronounced defunct by the accompanying mechanic. He also traced the recurring problem to a faulty installation of the transmission by the builders of the boat. Apparently the transmission had been driving the boat in reverse gear ever since it had been installed five years previously, forward gear being engaged only when the gear was shifted in reverse. With less than 24 hours to go before the start of the final leg, Roger and Moira had to take the painful decision to withdraw. It was a cruel disappointment to both of them after having worked against all odds to complete the rally.

Jake McCullogh of *Jakes Fantasia*, who had had his fair share of breakages, had a profoundly philosophical attitude. 'I honestly don't have any regrets about whatever breakages we've suffered. It's all character building.' He then described how they had to cook on a one-burner gas cooker steadying the pots with G-clamps when the generator broke down during the Atlantic crossing rendering their all-electric galley useless. The repair in St Lucia did not last long and the generator went down again on the way to Panama, but in typical fashion, Jake persuaded the captain of a US warship patrolling the area to send over a boarding party who fixed his generator.

For Mario Filipponi, such intervention was of a higher order: 'My yacht is called "Laura" after my younger daughter and this brings me luck. On *Laura* nothing ever breaks!' True to form, *Laura* finished Leg 13 without any problems at all. The Eye of Ra was obviously looking the other way.

14
THE RED SEA

Leg 14: Djibouti to Port Sudan

Due to the lighter than expected winds and the host of problems, the start of the leg to Port Sudan was postponed by two days. Despite this not all the yachts made it to the start line. *Jakes Fantasia* and *Brydie* had stopped in Aden to fill up with fuel and then the weather turned against them. The two skippers therefore decided to join the fleet as it passed through the Bab el Mandeb Strait. *Eye of Ra* arrived in Djibouti the day before the start, but had to repair their propeller shaft after it had been damaged in the collison with a whale. *Trillium* also arrived the day before and *Laura* on the day of the start, and although both yachts left Djibouti late, they caught up with the fleet in Port Sudan.

Strong southeasterly winds made for an exciting windward start. Competition to be first across the line was keen among the leading yachts, *Gulliver* and *Who Dares Wins* being so involved in the pre-start manoeuvres that *Cacadu* and *Elan Adventurer* were the first across. With air connections between Djibouti and Port Sudan both circuitous and unreliable, for the first time Andrew Bishop sailed with the fleet and was offered a lift to Port Sudan on *Bluewater*. For similar reasons, I persuaded Leo Birkby to leave Djibouti two days before the rescheduled start trusting him to get *Locura* to Port Sudan ahead of the fleet.

After the start, the yachts had to beat to a buoy off the Musha Islands, a group of small islands in the centre of the Bay of Tadjoura. Having rounded the mark, the yachts could then lay a course for the Bab el Mandeb Strait where a strong current gave a welcome boost of speed. All participants had been advised to keep well off the western shore, which was controlled by the rebel forces involved in the internal struggle in Djibouti. The organisers had been warned that in order to attract international attention, the rebels might attempt to seize one of the EUROPA yachts. The dangerous coast was passed safely, however and, helped by the favourable wind and current, the boats left Bab el Mandeb speedily behind and started on their 1200 mile long battle against the Red Sea.

My presence on *Locura* did not result in a change in her fortune and wind conditions throughout the passage to Port Sudan were consistently worse than those encountered by the rest of the fleet sailing a few hundred miles behind us. Contrary winds were the order of the day from the moment we left Djibouti and by the time we approached Bab el Mandeb, the wind was blowing straight at us at about 25 knots. 'Well, they are called the Gates of Sorrow after all', I tried to joke, but my sense of humour was not appreciated by the rest of the crew. What was appreciated, though, was Leo's decision to anchor for the night in the lee of the Yemeni coast, after talking on the radio to an Australian yacht which was in the anchorage. It was already dark by the time we reached the bay but we were able to identify the anchorage with the help of the Australian boat, whose skipper switched on his decklights to guide us in. Early the following morning we left for the straits, but as the wind was still against us, we decided to use the narrow passage between Perim Island and the Yemeni shore.

Having sailed part of the rally on *La Aventura*, this was the first time that I had the opportunity to sail on one of the other EUROPA boats and I relished the occasion, especially on a large and potentially fast yacht such as *Locura*. Steve Dashew, who had originated the Deerfoot concept, had put much thought into creating a fast and comfortable cruising boat easily handed by a small crew. A welcome spell of southerly winds helped us maintain our headstart on the rest of the fleet, but then the winds switched to the north, as they did for everyone else, and we started on our long beat to Port Sudan. Hard on the wind, the flat bottomed hull hit the short steep seas with all its might making such a loud noise that the first time I thought we had hit something harder than water. 'You'll soon get used to it', Leo tried to reassure me, 'but even for us it gets too tiring after a while, so we end up easing the sheets to take the wind at a more comfortable angle.' We did this soon afterwards and the few degrees lost were more than made up for in comfort.

As we closed with the Sudanese coast, the wind fell light and, knowing how keen I was to get to Port Sudan, Leo turned on the engine and so we managed to arrive in Port Sudan two days before the first boat crossed the finishing line. To my great relief, as soon as we anchored we were visited by the skipper of an Italian charter boat who told us that everyone was looking forward to the arrival of EUROPA 92 and that the authorities had already made the necessary preparations for our arrival. The preparations amounted to shifting one or two small ships from an area which had been designated the EUROPA 92 anchorage so at least we could raft all the yachts together. Later we were visited by Captain Abdel Halim, the EUROPA 92 official agent, who went through the cumbersome entry formalities with us as he was to do with all the others.

Meanwhile the other yachts had passed through Bab el Mandeb and were making good progress towards Sudan. One night, the crew of *Gulkarna* heard a couple of loud bangs and on investigation discovered that several strands had parted in their starboard stays. A temporary repair was effected using a length of chain and spare halyards after which they proceeded under reduced canvas to Port Sudan.

Unwilling guests

On the fourth morning after the start from Djibouti, during the morning silent period on 4 MHz, Val Carter came on the radio and reported that *Jakes Fantasia* was being pursued by a launch with several armed persons on board. Every morning and evening, before the regular SSB radio net, a silent listening period was observed by all participants so that anyone who might be in an emergency situation could be sure of making contact with the rest of the fleet. Val's message was picked up immediately by Andrew Bishop sailing on *Bluewater* and also by myself on board *Locura* in Port Sudan. All other yachts were tuned in to this frequency, so participants were shocked to hear Val describe the occupants of the boat as being well armed and behaving in a threatening manner. Val then gave *Jakes Fantasia*'s position and as I plotted the position on a chart of the Red Sea I was surprised to see that the boat was well inside Ethiopian territorial waters, and was in fact sailing at that very moment between the coast and a group of offlying islands. All participants had been warned at the skippers briefing in Djibouti to keep well off the Ethiopian coast because of the ongoing conflict with the Eritrean rebel forces, but as Jake McCullogh had diverted to Aden and not called at Djibouti, he had been sailing in blissful ignorance. He later explained that he had not been aware of the dispute between Eritrean forces and the Government in Addis Ababa.

Val and Jake lived through some tense moments when *Jakes Fantasia* was seized by Eritrean forces.

Acting as Rally Control, Andrew Bishop instructed *Jakes Fantasia* to exit Ethiopian waters by the shortest possible route, but almost immediately Val reported that a shot had been fired across *Jakes Fantasia*'s bow. Andrew explained that this was the standard procedure indicating a request for *Jakes Fantasia* to stop. Obviously they did not do this because soon afterwards Val announced with an anguished voice that their pursuers were preparing their grenade launcher. Realising that things had gone too far, I broke in and ordered *Jakes Fantasia* to stop immediately and surrender. This advice was followed and the boat was boarded by two men who took control and ordered Jake to anchor close to Dahalak Island. *Jakes Fantasia*'s transmissions ceased when they were boarded.

As soon as *Jakes Fantasia* ceased transmitting, Andrew made arrangements for the frequency to be monitored permanently by one of the net controllers who were to call *Jakes Fantasia* at regular intervals. Meanwhile, I spoke to our agent in Port Sudan who informed me that the Eritrean People's Liberation Front had an office in Port Sudan and that relations between the local authorities and the rebel forces were excellent, as Sudan had helped the Eritreans during their struggle against the central government. Captain Halim agreed to see the Governor of Port Sudan immediately and ask him to intervene with the Eritrean representative on our behalf. Fortunately contact had also been established with two US warships which were sailing in the vicinity at that time. The radio operator on US warship 42 coordinated their actions with Andrew Bishop on *Bluewater* and also called *Jakes Fantasia* repeatedly, attempting to get a reply. Peter Bunting then managed to get through on *Gulkarna*'s radio to the World Cruising office in London via Portishead Radio, informing them of the incident and asking them to advise the British Foreign Office. We later found out that the US State Department had also been informed via the US Navy and was liaising with the British Foreign Office as to the best course of action. The US authorities were taking a particular interest as one of the crew, Susan Lawrence, was an American citizen. By that time, *Cheone* had already arrived in Port Sudan and Marcello immediately contacted an acquaintance in the Italian Ministry of External Affairs who started his own intervention. The Italian authorities were particularly well placed to help as they had built up excellent relations with the Eritreans. I later found out that the Eritrean representative in London was summoned to the Foreign Office and asked to release the British yacht and its crew as soon as possible. Under such a barrage of diplomatic activity, the message soon filtered through to Asmara that Eritrea could only gain from dealing with the matter in a reasonable manner and, indeed, the attitude of the authorities towards the captive crew was exemplary from beginning to end.

After spending a few hours at Dahalak Island, *Jakes Fantasia* was escorted to the port of Massawa on the mainland where the crew were interviewed by Navy and Immigration officials. The following day, having completed what appeared to be normal entry formalities, the crew were allowed to go into town. That evening Jake was informed that the authorities in the Eritrean capital Asmara had decided to allow them to go and that they could leave in the morning.

After two days of intense diplomatic activity in London, Washington, Rome and Port Sudan, *Jakes Fantasia* was indeed allowed to leave and sail to join the rest of the fleet in Port Sudan. News of their release reached the rest of the fleet one day later, everyone being astonished at the speed with which the entire incident had been resolved. It was a much speedier and happier ending than the fate of another British yacht, which had been seized in the same area the previous year and whose crew had not been released for over two months. The yacht itself had still not been released by the time Jake and his relieved crew were allowed to go. By the time *Jakes Fantasia* reached Port Sudan, the next leg was already underway, although there were enough Cruising Division boats left behind to give Jake, Val and Susan a warm welcome.

Muslim reception

Apart from this incident, the leg from Djibouti produced no more surprises and *Gulliver* took both line honours and won the leg overall in the Racing Division, while Enio Nardi, following local advice given in Djibouti concerning where to find stronger currents, brought *Lady Samantha* in to win the Cruising Division. At the prize giving party hosted by the Governor of Port Sudan province, *Gulliver* was presented with a beautiful sword, while *Lady Samantha* received a traditional dagger.

In spite of having serious worries about the Sudanese stopover, these proved to be largely unfounded and the EUROPA 92 stay in Port Sudan was much more pleasant and enjoyable than everyone had expected. In many ways, this was due to the efforts of Captain Abdel Halim, whose fluent English and Italian helped to smooth our way through the jungle of Sudanese bureaucracy. Also to be seen day and night in the port area was the Director of Tourism, Khalid Khalafalla, who arranged various tours for the participants. One of these was to the ruined city of Suakin followed by a barbecue at a local craft centre. There was also an evening of folk dances from various regions of Sudan. The authorities themselves were obviously pleased to see a prestigious international event stop in Sudan and tried to make the fleet welcome. The Governor of Port Sudan, Dr Said Abdelrahaman, invited everybody to a welcome and prize giving party which was held on a Friday after evening prayers and was attended by several high ranking officials all wearing immaculate white jellabahs and matching head dress. Sharia law is strictly enforced in Sudan and the observance of religious customs dominates every walk of life. Consumption of alcoholic drinks is prohibited and participants were even asked not to bring their empty beer cans ashore. Otherwise the short stay in Port Sudan passed off pleasantly, helped by the fact that a recent devaluation of the Sudanese pound made local prices ridiculously low, although there was very little to buy except for locally grown fresh produce.

Leg 15: Port Sudan to Suez

With the next leg declared non-competitive for the Cruising Division, there were only ten boats on the start line off Port Sudan on 22 February. An unexpected spell of SE winds gave them an excellent start and, although the winds soon reverted to their normal direction, most yachts recorded good times, *Gulliver* being the first boat to arrive in Suez, having completed the 680 miles in just over four days. All yachts in the Racing Division arrived in Suez in good shape, thus dispelling the doubts of those who would have preferred not to race this section but to take their time to reach Suez. This is precisely what the yachts in the Cruising Division did and, freed of the need to start on a given date or to arrive within a time limit, most attempted to cover the distance to Suez in a leisurely fashion. Unfortunately this proved much more difficult than most had expected as the consistently strong headwinds and rough seas made for some very slow passages as well as much broken gear. Every day the morning radio net revealed yet another minor disaster, whether blown out sails and a broken transmission on *Rockhopper* or a violent bout of seasickness for a new crew member on *Twilight*. The latter proved to be so serious, that the sick lady and her husband had to be disembarked at a fishing village on the Egyptian coast. Permission to do this without clearing in at an official port first was arranged by the Italian Embassy in Cairo, who also managed to get an Immigration officer sent out in a taxi from Hurghada to accompany the two castaways to the nearest airport.

After acquitting herself of her duties as Committee vessel, *La Aventura* left Port Sudan in the company of several boats in the Cruising Division. Having heard of the excellent diving conditions in the Red Sea, most intended to stop at some of the reefs off the Sudanese coast. The most famous among them is Sha'ab Rumi, where Jacques Cousteau had conducted some of his underwater studies. Before leaving Port Sudan, Abdel Halim, who had worked with Cousteau, described the best anchorage and also how to find Cousteau's underwater habitat. After anchoring inside the lagoon, we inflated the dinghy and went in search of the habitat, which we eventually discovered on the outside of the southern pass. The disintegrating aluminium structure was clearly discernible at a depth of 40 feet surrounded by colourful coral reef. Close by, the reef wall fell to a great depth and a lone black tipped shark circled his territory. After returning on board, we brought *La Aventura* over the spot and noted down the exact position (19°56.39 N, 37°24.20 E) on our GPS, which we then passed on to those following us.

Needing to reach Suez as soon as possible, we sailed from there nonstop, but a long spell of strong northerly winds made our passage on *La Aventura* slower than expected. Trying to make the best of the existing winds, we took a long tack towards the Saudi shore, then tacked back to the Egyptian shore when the wind presented us with a slightly better slant. However, progress was very slow, and once we reached the narrower Gulf of Suez, we gave up and started motorsailing. Constant winds over 30 knots, lots of shipping and a string of oil drilling platforms, some of them unlit, made for some exciting sailing, especially at night.

We arrived in Suez to find all the boats in the Racing Division comfortably settled in at the Suez Canal Yacht Club where moorings had been laid down to accommodate all EUROPA yachts. On arrival in Suez, *Who Dares Wins* protested *Gulliver* over the number of spinnakers carried by the Italian yacht. A Protest Committee was formed, but the protest was dismissed as the rally, although using CHS ratings, was not run under CHS Rules and therefore the CHS restrictions to the total number of spinnakers carried did not apply in this case. Following the dismissal of the protest, the results could be announced, *Gulliver* and *Soolo* winning their respective classes, which made the situation at the top of the table closer than ever before, with 2.25 points separating the leading yachts in Class I and only 0.25 separating those in Class II.

The evening after the protest meeting, the Governor of Suez, Mr Samih El Said, hosted a prize giving party at which the winners in the various classes as well as other participants were rewarded with various gifts by the Suez Canal Authority. There was also a special award for Dave Sutherland's *Tais* who, after crossing the finishing line in Port Sudan, had carried on sailing and so completed the section Djibouti to Suez nonstop. A consolation prize was also given to Giovanna Caprini who had flown in from the Maldives to join *Libertad* for the last two legs to Gibraltar. Meanwhile *Orchidea*, repaired and with a new rudder, was being sailed from the Maldives by the new skipper who was trying to catch up with the rest of the fleet in Alexandria.

As in Sudan, the stopover in Suez had caused us concern, but we found that the officials tried to make our stay in Suez as pleasant as possible. The Suez Canal Authority, who administer the yacht club in Suez, had put down moorings for every yacht and formalities were generally kept to a minimum. The Egyptian Sailing Federation had seconded Commodore Hassan Luxor, an ex-sailing champion of Egypt, to coordinate all EUROPA 92 activities. Sadly, the President of the Federation, Adel Taher, who had also been involved with EUROPA 92, died suddenly of a heart attack the day before the welcome party in Suez. It was therefore decided that a special trophy bearing his name should be awarded to the winner of the Alexandria–Malta leg.

Taking advantage of the convenient facilities in Suez and the safe moorings, most participants left their yachts there to visit other parts of Egypt: Sinai, Cairo, the pyramids at Giza or the ancient sites on the Upper Nile. Slowly, the yachts that had been delayed by weather or breakages on their way to Suez, joined the rest of the fleet. *Soolo* was the first yacht to transit the Canal and, despite delays due to strong winds and sandstorms, by the middle of March most yachts had transited the Suez Canal and proceeded to Alexandria in preparation for the start of Leg 16 to Malta.

Maintenance routines

Disasters always make the news in preference to happy stories and cruising is no exception. By the same token, the previous chapter dealt almost exclusively with the bad news, which hopefully did not create the impression that the round the world rally amounted to a nonstop sequence of breakages and unfortunate incidents. In fact, the majority of the boats sailed around the world with little or no problems and suffered far less breakages than had been expected. Although it is difficult to draw any overall conclusions, some obvious ones became instantly apparent. One first observation was the number of breakages that occurred during the Atlantic crossing. The 2700 mile long passage, with the winter trade winds blowing at their strongest, put both boats and crews to a real test. For most boats this was the first proper offshore shakedown and it brought out all the weaknesses hitherto undiscovered. The transatlantic passage not only taught participants how much they could expect from their boats both in performance and in ruggedness, but was also a useful and often costly lesson in how to avoid similar problems in the future.

Chafe and the damage associated with it was much more serious than most participants had anticipated and they quickly learned how to prevent or minimise its effects. Many also learned the value of regular maintenance as well as the utmost importance of frequent visual checks. The section of the survey dealing with breakages also dealt with maintenance schedules on the 36 yachts, various routines being applied on each yacht.

● **Standing rigging:** A thorough inspection was carried out before every leg and on almost every boat this included a trip to the top of the mast when all rigging and terminals were checked. At the same time, the points of attachment to the mast and spreaders were also inspected as were spinnaker blocks, sheaves as well as halyards. As Pasquale de Gregorio pointed out: 'It's at the top of the mast where things go wrong, so one cannot go up often enough.' This was not exactly the feeling on *Eye of Ra* where lots were drawn whenever an expedition to the masthead was due. As John Smith explained 'We are not the keenest mast climbers'. The crew of *Midnight Stroller* no longer had to be persuaded to make the trip as they had discovered various things which could have had a disastrous ending if not discovered in time, thus showing the value of such regular inspections. On one occasion, Frank Wilson noticed that a bolt securing a running backstay had almost sheared through and could have had grave consequences if it had not been dealt with immediately. Dino Blancodini made a quite unexpected discovery on his last visit up *Twilight*'s mast before the start in Gibraltar. Dino had somehow forgotten that he had his passport in his back pocket and only noticed this as he saw it flutter down and disappear in the depths of Marina Bay. With the rally starting the following day, he decided to leave for Las Palmas after being told that there was an Italian consul there. The stop in Las Palmas proved to be too short for the new passport to be issued, so he carried on to St Lucia, where the story was repeated. Amazingly, Dino managed to sail from country to country with only his ID card, as at every stop the organisers assured the local Immigration officials that the passport was bound to arrive any day. Finally, a new passport did catch up with Dino, but only when the round the world rally had reached its halfway mark in Fiji.

Besides regular visual checks, several skippers described their preventive maintenance routine. Much of this concentrated on the rigging. On *Ambler*, the swaged terminals were sprayed regularly with WD40. All rigging as well as the furling gear were checked daily on *Gulliver* and turnbuckles rinsed and oiled regularly. Rigging tension was another item checked regularly at the same time as inspecting the standing rigging. Very little if any maintenance was needed on boats with rod rigging. On *Locura*, the silicone grease was replaced regularly inside the terminals and the threads were also lubricated.

- **Running rigging:** Visual inspections were carried out frequently, usually at the same time as those for the standing rigging. Halyards were either changed or shortened occasionally. This also applied to sheets which were in constant use, especially spinnaker sheets. Whenever possible, sheets were rinsed in fresh water.
- **Furling gear:** The lower assembly was flushed out with fresh water as frequently as possible. On *Dafne*, a silicone spray was used to lubricate the gear and boltrope groove.
- **Sails:** These were checked after each leg and any necessary repairs carried out immediately. Whenever possible, the sails were rinsed off in fresh water. The seams had to be restitched on some

of the older sails and, as the mileage added up, so the sails needed more attention. Frequent visual checks were made on most boats. Rather than wait until it may be too late, *La Aventura*'s furling yankee was completely serviced in Darwin and all suspect seams were restitched.

- **Chafe:** A lot of thought had gone into chafe prevention and, from their comments, it would appear that most skippers were happy with the results. On *Amadé* leather guards were fitted on the pulpit and lifelines where the genoa rubbed against the lines. On *Bluewater* spreader patches had been added to all sails, while on *Eye of Ra* there were rollers on all shrouds. On *Sojourner* chafe guards were added on the aft lower shrouds and also on the back of the spreaders. A strop was also added to the furling jib so as to take it above the pulpit. As a final precaution against chafe, Rick Palm decided to run his spinnaker halyards on the outside of the mast. Special sheet leads were added on *Tais* to avoid unnecessary chafe. Due to heavy use, the Spectra sheets on *Who Dares Wins* only lasted a few months and had to be replaced when they chafed through.

On *Octopus*, the furling genoa had been strengthened at the height of the first set of spreaders, while the mainsail batten pockets had their thickness doubled. On *Oyinbo*, Richard Goord had abandoned the old fashioned baggy wrinkles as they were getting wet and dirty, and replaced them with lengths of PVC hose which

Rinsing the sails with fresh water helps extend their lives.

were pulled over the aft shrouds. Chafe caused much damage on *Rockhopper* early in the voyage, but as Roger Gold explained: 'We're getting better as we gain experience.' When asked if he had made any provisions against chafe, Jake McCullogh replied: 'Yes, him' and pointed to his crew Alan, a professional upholsterer who had sewn leather anti-chafe patches everywhere on *Jakes Fantasia*.

- **Engine:** Main engines and diesel generators were maintained and serviced regularly on all boats, the task made somewhat easier by the fact that certain jobs, such as oil and filter changes, had to be done whenever the unit had run for a given number of hours. On some boats, the engine had a professional service every six months. On *Ambler*, all fluid levels were checked whenever the engine had been running for more than six hours. On *Rockhopper*, if the engine had been running continuously for 48 hours, the engine was turned off for one hour and everything checked thoroughly. Also, audible alarms had been fitted to all critical instruments, so the crew on watch could monitor everything. On *Daughter of Baltic* the engine compression was tested regularly as an early indication of possible problems. Belt tension was also checked frequently on most boats. Wilhem Greiff of *Octopus* also suggested thoroughly inspecting the engine after it had been idle for a long time, whether at sea or in port. On such occasions, one should check cooling water and oil level, seawater filters, and also check for possible leaks for water ingression through the exchange cooler, or via the exhaust system.

On *Oyinbo*, when the engine was running, the person on watch had to record every hour in the log the following information: oil pressure, temperature, starting battery voltage, gear box oil pressure and temperature, fuel filter pressure. On *Locura*, separate logs were kept for the engine, generator, watermaker and diving compressor, so that an accurate record could be kept on what should be serviced and when.

Participants were also asked to elaborate on their maintenance routine, particularly if they followed a daily, weekly or monthly routine. For Paul Skilowitz the question was superfluous: 'I'm an obsessive fiddler, so I keep a permanent eye on things.' Probably the best organised yacht in this respect was *Oyinbo* where printed schedules had been prepared for everything, the crew ticking off the various jobs on a daily, weekly or monthly basis. Richard Goord had prepared a crew information booklet which listed all that they needed to know about every aspect of the yacht. Before the voyage Richard had also bought all consumable items needed for the routine maintenance of all equipment on board for the entire voyage.

- **Daily routine:** Such a routine was followed on all boats, especially at sea. On *Cacadu*, the last watch before sunset checked everything, all ropes were coiled and the boat tidied for the night. The sunrise watch had to tidy up and clean up everything for the day. On *Lady Samantha*, Enio Nardi walked around the deck every evening and checked that everything was in order. Also as part of the daily routine, the position of the spinnaker halyard was changed if the spinnaker had been in use for a long period.

Wilhelm Greiff also made it a habit of checking everything on deck before dark, particularly the state of the pins in the various turnbuckles and the bolts securing the forestay and jib furling gear. A thorough daily inspection was also the routine on *Who Dares Wins* when everything was checked on deck, such as sails, ropes and sheets, as well as anything else that was likely to wear.

The things which were checked daily on the various boats varied, with some skippers spending as much time in their engine rooms as on deck, while others relying more on their instruments to tell them if anything was wrong. Among the things checked daily was the battery voltage, an important aspect bearing in mind the amount of electricity consumed on most boats. The bilges were also frequently checked, especially on boats with persistent leaks. Cooling water level, plus a visual check to see if water was coming out of the exhaust, was another item which was checked regularly. As this is rather difficult to check, especially if the exhaust is concealed under the stern, on *La Aventura* an additional small diameter pipe carries exhaust water to the port side of the hull from where it is easily seen by the helmsman.

- **Weekly routine:** Several skippers conducted a more thorough inspection at least once a week. On long passages, this usually included a trip to the top of the mast. Peter Bunting praised the scavenger pump on his Hallberg Rassy 45 which was operated as part of the weekly routine. The pump draws a sample from the bottom of the fuel tank and, if this is not clean, the sludge is pumped out until clear fuel appears in the sighting tube. The batteries were checked on *Jakes Fantasia* as part of the weekly routine when terminals and contacts were inspected and also the acid level in each cell.

- **Monthly routine:** Engines and generators were serviced once a month unless such a service had been due because of the number of hours that the equipment had been in use. Among the items serviced on a monthly basis also were winches and windlasses.

As part of the general preparations for the rally, Richard Goord had compiled a comprehensive list of all equipment on board, not an easy task on a yacht with such complex equipment as *Oyinbo*. Richard went

On most boats the winches were serviced as part of the monthly maintenance routine.

through all the various equipment manuals extracting the essential information, sometimes having to contact the manufacturers to obtain additional information. The data was fed into a computer and printed out so as to be available whenever needed. All this information was put together in a book which was handed to any new crew joining the boat. It contained clear instructions on how to start, operate and stop every piece of equipment on board, as well as how to maintain it and what spares were necessary for routine servicing.

Just as the boats which had been best prepared suffered least breakages, those on which maintenance was carried out properly rarely suffered delays. 'Prevention is the best cure when cruising', commented Paul Skilowitz who spent much of the time in port inspecting the various systems on his boat and, as a result, encountered very few problems at sea and could enjoy the rally so much more. It also brought him the satisfaction of putting *Bluewater* at the top of the Cruising Division early on in the rally where it stayed right to the end.

15
THE MEDITERRANEAN

Leg 16: *Alexandria to Malta*

Facilities in Suez were so much better than expected, so most participants decided to visit the splendours of ancient Egypt before transiting the Canal. All arrangements for the transit were made by the Prince of the Red Sea agency, whose founder, Fathi Soukar, I had met when I first transited the Canal ten years previously. His two sons now run the business and dealt with all formalities with the utmost efficiency, both clearing the boats into Egypt and arranging the Canal transit. The largest convoy of eleven yachts was delayed in Suez for 24 hours due to a southerly gale accompanied by sandstorms which greatly reduced visibility. Each boat accompanied by a pilot, the convoy made their way to Ismailia, where they had to spend the night at anchor as small boats are not allowed to transit the Canal in the dark. On the second day of the transit, four of the slower yachts were stopped south of Port Said due to the late southbound convoy, which meant they had to spend an extra night in the Canal. In EUROPA fashion, an impromptu party was organised on board *Lady Samantha*, each crew contributing a different dish.

Last stop
After dropping off their pilots in Port Said, boats proceeded without stopping to Alexandria in preparation for the penultimate leg to Malta. For various reasons, a few skippers decided to bypass Alexandria and sail directly to Malta. The EUROPA 92 base in Alexandria was the Yacht Club of Egypt, whose management had agreed to host the rally, but appeared to be interested only in making as much money out of the event as possible. A new menu was prepared in the club restaurant with prices for visitors four times more than those for local members. One of the most frustrating difficulties was in obtaining fuel and this was only resolved on the morning of the start, which meant delaying the start by four hours. One problem which could not be resolved was to obtain permission for the rally officials to go on board the Naval vessel which had agreed to act as the Committee vessel. In the end Dino Blancodini offered *Twilight* as the Committee vessel and the start finally got underway.

A strong northwesterly wind was blowing as the boats lined up for the start outside Alexandria harbour. They were later joined by *Octopus* whose anchor had got entangled with the moorings of local fishing boats. Another boat which took a late start was *Orchidea* which had sailed virtually nonstop from the Maldives to Suez after having had its rudder replaced in Malé. After the start, *Twilight* lost no time in returning to drop off the rally officials before battling their way into the open sea for the second time. Both participants and rally officials were visibly relieved to bid Alexandria goodbye, which later was voted the worst stop of the entire rally. The main culprit was the yacht club whose unwelcoming attitude spoilt everyone's impression of this interesting country.

Strong winds from the northwest characterised the first three days of the passage, but by now the yachts had become hardened to the inclement weather. The winds gradually improved and then the majority of the boats had good sailing in 12 to 20 knot winds from the southerly quarter. *Gulliver* was the first to arrive in Malta, sailing the 900 miles in 5 days and 18 hours. They finished over ten hours ahead of *Who Dares Wins*, *Gulliver* winning the leg overall and the Adel Taher Memorial Trophy. As on many previous occasions, the leading boats managed to get the best winds and, after the first yachts had arrived in Malta, the weather deteriorated forcing some of the boats in the Cruising Division to heave to. There were several close encounters with ships, although in most cases the ships' radio officers were helpful, often giving the yachts weather information. The strong winds were also taking their toll on sails and *Libertad* blew out most of theirs on this passage. The French yacht then ran out of fuel, but managed to get some from *Amadé* shortly before arriving in Malta. *Amadé* went on to win the Cruising Division overall for this leg.

The Maltese authorities had made great efforts to welcome the fleet and the management of Msida Marina arranged for one pontoon to be completely cleared of other boats and reserved for EUROPA 92. This was the first time that the yachts had been together on one dock since Darwin and it created an excellent atmosphere. After three difficult legs, many skippers took advantage of Malta's excellent repair facilities. Some of the late starters from Egypt caught up with the fleet here, while five American yachts, *Brydie*, *Kite*, *Sojourner*, *Trillium* and *Scorpio*, confirmed their withdrawal after having decided to spend time cruising in the Eastern Mediterranean.

The Royal Malta Yacht Club welcomed all participants in its historic setting in Fort Manoel. A lecture on the history of Malta was well attended and gave participants an added interest in visiting Valletta and the rest of the island. The yacht club was also the venue for a successful party organised by the German speaking contingent in reply to the British party in Papeete, the Italian spaghetti dinnner in Musket Cove and the American party in Bali. Wilhelm and Astrid made special sausages on board *Octopus*, while Fabienne and Roland of *Oingo Boingo* had raclette machines and two huge cheeses flown in from Switzerland. Brunhilde and Walter of *Amadé* generously picked up the tab for the wine and beer assisted by Arne of *Cacadu*.

The prizegiving for the Alexandria to Malta leg was hosted by the Minister of Transport and Communications at the Hotel Les Lapins, while the Minister of Tourism hosted a farewell reception in the Mediterranean Conference Centre set in the huge vaulted rooms, which once had been a hospital of the Knights of Malta. Twenty four school children from Pederobba, a small village near Treviso, home town of Enio Nardi, had a trip of a lifetime when they visited the fleet in Malta. The Italian children had been following *Lady Samantha*'s progress throughout the rally. For all of the children this was their first aeroplane flight and their first time outside of Italy. Hosted by the Ministry of Education, they had a full programme besides visiting the yachts, including an audience with the President of Malta. They stayed for the start, cheering *Lady Samantha* and the rest of the fleet as they crossed the line set between Fort Manoel and the ramparts of Valletta.

Final leg: Malta to Gibraltar

Brilliant sunshine and a good breeze made for an exciting start to the final leg to Gibraltar against the magnificent backdrop of Valletta, watched by many spectators on both sides of the harbour. Due to the short start line and restricted manoeuvring space, the Racing Division started 15 minutes before the Cruising Division. The start was made more dramatic by the firing of a gun by the Malta Regiment on top of Fort Manoel and it was the first time since Las Palmas that the start had been given on land. As the boats reached the entrance to the harbour and were hit by stronger gusts, there were several near broaches, the most spectacular by *Gilma Express*.

After four successive wins, *Gulliver* was only one point behind *Who Dares Wins* and either boat had to win this last leg if they hoped to win the event overall. In Class II, *Soolo*, by winning the two Red Sea legs, had reduced *Oingo Boingo*'s lead in this class to 1.25 points and this could still be overturned. *Orchidea*, fully repaired and aggressively sailed by her new skipper Luca Repeto, threatened to put a spanner in the works. As the fleet left Malta everyone was waiting for the daily radio positions with bated breath.

Strong winds from the southeast only lasted for one day after the start after which the winds settled in the northwest. With the winds then blowing at 25 to 45 knots from either SW or NW, the yachts had to tack and chose different routes, some to the north and some to the south. Pasquale de Gregorio kept *Gilma Express* close to the African coast and

Gulliver crosses the finishing line off Europa Point to be the first boat to return to Gibraltar at the end of the round the world rally.

managed to pick up a favourable current. Although *Gilma* was rapidly gaining on the other front runners, it was too late and at 0840 on Saturday 11 April *Gulliver* crossed the finishing line off Europa Point being the first boat to complete the rally. His Excellency the Governor of Gibraltar, Admiral Sir Derek Reffell and Lady Reffell were among the first people to greet *Gulliver* in Marina Bay Marina. However, for owner Francesco Casoli and skipper Alessandro Mosconi there followed an anxious few hours until they were sure that they had also beaten *Who Dares Wins* on corrected time. In Class II, Roland Schlachter brought *Oingo Boingo* across the finishing line under spinnaker to win his class overall and gave spectators a colourful sight. Christian Philibert's *Libertad* won the Cruising Division for this leg, pushing *Bluewater* into second place, although Paul Skilowitz's impressive lead meant that *Bluewater*'s overall win had never been in doubt.

Anxious not to miss the partying in Gibraltar, some of the Cruising Division boats were burning up fuel fast and called in to refuel along the southern Spanish coast, *Gulkarna* achieving this in 40 minutes flat. There were few dramatic incidents in this last leg, although both *La Aventura* and *Bluewater* fouled fishing nets at night and had to wait until daylight for a member of the crew to dive and free them.

At a cocktail reception given by the hotel management on the top floor of the Holiday Inn, the participants had a splendid view of the Bay

Karen and Paul Skilowitz's overall win in the Cruising Division was largely due to thorough preparation.

of Gibraltar and watched the last two boats arrive, *Wachibou* towing a disabled *Octopus*. In order to confuse everyone, *Jolly Joker Again* had reverted to being *Wachibou* again, both Guy Libens and András Jójárt having sailed the last leg together.

Marina Bay Marina had kept the visitors dock clear and so all the yachts could be berthed close together. It also made it easier for the many impromptu parties that were thrown by various boats, either on the dockside, on boats or in the nearby restaurants. The final leg had been sponsored by Saccone & Speed (Gibraltar) Ltd, who hosted the final prize giving on 19 April at the Caleta Palace Hotel. The timing of this for the Easter weekend meant that many families, friends and crew could fly in from all corners of the globe and over 250 people attended the party. Most of those who had been unable to complete the rally arrived in Gibraltar by air, among them John Rose, Marcello and Sabrina Murzilli, Moira and Roger Gold. Nicola Borsó, whose *Dafne* had had to divert to Crete with several problems on the leg from Alexandria, flew in from Italy, while Richard and Susan Goord had left *Oyinbo* in New Zealand to rejoin the many friends they had made during the rally.

The overall winners, *Gulliver* in the Racing Division and *Bluewater* in the Cruising Division, were presented with special Rock of Gibraltar trophies by the Minister of Tourism, the Hon Joe Pilcher. *Gulliver* also received the Commodore's Cup awarded by Micko Sheppard-Capurro, Commodore of the Royal Gibraltar Yacht Club, for line honours in the final leg. Having won line honours in nine out of 17 legs, Pasquale de Gregorio received the Navigator's Cup. There were many other special awards, including EUROPA 92 Junior Cups for Stacey and Scott Birkby of *Locura*, and a special Doublehanded Award for Astrid and Wilhem Greiff of *Octopus* for having completed the whole rally with no additional crew. The Panu Harjula Memorial Trophy for the best crew was awarded to John Driscoll, who had sailed from Gibraltar on *Tais*, then skippered *Elan Adventurer* when Julian Wilson was ill and finished the rally on *Twilight*, being particularly helpful on the radio net. At the end of the evening, the Governor of Gibraltar, Admiral Sir Derek Reffell, presented the main perpetual award, the Concordia Cup, to the crew who had best reflected the spirit of the event. This had been a difficult choice as many participants fulfilled the criteria in different ways but the final choice of Brunhilde and Walter Gollhofer of *Amadé* proved a popular decision. In Class I of the Cruising Division, *Amadé* had sailed every leg and taken every start. They joined wholeheartedly in all activities, were always goodhumoured and mixed socially across the whole spectrum of participating nationalities.

The crew of *Amadé* are congratulated by HE the Governor of Gibraltar for winning the Concordia Cup.

The prize giving party went on into the early hours as if no one wanted it to stop. The following day, on Easter Sunday, Sir Derek and Lady Reffell invited the skippers and their wives to a reception in the beautiful garden of their official residence. It was a moving and fitting farewell to EUROPA 92.

Conclusions

With the yachts gathered together for the last time it was an appropriate moment to ask some of the skippers for their final comments on both the rally and their boats. Although some of the comments had been made earlier, it was remarkable how very few had changed their views. The last conversations in Gibraltar either confirmed or reinforced earlier statements when skippers had been asked to comment on various features of their boat such as deck layout, livability below on passage, crew comfort or seaberths. They were also asked for their comments on the builder's aftersales helpfulness and, finally, if they felt that their choice of boat had been right for the rally.

After some of the critical remarks mentioned in the foregoing pages, I was surprised to find that the majority were in fact pleased with their choice and, although certain features of their boats had attracted some criticism, there were very few boats which had failed their owner's expectations. Indeed, this is probably the main reason why, in spite of all the problems and the sustained rhythm of the rally, so many boats completed the circumnavigation and returned to the point of departure barely fifteen months after setting off on this epic voyage. It was in this last section of the survey that the seriousness of their preparations became evident and also how much thought skippers had paid to optimising their boats for the round the world rally. All these observations were born out by the results themselves, as all the boats which had done well from the performance point of view were also those whose owners had had both time and money to prepare the boats well for the rally.

The winner of the Cruising Division was a good example in this respect. Asked if he liked *Bluewater*'s deck layout, Paul Skilowitz exclaimed 'Of course I do, I designed it!' Indeed, the layout was well thought out and worked well. 'We have a single line reefing system led back to the cockpit, as do all halyards and furling lines. So there is no reason to go forward to shorten sail, which makes life very easy.' Rick Palm made the same comments when we discussed the other Tayana in the fleet, *Sojourner*. 'The deck layout is perfect. One can run the boat without going forward of the mast, although most of the sail handling is done right from the cockpit.'

This was one aspect on *Dafne* criticised by Nicola Borsó. 'The deck layout is bad. Some halyards are on the mast, while others are led back to the cockpit when ideally all should be brought aft.' Although generally pleased with his deck layout as well as *Kite*'s wide side decks, Dick Wilson disliked the fact that someone had to go forward to reef the mainsail and felt that being able to reef from the cockpit would have been a great bonus. Nor was András Jójárt content with the layout of his *Jolly Joker*. 'The boat was designed as a racing boat with a crew of 8 or 9 and therefore was very difficult to be handled by only 4 or 5. The cockpit was also badly designed, there was no backrest, so one had to sit on the floor. It was also extremely wet. The situation was just as bad below and the boat was very uncomfortable on long passages.'

Livability below, crew comfort and privacy generally were other aspects on which the skippers were asked to comment. One of the happiest owners in this respect was Pasquale de Gregorio. 'Although *Gilma Express* was built without bulkheads to save weight, it can easily be partitioned off to ensure privacy.' The importance of this aspect was stressed by several skippers, including Julian Wilson. 'There is no hot bunking on *Elan Adventurer*, which is not bad for a crew of six on a 43 foot boat.' Although the crew was smaller and there were five seaberths on *Eye of Ra*, John Smith felt that there should have been leecloths in both the aft and foreward cabins, but they were not easily installed on his type of boat. *Ambler* was one of the few boats without proper sea-berths, but as John Papp explained, 'There are so many berths on the boat anyway, that one can always find an empty berth on the lee side.'

Comfort on passage

Several boats had been fitted with seaberths for the rally, but undoubtedly the best ones were those on *Cacadu* which had been specially made by two Finnish sailors who had sailed in the Whitbread. The berths were provided with strong leecloths, the shape and angle of which could be adjusted by the occupant with the help of a block and tackle. Apart from wanting a fast yacht, Arne Blässar also wanted a boat with three separate cabins, which would allow the crew off watch to sleep undisturbed without the need to use the bunks in the main saloon. The choice among existing 50 footers was rather limited and Arne never regretted his choice of a Bénéteau 51. 'The French know how to build boats. So far I am very happy with *Cacadu*. I hope it will last.'

Cheone's crew undoubtedly slept in the most elegant surroundings as the yacht has four separate cabins with two berths each as well as individual bathrooms. Marcello described *Cheone*'s degree of comfort as 'perfect' and he could only think of one criticism. 'The cockpit is just as comfortable but it needs a bimini. I never liked biminis, but when you're sailing around the world, you need one. You also need a dodger over the companionway to stop rain coming in.'

Octopus was one of the few boats built by their owners. It had taken Wilhelm and Astrid Greiff five years and 6000 hours of work to fit out their dream boat. At the end of the rally both agreed that the choice had been right, although they would have preferred a faster boat. Experience also showed them the mistakes they had made. They found, for instance, that although it was easier to steer the boat with a tiller, a wheel would have been better as the tiller always got in the way. The positioning of the winches was also ergonomically wrong as one had to lean over too much when grinding. Wilhelm also had doubts about the wisdom of bringing the mainsail halyard back to the cockpit, as one had to go to the foot of the mast anyway to handle the fully battened mainsail whose travellers tended to jam in the track. On the other hand, having the spinnaker halyard led to the cockpit proved to be a good idea as it allowed the person steering to raise the spinnaker while the other person was handling the douser on the foredeck.

One of the boats which had been designed and built for safety and comfort was *Lady Samantha*. 'The deck layout is absolutely safe. You cannot trip over anything. For added safety, both the gunwhales and lifelines are higher than normal.' Although *Lady Samantha* sailed around the world with a crew of eight, in fact she had been designed to be sailed by just Enio and his wife Ksenjia, so the sails had been kept small. Having sailed 100,000 miles on *Lady Samantha*, Enio was as happy with the boat as on the day of her launch in 1985. One of the few things he regretted not having was a wheelhouse, which the designer refused to accept as he considered it would have spoilt the lines, although Enio felt that he should have insisted. One of the things he would not have, if he were to build such a boat again, was a centreboard as it only caused problems. 'The advantages of a shallow draft do not warrant a centreboard, so another time I would definitely go for a fixed keel.' Although initially Enio had wanted a cutter, he was happy with the ketch rig which allowed him to set the sails so that the boat steered by herself. Having had fibreglass, aluminium and steel boats before, Enio felt that the West System was the best. '*Lady Samantha*'s hull is light and strong. For added strength the hull was sheathed in Kevlar, which was then covered by one layer of fibreglass to protect the Kevlar from the sun, so maintenance is kept to a minimum.'

Another owner who had absolutely no doubts about his hull material was Walter Gollhofer. 'I was happy with aluminium before, but after running on a reef in Tonga I fell totally in love with aluminium. Otherwise I wouldn't have a boat at all.' Walter also commented on *Amadé*'s unpainted aluminium hull, which although easier to keep clean if it were painted, was so much easier to maintain in its unpainted state. Although generally very pleased with his Levrier de Mer, Walter also had some complaints, such as the poor ventilation inside the boat. In strong winds all hatches and portholes had to be closed which made it very stuffy below.

As to be expected, one of the most satisfied owners was Francesco Casoli, who had ordered his Swan 59 *Gulliver* especially for the rally and had the satisfaction of winning the event. Although the basic design was not altered, the rudder had been slightly enlarged and the rig made taller. The alterations were inspired and both these features helped *Gulliver* perform better in the light winds encountered on some legs, although the rally was eventually won by *Gulliver*'s better performance in the final three legs when windward conditions gave her an advantage over all other boats, her nearest rival included, the Swan 53 *Who Dares Wins*. The ex-*Crackerjack*, a well known yacht on the international racing circuit, had been bought by Ian Kennedy only six weeks before the start to replace his Swan 36, which was too small for the rally. The boat was refitted in Palma de Mallorca, where the Swan Nautor agent was very helpful in getting the boat ready in the short time available. Generally, Ian was happy with his choice, but pointed to the dilemma caused by the choice to be made between cruising and racing. 'One had to decide before the start what sails to carry. You don't want to carry too much and end up too heavy, but you don't want to be left without some essential sails either.'

Ian also commented on the difficulties of sailing such a boat efficiently with a small crew, which is what he did at the start of the rally. 'The rig is so tall that the running backstays were used all the time. Even a crew of five was not enough when gybing such a big mainsail, so our original crew of five was totally inadequate. This may not sound like a comment on the actual design of the boat, but how could one be expected to do well unless you have a large crew?'

Guy Libens came to virtually the same conclusion. '*Wachibou* falls somewhere between the Racing and Cruising Divisions, but it didn't really fit into either one or the other. To be more competitive it should have had more and better sails, as well as a larger crew. Overall, however, the choice was probably right.' Guy had bought the Meridien 53 in 1990 after the boat had been impounded for several years in Amsterdam for drug smuggling. While fitting out the boat for the rally, Guy tried to contact the French builders, but they had gone out of business, so the question concerning aftersales service did not apply.

Among the new production boats, *Cacadu* had had a lot of modifications carried out by Bénéteau before the rally and Arne Blässar was very pleased with all of them. He also praised Bénéteau's attitude afterwards as everything that broke or did not work as expected was replaced promptly without any questions. When Arne complained about the quality of the antifouling paint after the Atlantic crossing, Bénéteau advised him to sail to Guadeloupe where the boat was repainted free of charge. Earlier, on his maiden voyage to Finland, Arne had complained to the builders that the cabin heater was too efficient and was making the boat too hot, so Bénéteau paid for a smaller heater.

Aftersales service

Another well known French builder, Amel, received less praise from Christian Philibert, the owner of *Libertad II*, an Amel Mango he had bought new in 1988. Although Christian was generally pleased with the boat and its performance, he described Amel's aftersales service as 'not too helpful'. Even less helpful were Gibert Marine, the builders of the Gibsea 442 *Oingo Boingo*, who refused to replace a set of damaged sheaves and demanded payment, although they were still under guarantee. The badly designed masthead sheaves caused Roland Schlachter a lot of problems and he had to lower the mast on three separate occasions to replace the sheaves. Nevertheless, he was very happy with the boat itself which, after all, helped him win Class II in the Racing Division.

As a Tayana dealer, Paul Skilowitz had received a tremendous amount of help from Tayana. To his knowledge, the factory never refused a warranty claim from any of its clients, provided it was done in the right and proper way.

Not surprisingly the owners of boats which were bought second hand, or which were no longer under guarantee, could not expect as much help from the builders as those who had just taken delivery of their yachts. However, this was not necessarily the case. Leo Birkby, whose second hand Deerfoot 72 had been built in 1985, found the builders extremely helpful when he approached them for advice and he ended up using them to order any spare parts he needed during the rally. At the end of the rally, *Locura* was sailed to Deerfoot's new boatyard in Maine, where she was going to undergo a major refit.

Alan Spriggs, who had bought *Pennypincher*, an Oyster 46, from Arne Blässar, found Oyster very helpful whenever he contacted them for help. Although both he and Penny are competitive sailors, they felt that a comfortable cruising boat was better suited for a voyage along the route taken by EUROPA 92 and considered their choice as 'absolutely' right. What they particularly liked on their boat was that the hull had not been gelcoated but painted with International 709. 'The hull always looks good, it never dulls, as gelcoat does, and maintenance is minimal.'

Also bought second hand was *Oyinbo*, a Nordia 61 built in 1985. Richard Goord took the yacht back to the yard for a refit and he found the builders extremely helpful, both at the time and on subsequent occasions. However, Richard found the manufacturers of some of the equipment less obliging when he tried to order the various spares he considered necessary for his voyage. He compiled a list of such essential spares and ordered them by telex or fax from the manufacturers, but found it very frustrating not to receive an answer even after three or four faxes. He ended up visiting some manufacturers personally in the UK and New Zealand and, after telling them about the round the world rally, they usually became more cooperative.

One of the oldest boats in the fleet was *Tais*, a Rival 41 built in 1978 and bought second hand by Dave Sutherland one year before the rally. Although he was 'reasonably happy' with his choice, Dave considered the elderly design as rather old fashioned with a lot of wasted space which could have been put to better use. Dave found the builders very helpful when he contacted them for advice on the osmosis treatment he carried out on the hull before the start.

'Hinckleys are unbelievable. All I have to do is just call them from wherever I am and they'll send anything I need.' Brad Bernardo's enthusiasm was justified and this I could testify myself when a small but weighty parcel arrived from Hinckleys in St Lucia after *Brydie* had already left for Panama. Thinking that it was some essential equipment and as I was going there myself, I decided to take the parcel with me. And so it flew from St Lucia to London, then to Miami, and finally Panama, where a rather embarrassed Brad opened it in front of me to expose two ordinary zinc anodes. Needless to say, he could have bought a ton of them from the nearest chandlery in Panama!

Brydie's delayed package was one of countless examples of a late delivery by an international courier company. This was a major problem throughout the rally and, having either suffered ourselves from such lack of efficiency, or watched frustrated participants miss a start because of a delayed or lost package containing some essential spares, I was forced to draw the conclusion that most courier companies are unreliable, if not outright dishonest, and often take at least twice as long to deliver a package than they promise. Also, in most countries their arrangements at incoming airports are poor or nonexistent and couriered consignments end up being mixed up with ordinary airfreight. The only solution is to go to the airport and look for the consignment oneself, or employ the services of a local customs agent. Naturally, there were a few exceptions, such as the DHL branches in St Lucia and Panama, but overall the service was disappointing. A more reliable service, where it exists, is the courier service run by the post office itself, such as Datapost.

Such delays were not always to be blamed on the courier companies as some builders or manufacturers sometimes took too long to deal with the freighting of essential spares. One of the companies which always appeared to deal promptly with requests from its customers was Swan Nautor. The Finnish company attracted the praise of Francesco Casoli for their attention to detail. He also pointed out that the company sent one of its representatives to Gibraltar before the start to ensure that everything was working well.

Another boat ordered for the rally was *Gulkarna II*, Peter Bunting's Hallberg Rassy 45. Peter was generally very pleased with the boat, but also had some criticism. In particular he found the working area of the cockpit too small with insufficient space for the various halyards and other lines which had been led aft. Also he considered the number of winches, stoppers and cleats insufficient. Having gone to Sweden to take over the boat, Peter found the handover system at Hallberg Rassy's unsatisfactory. 'It was a sloppy handover and it was obvious that they just wanted to get rid of me and get on to the next customer. Also the handbooks and manuals were terrible, with few instructions in English and several missing, such as the one on the Maxprop. Also there were no wiring or plumbing diagrams to show any modifications, which caused a lot of trouble later when we tried to trace a problem.' Peter was clearly unhappy about this attitude, although later in the rally he admitted that the company dealt promptly with all his requests. However, he felt that, 'Now that Hallberg Rassy have gone to German Frers to design a boat that *can* sail, experienced sailors like myself who buy Hallberg Rassy boats will have higher demands.'

'We wanted a fast boat which is also very comfortable – and that is what *Amadé* is. We couldn't have made a better choice' stated Walter Gollhofer at the end of the rally. 'However, we were often frustrated at not being able to sail the boat at her full potential, for which we would have needed a larger crew. This is why we decided to join the Cruising Division.'

Pasquale de Gregorio, whose *Gilma Express* won line honours in nine out of 17 legs and finished third overall in the Racing Division, had no doubts about his choice. 'I am convinced that a ULDB is the perfect boat for both racing and cruising. With a light and easily driven hull, you only need to have small sails. Also the boat rarely sails heeled over as you always have the right amount of sail up. Therefore the boat always sails well and is also comfortable.'

'The Morgan 41 is a comfortable boat and generally sails better than I had thought, but on the wind – forget it!' were John Papp's comments on *Ambler*'s sailing performance.

'I am as excited about this boat now as I was when I ordered it' said Brad Bernardo who nevertheless had second thoughts about his choice when he commented on *Brydie*, a Hinckley 42. 'If I knew when I planned this boat that I was going to sail around the world, I would have gone for a bigger boat.'

Nicola Borsó, who had done a lot of racing in the Mediterranean and who bought ten year old *Dafne*, a Nautic Saintonge 44 especially for the rally, did not mince his words. '*Dafne* is too slow for my taste. It would have been better to have had a faster boat so as to spend less time at sea – such as a 45 ft long *Amadé*.'

Although sailing in the Cruising Division, Ismo Nikola's comments were similar. '*Daughter of Baltic* is a very comfortable boat. So from this point of view the choice was right, but not if we wanted better performance.'

Julian Wilson had no doubts about *Elan Adventurer*, which was entered in the rally by Adventure Sailing, an offshore charter company taking on fee paying crew and the yacht had been sailed as far as Panama by David Miles of Adventure Sailing. 'The choice was definitely right as the Elan 43 is a very fast boat. Unfortunately we did slow her down as we carried too much gear.' This observation was made by several skippers who felt that their boats would have performed much better if only they could have kept weight under control. In spite of his concern about saving weight, Julian would have liked to have carried a sewing machine on board. 'Having stitched three blown spinnakers by hand and then spent over one thousand dollars on another repair job, a sewing machine should be a must on such a voyage.' Another suggestion he made was to carry sufficient Camping Gaz bottles to last three months, as well as the necessary adaptors so that they could be filled anywhere in the world.

John Smith, who had owned his Moody 419 *Eye of Ra* since 1986, was quite candid about his choice of boat for the rally. 'It's what I had and I couldn't afford anything else, but a boat should be at least 45 ft long for this kind of voyage.' *Eye of Ra* had undergone various modifications for the round the world rally so I asked John if he should have added anything. 'Yes indeed. An electric windlass, a freezer and a watermaker.'

Jake McCullough was 'more than happy' with his choice although he would have preferred to have had more time to prepare the boat properly for the rally. Jake also felt that in a boat heavy and difficult to manoeuvre, such as his, a bow thruster would have been invaluable.

John Rose, who also bought a second hand boat for the rally, was very happy with his Trintella 53, although he had some second thoughts, '*Midnight Stroller II* is extremely comfortable and although I am very happy with this degree of comfort, perhaps I should have been more interested in the racing side of the event. In that case I should have gone for a Bénéteau 51.'

Roger and Moira Gold were also pleased with their choice, a Roberts 435 built in the USA in 1987. 'The boat is extremely comfortable, stiff and steady. We had 45 people on board at a party in St Lucia and the boat didn't even move.' They had good reasons why they wanted this kind of boat. 'We wanted something inherently safe bearing in mind the inexperienced crew we were going to have. The boat was frustrating at times, but very safe.'

The owner of another steel boat, Wes Harris, had similar feelings about his *Scorpio II*. 'A steel hull is perfect. In Fiji, we hit an uncharted reef at 6 knots. A fibreglass boat would have been in trouble, but we came off in 30 seconds.' Yet Wes admitted that safety should not be allowed to become the one and only consideration. 'Although I am happy that we came off that reef with only a scratch, sometimes I wish I'd joined the rally in my previous boat, a Peterson 44, which was so much faster. If I ever did this again I'd come in a faster boat and do proper racing.'

Another Californian just as keen on racing was Dick Wilson, who took a philosophical attitude. 'Some boats are faster, but do not have the luxuries. Everything is a trade off. *Kite* may not be one of the fastest boats, but we are very comfortable.'

So did a consensus emerge from all these comments and observations? From the remarks quoted above and statements made throughout the rally, one can say that most owners would have preferred to own potentially faster boats. It was interesting to note that even some of the dyed in the wool cruisers gradually modified their views after seeing their colleagues in the Racing Division sail faster and better under any conditions. Only by such direct exposure can one see for oneself how much more fun it is to sail fast and well. Even I came to reconsider some of my views and concluded that the trend towards faster, more efficiently sailed cruising boats is irreversible. This need not be a contradiction, as in the point made by Dick Wilson, for indeed in both racing and cruising one should always aim for that elusive ideal, even if one ends up with a compromise. 'No one is ever completely happy. You always see something you like better, but either you are not ready for it or cannot afford it', commented Dutch Taylor.

The first round the world rally has taught everyone – participants, organisers, designers, boatbuilders, any interested sailor – many useful lessons. It has also shown that however good the boats, it is the people who sail in them who really matter. Even in today's world of technological wonders to sail around the world is not just a great adventure but a major achievement. Let no one forget that.

16
MORE STORIES FROM THE SOUTH SEAS

Only the winning stories were printed in Chapter 8, but as there were many other talented entries, they should not be condemned to oblivion such as Doina's little story which started the whole idea.

Gulliver's Aventura

Gulliver was a *bluewater ambler*. His friend *Jake's fantasia* was to make a *sojourner* on the island of *Wachibou* in the *Oingo Boingo* Sea, so he could fly his *kite*.

As they landed on the beach, under the scorching *Eye of Ra*, far off they heard the red tufted *Rockhopper* make its distinctive call, '*cheone, cheone*', answered by the blue-billed *Cacadu* with a shrill '*trillium, trillium*'.

There before them stood the beautiful *Laura, Daughter of Baltic*, the infamous giant from the land of *Gulkarna*. *Gulliver* was bowled over. '*Oyinbo*', he greeted her, and asked 'Won't you be my *brydie*?' as he picked her an *orchidea*. She replied 'Oh yes, but first you must vanquish the giant *Octopus*, in the Cave of a Thousand *Scorpios*.'

He did this with the *elan* such an *adventurer* has, and they were soon married, taking their honeymoon on the *Gilma Express*, in a special compartment with music laid on by *Amadé*.

The happy couple visited the wise soothsayer *Lady Samantha*, who shuffled the cards and pulled a *Jolly Joker*.

But *Gulliver* was rather a *midnight stroller*, and *Laura* got *locura*. 'I'd rather be *soolo*!' she cried. 'I want my *libertad*!' And she walked off into the *twilight*.

Gulliver sighed. '*Who Dares Wins . . .*' He thought her a bit of a *pennypincher* anyway . . . and *Dafne*'s charms were beginning to tempt him.

Doina Cornell,
La Aventura

EUROPA 92 Makes Landfall

Amadé (I'm a day) late on this *Rockhopper Sojourner* over *Bluewater* so will be disqualified, 'Tis sad! So, *Laura*, instead of a *Twilight* saunter through the *Clover* how about a *Midnight Stroller* down to Club *Jakes' Fantasia* for some *Locura* and coffee? Maybe we'll do some *Dancing* . . . *Waves* and *Octopus* are playing and I hear *Oingo Boingo* does a great drum *Soolo*.

Coming back on the *Gilma Express* I overheard an *Elan Adventurer* telling some *Jolly Joker* there was quite a party at Jakes a few nights ago. Seems *Brydie*, *Gulliver* – oh, and *Libertad II*, were drinking hard and high as a *Kite*. They joined a high stakes poker game shouting *Who Dares*, *Wins* all and began buying rounds for the bar. Acting like they were *Trillium*-aires. Old *Gulkarna II* got really carried away plied by their drinks. His *Lady*, *Samantha*, is such a *Pennypincher* he'll soon be living with his *Daughter of the Baltic* or maybe Siberia.

Let's *Ambler* over and see what *La Aventura* is happening tonight. *Oyinbo!* Do you see *Cheone* doing the *Cacadu* with hip swinging, bosom flinging, luscious Miss *Orchidea*? Ha, the jaded *Eye of Ra*-chelle is glaring more sharply upon them with every shake and shimmy. I've heard she's a *Scorpio II* and if you know star signs his Yachting World days are over. Ah, but look to the lovelorn sweet *Dafne*. Bet she *Tais* pity upon him, I can see it in her starry eyes. *Wachibou* wiggle out of this one. Come on *Laura*, let's get them to teach us this new crazy bird dance. (Runner up – short category)

Pat Taylor
Trillium

La Ventura of Jake, A Sailing Fantasia

Jake Stroller was an *Elan Adventurer*. During his youth he had spent his life at sea in pursuit of bacchanal pleasure. Now at age 35 he began to feel an unbearable loneliness. He needed a special woman to share his life. He began his search in earnest January 6, 1991, in Gibraltar.

As a youth, in French Polynesia, he spent his time chasing *Octopus* in tide pools and playing with his canaries and his pet rooster *Cacadu*ldo. As a young *Jolly Joker* he played tricks on his friends, and dreamed of seeing far off lands, but never a thought for the girls. As Jake grew older he was more discontented with his life. He longed for excitement and adventure. As a child, flying his *Kite* Jake had learned to read the wind, so his father, his Excellency the *Wachibou* of New Zealand, *Maid* a suggestion to buy a sailboat and seek his fortune at sea. Jake agreed.

To find the perfect yacht Jake consulted World Cruising Ltd President Jimmy Cornell who referred him to a St Lucia yacht broker. There he found a sleek sloop named *Libertad II*. She had a *Hypatia*us interior and required a EUROPA 92 feet to hoist the mainsail.

'Doina you think she's a beauty?', asked the broker. To which Jake responded, 'Gwenda you think she'll be ready to sail?' 'At *Twilight*', he replied. As his Visa card was extended he decided to challenge the yacht broker. 'Are you a gambling man? Double or nothing', said Jake. 'Give me *Libertad* or give me debts.' He lost the bet but by *Kite*ing his check it floated as well as the boat.

Being a *Pennypincher*, and to reduce provisioning expenses, he opted to *Soolo* hand his boat. For provisions he stowed a crock of *Gul liver* pate and s*Oy in Bo*ttles. Later he would s*Locur A* lot of ham. He bought a *Tais* deck to listen to *Oingo Boingo* on long, lonely watches. Jake sailed on the morning tide eager to see the world.

As a *Sojourner* he met many people in exotic lands. One evening, in a bar in Panama, he met a woman named *Laura*. She asked him how long until *Midnight*. *Stroller II* soon realised they would never have *A Made* in heaven relationship when she rejected his offer to share *A Meli A Viking* would enjoy.

He awakened the following morning. A strange mood enveloped him. What was missing? Why did he feel so *Blue*? *Water* under his keel had always satisfied him before. But with *Laura*'s rejection he realised he was tired of sailing *Soolo*. It was January 5, 1991, tomorrow he would be 35.

To solve his dilemma he sought advice from *Brydie* Murphy. She had had many lives and was surely wise. She told him to consult an astrologer whose sign was *Scorpio*. Jake's sign was *Scorpio, II*, so he had confidence in his wisdom. The astrologer said, 'I have a friend named Rahmond, who has only one eye. Look into the *Eye of Ra*hmond, and he will tell your horoscope.'

Jake found Rahmond overseeing the preparation for a large celebration in *Gulkarna*, a mythical island off the coast of Gibraltar. Rahmond said. 'Be an *Ambler* my son, *Bluewater* voyaging is exciting, but costly. Look for a rich wife as *Soolo* sailing may make you *Dafne*. Be a guest at my party in *Gulkarna, II* see if you'll find whom you seek.'

As time was of the essence, Jake took the *Gilma Express* overland railroad. Upon arriving at the party he saw the most incredible woman he'd ever seen. This is the biggest *Gull I Ver* saw, Jake visualised. She was the *Daughter of Baltic Cheone*, the governor of the Galapagos Islands. Her name was *Orchidea*

Cheone, and her voice was *Trillium* enough to break glass. Her biceps measured 15 inches. A woman like this could be heard from the foredeck and turn a winch one handed. He had to have her as his mate.

But first he had to have approval of her mother, *Lady Samantha*, the champion *Rockhopper* of *Gulkarna*. *II* hop rocks she would stand on one foot, leap from one rock to another yelling *'Who Dares Wins'*. Jake won her respect, as well as her daughter's hand and dowry, as he outleapt her over the Tonga Trench. *Orchidea* was destined to sail the seven seas as the *Brydie* of Jake and *Jake's Fantasia* was a reality. She reprovisioned the boat with cabbage, onions, hot dog sausages and beans. With this fare they were destined to always have wind at their backs. (Runner up – most original)

Lona Wilson
Kite

Pacific Paradise for EUROPA 92 Participants

At sunset in the South Pacific the jungle becomes alive to the shrill call of the *Cacadu* and the shriek of the *Kite* hawk. There is the distinctive noise of the *Oingo Boingo*, the mating cry of the *Bluewater* bird, the grunt of the *Tais* and the squawk of the *Rockhopper*. Occasionally the rare *Wachibou* may transfix one with its *Eye of Ra* like stare, whilst the *Cheone* can be heard flapping noisily overhead.

Along the seaside *Brydie* path that renowned *Pennypincher* Lord *Gulliver* was enjoying a *Twilight Ambler* during his *Soolo Sojourner* on the remote paradise island of *Gulkarna* when he made the mistake of treading on a *Scorpio*, slipped and fell into the water, where he was quickly engulfed in the tentacles of a giant *Octopus*.

This startled *Lady Samantha* who with *Dafne, Daughter of Baltic*, was embarking on a *Midnight Stroller* to admire the strange night *Orchidea*. She let out a *Trillium* cry!

Fortunately the *Elan Adventurer* appeared at that precise moment and with a shout of '*Oyinbo!*' dived into the swirling water. To his astonishment he found it was actually the lovely *Laura* embracing her lover. The *Jolly Joker* had got there first with a call of '*Who Dares Wins*'! What a *Libertad*!, he thought and 'what *Locura*', he breathed.

Alas it had only been *Jakes Fantasia*. It was in fact *Amadé* on the *Gilma Express* on the way to the city. He had been daydreaming.

What a *L'Aventura*, he sighed . . .

Richard Goord
Oyinbo

The Adventures of Dafne

'Ah! Sweet *Libertad*! Free at last' thought *Dafne* as she slid down from her second story bedroom window. *Dafne* was the sixteen year old *daughter of Baltic*, J C Baltic, that is, heir to the vast *Gulkarna* pharmaceutical fortune. She had everything a young girl could ask for, but as with many young girls, something was missing. Since the disappearance of her mother when she was eight, her father had been overly protective of his only daughter. She was never alone except at bedtime. She spent this time reading books of *Elan* and his *Adventurers* and dreamt of having adventures of her own.

'And now here I am, she thought, on my own, a *soolo* act, an *ambler*. I'll have to get a job and make some money, that will be adventure #1', she laughed. 'But first I have to get out of this town unseen', and off she headed for the bus depot. Once there she really had no idea where to go. She got on the biggest bus, the one with '*Gilma Express*' painted in big black letters down the side. 'This looks like the fastest way out of here', she thought, and settled in for a long ride, wherever. She slept most of the night and was awakened by a gentle tapping on her arm.

'Hi! My name is *Laura*', said the girl sitting next to her, 'I'm going to visit my dad, he lives in California.'

'Oh my!, is that where I'm going?' *Dafne* thought. Well at least it was a bigger more exciting place than the small town of *Tais*, where she was from. There, everybody knew your business before you did. 'What does your dad do?' *Dafne* asked *Laura*.

'He makes jewelry, see this locket he gave me? It's the *Eye of Ra*, a good luck charm. It's worth a *trillium* dollars.'

'I'll bet it is', *Dafne* said and went back to sleep.

It was two in the afternoon the next day before they finally reached San Francisco and once off the bus *Dafne* realised she hadn't a clue what to do next. It was a beautiful warm summer day and a walk through the park to the bay was definitely in order. There were many people in the park enjoying the day. Kids on bikes, roller skates and skateboards. One boy was flying a *kite* that looked like a dragon. Down by the water a man with his face painted half white and half black was doing pantomime. *Dafne* stood and watched as he did his routine and as he finished, came over to her and handed her the *orchidea* from his lapel. She blushed, said thank you and went to sit by the water.

As she sat staring out over the great *bluewater*, she spied a beautiful old schooner tied to the end of the pier. The name painted on the side in bright gold letters was '*Lady Samantha*'. It was like something out of a dream. 'One day', *Dafne* thought, 'I'll see the world from that boat. Right, dream on, first I need a place to sleep and a job to pay for it.' So off she walked in search of one or the other.

San Francisco was a big city away from the water. Quite different from what she was used to. It was starting to get late and *Dafne* was tired. She had no idea where to go so she thought maybe she'd sneak into a movie theater and sleep a little there. There was only one theater on the street she was on. The name on the marque was '*Jake's Fantasia*', rated X. 'Funny, I thought that was a Disney film', she sighed, and walked on into the night.

'Just as she thought all was lost *Dafne* came upon neon lights, '*Oingo Boingo* Bar and Grill', it flashed.

There was a small sign below it saying, Help wanted. Brilliant! and just in time too. It was getting towards 1 am and the street corners were buzzing with strange people, mostly the *midnight strollers* and other lost souls of the *twilight* hours.

Once inside she was met by a rather large man with an *octopus* tattooed around his forearm and a white *cacadu* named Fred perched on his shoulder. 'Good Lord', she thought, 'this should be a real adventure.'

'*Cheone, Cheone*, chow bella', the bird squawked.

'My name's *Dafne*', she said to the man and 'I'd like the job.'

'It doesn't pay much', he said with a gruff voice, 'but you keep the tips and if you need a bed there is a room in the back.'

'This is perfect', she thought, and said quickly before he changed his mind, 'I'll take it! When do I start?'

'No time like the present', he said and turned and walked away.

'Fine, now what do I do?,' she said to herself as she scanned the smoky room full of colourful people. Sitting at the corner table, a strange little man with a fuzzy red tuft of hair on top of his head, whistled at her and shook the cubes in his empty glass trying to get her attention. What a funny looking character he is, she laughed, and he looks like a little *rockhopper* all dressed in his black suit and bow tie. She walked over and took his glass and brought back a refill. He paid her and told her to keep the change, which was only a dime.

'Boy, what a *pennypincher*', she thought hoping this wasn't a sign of things to come.

Over by the window a man was playing the piano. *Dafne* walked over and introduced herself. She was a litle surprised when in a very feminine like voice he said, 'Hello *Dafne*, my name is *Amade*us, but you can call me *Amadé*. I'm a *Scorpio*. What's your sign dear?'

'Oh!, well I'm a *Scorpio* too', she said trying to hold back a laugh. They talked for a while and she found that because he was such a *jolly joker* you really didn't mind how bad he played the piano.

As the last customer left the bar, *Dafne* went to the backroom to meet 'the boss'. She had heard from the bartender that he had been nicknamed the 'Great *Oyinbo*' by the natives from deep in the jungles of *Wachibou* where he hunted regularly. *Dafne* noticed a plaque on the wall wedged between a tiger and a bear head which said '*Who Dares Wins*'. She was finding out that it wasn't far from the truth.

Over the weeks they talked of his travels and adventures. Fred would sit on her shoulder and call her *Cheone* and each day she would go to the pier and look at *Lady Samantha* and dream of being a *sojourner* like her boss.

One afternoon during one of her daydreams a man came up to her. His name was *Gulliver*. 'Chow bella' he said. 'Did it ever *locura* toa you that I could taka you on *laventura* of a lifetime. Coma sail away with me and be my *brydie* and I'll show you the world!'

She awoke with a start to the squawking of Fred, '*Cheone*, chow bella!'

'The name's *Dafne*, Fred,' she sighed and got up to go to work at the *Oingo Boingo* Bar and Grill.

Bluewater

Lou Midnight

Jakes Fantasia was a Western style dude bar just outside Scunthorpe. Our eponymous landlord and customers, including the regular loser Boo, had been playing *Soolo* since *Twilight* and Boo was again in debt.

'*O!Bimbo*' wailed Boo 'I had the *Key only I made a* mistake playing the *Jolly Joker*. Will you take a cheque?'

'You'll fly no *Kite* with me Boo,' snarled Jake.

'Honestly, Jake, my cheque won't go *Oingo Boingo*', pleaded Boo.

'*Who Cares? Win* some lose some. *Cash'll do* or if it would help *Gilma Express* will do nicely.'

Mac*Pennypincher*, the Scottish moneylender, was in the dark corner where he used to *skulk*. '*Canna too* be helping with a loan?' he offered.

'Thanks a *Trillium*' replied Boo making a move for his gun.

'*Watch it Boo*' snapped Jake drawing his *Octopus* 45 with *Elan*. 'This is no place to die. You'll get no *orchids here*.'

Desperately Boo suggested a dea*l*, '*A, a, a, ventura, a . . .* ' he stammered.

'Don't take *libertad*s with me, I haven't fallen for that line since the Dowager *Lady Samantha* was a blushing *Brydie*.'

'I'll give you my medals,' Boo tried, '*R*emember I was awarded the *DOB* after the *Scorpio* affair. Or double or quits on this riddle. What kind of bird is a *Rockhopper?*'

'It's a *Gull. I've hea*rd it before, you lose again Boo.'

Just then Boo looked at *Daphne* and *Laura* the local *Midnight Strollers* who had just *amblered* up to the bar.

'Take your *eye off tha*' ' Jake ordered.

'I'm leaving town,' sobbed Boo.

'*So journey* with me, but buy me a drink first.'

'Just name your poison.'

'A *Locura & Bluewater*, it may sound awful, but I like the *Tais*.'

Note: Sadly not all boats are included, apologies have been received from *Amelia Viking*, who has acute *Hypatia* and has been put out to *Clover*. He hopes to be fit for the formation surfing competition as part of the *Dancing Wave* team.

Pennypincher

Rockhoppers Top Cheones in Worldball Debut

Since cruising in the Pacific, several international events have bannered the world's headlines. None have been so captivating as the revival of Worldball, a new *Aventura* in international sport and the most recent attempt to spread the fame and glory of American-style football.

The debut season culminated recently in the SuperBowl between the *Bluewater Rockhoppers* from Antarctica and the

America Indian *Cheone*s from the Western United States (but manned by Italians shouting '*Cambio! Cambio!*' in pursuit of the turnover).

Achieving the heights of the SuperBowl was no easy task as the *Rockhopper*s beat the genetically-superior *Oyinbo* team from Africa and toppled the harmonic *Amadés* from Austria.

As the crowds filled the stands, the cheerleaders began their antics to heighten the spirit of the day. Who could fail to respond to the cheers led by an international bevy of beauties . . . *Dafne, Laura, Brydie* and *Lady Samantha*. The latter was a true *Daughter of Baltic* with her blonde hair and *Orchidea* pinned to her bouncing breast.

When the last *Ambler*, a *Midnight Stroller* among the taverns the night before, found his seat in the stadium, the teams rushed on to the field with the *Elan* of an *Adventurer*. Under the *Eye of Ra*, the players flexed their muscles to ready for the *Tais* (toss) of the coin.

The *Rockhopper*s stormed the field. A veritable *Gilma Express*. Unstoppable. Quarterback *Gulliver* faked, then threw the ball, blasting it into the ozone where it hung like a *Kite*. After a momentary pause that stunned the *Cheone* defence, the ball returned to the *Octopus* arms of the *Soolo* wide receiver who walked into the end zone like a *Sojourner* on a Sunday afternoon promenade.

The *Rockhopper* fans cheered wildly sounding like a *Trillium Cacadu*s in a tropical jungle. The *Cheone* fans clamoured for revenge and *Libertad* from the looming stigma of being a loser.

Both sides went crazy, a *Locura* of international chants that merged in mingled energy and emotion. One side screamed, 'Watch your back!' The other countered with repeated 'Boos'. The effect was a somewhat garbled, '*Wachibou*'. But through all the cheering, the message was clear . . . 'He *Who Dares Wins*.'

The *Cheone* team took to the field, no longer the *Jolly Joker*s of the pre-game festivities. Back and forth, the two teams struggled. Like a *Scorpio*, the *Rockhopper* defense stung again and again. Jake, the *Cheone* captain, fumbled a handoff and watched the ball bounce, helter skelter, *Oingo Boingo*, across the turf. *Jake's Fantasia* of being the hero of the game and the focus of future commercial endorsements vanished. His *Gulkarna* was gone. The stingy *pennypincher* defence of the *Rockhopper*s had held.

As *Twilight* fell, the teams left the field . . .
*Rockhopper*s victorious.

Sojourner

The Adventures of Captain Tais

In the *Twilight* of his life, Captain Jake *Tais* was used to spend the summer nights on the terrace of his green windowed house, overlooking the bay and the lights of the fishing boats, fading away . . .

He was wandering in the memories of the past, when he was an *Elan Adventurer*. All his friends loved to listen to *Jake's Fantasia*, telling them about his voyagers (*Gulliver*'s travels compared to his were nothing).

At 24 he had a flower shop at Cape Town. There he met his first love: *Laura* was her name and she became his *Brydie*. The day of the wedding he gave her the most beautiful *Orchidea* anybody had ever seen, but she was allergic and she died of sneezing. He was in despair.

'*Oyinbo*! *Oyinbo*!' the locals were calling him in vain, in that dusty afternoon . . . he was *Soolo* now, and an *Ambler*. With the name of his *Brydie* tattooed on his arm he left and he became a capable sailor. *La Aventura* of his entire life, sailing across the *Bluewater*, was full of exciting events.

Once he met a giant *Octopus* in the land where the *Rockhopper* lives . . . He kissed one of the *Octopus'* tentacles and it turned into a wonderful lady:

'Call me *Samantha*' she murmured, embracing him tightly. And the duel with terrible pirate *Scorpio Two*? From whom Captain *Tais* stole his best *Kite* in order to bring a gift to the splendid *Dafne*, the *Daughter of Baltic* he met in the land of *Gulkarna* at the beginning of the spring. The fight with *Scorpio* was bloody and terrific, but in the end, blessed by the *Eye of Ra* and the god *Cheone*, Captain *Tais* handled the thread of the *Kite* and crying '*Who Dares Wins*' ran away riding a wild *Oingo Boingo*, reaching his new flame.

And the dancer he met in Bahia? He landed that night with his vessel, and went downtown, to the most famous nightclub of the Atlantic coast, the '*Cacadu*' – and there he saw her dancing: *Gilma Express* was her name, an ecstasy! She was a complete *Locura* for Captain *Tais*. He became a *Midnight Stroller* along the dark roads of the sleepy Bahia, trying to find out where her manager, *Jolly Joker*, was keeping the sensual dancer. In the end he found them: they were listening to some classical music written many years before by a famous European musician. Captain *Tais* couldn't remember his name, he had it on the top of the tip . . . something similar to *Amadé*. Anyway, he finally had found *Gilma*. He realised that the manager was barely a *Pennypincher* and he gained *Gilma's Libertad* with a bottle of

Cachaca and a few coins he had won playing darts at the *Cacadu*. When he finally had her in his arms, he realised she was not the beautiful and young lady he thought. He pronounced the magic word '*Wachibou*' and she was turned into a *Trillium*. So he rose his sails again, and he went on being a *sojourner*.

These and other stories Captain *Tais* was telling every night, overlooking the bay and dreaming of a travel around the world with his imaginary vessel.

Simona Oreglia
Leg 7 on *Brydie*

EUROPA 92 OVERALL RESULTS

Racing Division

Boat	Class	Leg 1	Leg 2	Leg 3	Leg 4	Leg 5	Leg 6	Leg 7	Leg 8
Gulliver	I	6.00	4.00	0.75	0.75	0.75	0.75	2.00	8.00
Who Dares Wins	I	3.00	0.75	3.00	4.00	2.00	3.00	3.00	0.75
Gilma Express	I	11.00	3.00	7.00	5.00	3.00	2.00	0.75	9.00
Oingo Boingo	II	0.75	9.00	9.00	8.00	6.00	7.00	4.00	2.00
Soolo	II	5.00	5.00	4.00	2.00	5.00	9.00	7.00	5.00
Cacadu	I	2.00	2.00	2.00	3.00	7.00	9.00	5.00	3.00
Orchidea	I	8.00	10.00	5.00	6.00	4.00	4.00	6.00	10.00
Wachibou	II	7.00	7.00	11.00	9.00	9.00	10.00	9.00	4.00
Elan Adventurer	II	9.00	6.00	8.00	12.00	12.00	11.00	11.00	11.00
Octopus	II	12.00	11.00	13.00	12.00	12.00	10.00	10.00	14.00
Locura	I	14.00	14.00	13.00	12.00	12.00	5.00	11.00	12.00
Dafne	II	4.00	8.00	6.00	7.00	8.00	6.00	8.00	7.00
Sojourner	II	14.00	14.00	13.00	12.00	12.00	11.00	12.00	6.00

Cruising Division

Boat	Class	Leg 1	Leg 2	Leg 3	Leg 4	Leg 5	Leg 6	Leg 7	Leg 8
Bluewater	I	0.75	0.75	2.00	6.00	0.75	0.75	0.75	11.00
Libertad II	II	5.00	2.00	3.00	13.00	7.00	5.00	2.00	13.00
Lady Samantha	II	2.00	3.00	8.00	2.00	14.00	2.00	10.00	5.00
Midnight Stroller	I	7.00	5.00	4.00	12.00	8.00	11.00	3.00	6.00
Amadé	I	9.00	6.00	15.00	9.00	12.00	8.00	9.00	16.00
Tais	III	8.00	9.00	13.00	3.00	5.00	20.00	17.00	14.00
Pennypincher	II	6.00	8.00	6.00	15.00	18.00	20.00	5.00	0.75
Twilight	I	10.00	10.00	16.00	23.00	11.00	4.00	4.00	15.00
Laura	III	3.00	7.00	17.00	4.00	16.00	10.00	20.00	17.00
Gulkarna II	II	11.00	4.00	11.00	11.00	15.00	18.00	11.00	9.00
Eye of Ra	III	15.00	11.00	14.00	18.00	13.00	14.00	15.00	12.00
Daughter of Baltic	III	13.00	12.00	19.00	19.00	21.00	16.00	13.00	8.00
Jakes Fantasia	II	14.00	18.00	21.00	22.00	23.00	20.00	22.00	20.00
Cheone	I	12.00	13.00	0.75	21.00	10.00	13.00	14.00	2.00
Rockhopper	III	17.00	16.00	20.00	20.00	22.00	19.00	21.00	20.00
Kite	II	19.00	18.00	23.00	24.00	0.75	6.00	8.00	4.00
Brydie	II	19.00	18.00	18.00	8.00	9.00	15.00	12.00	7.00
Scorpio II	III	19.00	18.00	23.00	24.00	25.00	12.00	19.00	18.00
Trillium	III	19.00	18.00	23.00	24.00	25.00	17.00	18.00	10.00

A points system was used to calculate results in the two divisions. The winner in each individual leg was awarded $\frac{3}{4}$ point, the second 2 points, the third 3 points, and so on. The boat with the lowest total won the respective class or division.

Leg 9	Leg 10	Leg 11	Leg 12	Leg 13	Leg 14	Leg 15	Leg 16	Leg 17	Total
0.75	2.00	2.00	2.00	0.75	0.75	0.75	0.75	0.75	33.50
2.00	0.75	0.75	0.75	2.00	2.00	2.00	2.00	2.00	33.75
3.00	4.00	3.00	5.00	6.00	5.00	3.00	5.00	4.00	78.75
4.00	7.00	4.00	3.00	3.00	4.00	5.00	3.00	5.00	83.75
5.00	8.00	6.00	4.00	4.00	3.00	4.00	4.00	6.00	86.00
7.00	5.00	6.00	8.00	7.00	6.00	6.00	7.00	6.00	91.00
8.00	3.00	5.00	10.00	7.00	7.00	7.00	6.00	3.00	109.00
9.00	8.00	6.00	12.00	7.00	6.00	6.00	7.00	6.00	133.00
11.00	8.00	6.00	7.00	5.00	6.00	7.00	8.00	6.00	144.00
10.00	8.00	6.00	11.00	7.00	6.00	6.00	7.00	6.00	161.00
12.00	8.00	6.00	13.00	7.00	7.00	7.00	8.00	6.00	167.00
6.00	6.00	6.00	6.00	7.00	6.00	6.00	8.00		
12.00	8.00	7.00	9.00	7.00	6.00	7.00			
3.00	0.75	2.00	2.00	0.75	2.00	2.00	4.00	2.00	41.25
4.00	3.00	2.00	3.00	2.00	4.00	2.00	7.00	0.75	77.75
9.00	6.00	2.00	7.00	3.00	0.75	2.00	2.00	4.00	81.75
2.00	2.00	2.00	12.00	5.00	9.00	2.00	8.00	12.00	110.00
8.00	10.00	2.00	0.75	4.00	3.00	2.00	0.75	5.00	119.50
5.00	15.00	2.00	6.00	6.00	5.00	2.00	5.00	12.00	147.00
16.00	9.00	2.00	11.00	10.00	6.00	2.00	11.00	6.00	151.75
10.00	4.00	2.00	10.00	11.00	8.00	2.00	6.00	7.00	153.00
12.00	12.00	2.00	9.00	10.00	13.00	2.00	3.00	3.00	160.00
6.00	14.00	2.00	14.00	7.00	14.00	2.00	11.00	9.00	169.00
7.00	8.00	2.00	4.00	10.00	14.00	2.00	11.00	8.00	178.00
14.00	11.00	2.00	17.00	10.00	14.00	2.00	11.00	10.00	212.00
15.00	19.00	2.00	18.00	10.00	14.00	2.00	11.00	11.00	262.00
0.75	7.00	2.00	13.00	10.00	11.00	2.00	9.00		
13.00	13.00	2.00	16.00	9.00	12.00	2.00	11.00		
11.00	5.00	2.00	5.00	2.00	7.00	2.00			
17.00	17.00	2.00	8.00	10.00	14.00	2.00			
16.00	16.00	2.00	15.00	8.00	10.00	2.00			
17.00	19.00	2.00	19.00	10.00	14.00	2.00			

The following yachts withdrew during the rally: *Amelia Viking* (Las Palmas), *Hypatia* (St Lucia), *Oyinbo* (Fiji) and *Ambler* (Australia). *Kite*, *Brydie*, *Sojourner*, *Scorpio II* and *Trillium* left the rally in Egypt to cruise in the Eastern Mediterranean. Technical problems stopped *Midnight Stroller II*, *Tais*, *Dafne*, *Cheone* and *Rockhopper* from completing the last leg.

INDEX